RESTORATION DRAMA

THE
MAGILL
BIBLIOGRAPHIES

Other Magill Bibliographies:

The American Presidents—Norman S. Cohen
Black American Women Novelists—Craig Werner
Classical Greek and Roman Drama—Robert J. Forman
Contemporary Latin American Fiction—Keith H. Brower
Masters of Mystery and Detective Fiction—J. Randolph Cox
Nineteenth Century American Poetry—Philip K. Jason
Twentieth Century European Short Story—Charles E. May
The Victorian Novel—Laurence W. Mazzeno
Women's Issues—Laura Stempel Mumford

RESTORATION DRAMA

An Annotated Bibliography

Thomas J. Taylor

SALEM PRESS

Pasadena, California   Englewood Cliffs, New Jersey

Library of Congress Cataloging-in-Publication Data

Taylor, Thomas J. (Thomas James), 1937–
   Restoration drama / Thomas J. Taylor
      p.   cm.—(Magill bibliographies)
   ISBN 0-89356-657-8
   1. English   drama—Restoration,   1660-1700—
History and criticism—Bibliography. 2. English
drama—Restoration,   1660-1700—   Bibliography.
I. Title. II. Series.
Z2014.D7T39   1989
[PR691]
016.822 ' 409—dc20   89-10852
                                         CIP

CONTENTS

	page
Introduction	1
General Studies	8
Aphra Behn	53
Colley Cibber	58
William Congreve	
General Studies	61
The Double-Dealer	70
Love for Love	72
The Mourning Bride	75
The Old Bachelor	75
The Way of the World	77
John Crowne	82
John Dryden	
General Studies	83
All for Love	91
Aureng-Zebe	93
The Conquest of Granada	96
The Indian Emperour	97
The Indian Queen	98
Marriage à la Mode	98
Sir Martin Mar-All	99
The Spanish Friar	100
Tyrannic Love	100
George Etherege	
General Studies	102
The Comical Revenge	107
The Man of Mode	109
She Would If She Could	111
George Farquhar	
General Studies	114
The Beaux' Stratagem	117
The Constant Couple	118
Love and a Bottle	119
The Recruiting Officer	119
The Twin Rivals	120
Nathaniel Lee	121

	page
Thomas Otway	123
Thomas Shadwell	127
John Vanbrugh	131
George Villiers	135
William Wycherley	
General Studies	137
The Country Wife	142
The Gentleman Dancing-Master	145
Love in a Wood	146
The Plain Dealer	148
Index	153

EDITORIAL STAFF

ACKNOWLEDGMENTS

In the process of getting to this book (in the metaphysical sense) I have enjoyed four kinds of support: professional, pedagogical, technical, and personal. I want to acknowledge them each:

Professors William Macintosh, Robert McLaughlin, Robert Merrix, John O'Connor, Jim Wise, and Anthony York, for sustaining their collegiality in defiance of better judgment;

Students Suzanne Fox, Madeleine Pabis, Elizabeth Rieser, Amy Reeder, Chuck Strubbe, and Robert Walsh, for making believe there is such a word as dramaturgy;

Editors Ellen Reinig and Chris Moose of Salem Press, and the Humanities Library staff of Purdue University, especially the Circulation and Interlibrary Loan departments.

This and all my work is lovingly dedicated to my wife and son, Bobbie and Beckett, without whom I would be a bum sitting on the curb in San Francisco.

RESTORATION DRAMA

INTRODUCTION

This bibliography is by way of invitation.

It invites the student scholar to discover among these entries a lost city, buried for almost three centuries under the weight of the science of scholarship in its infancy, ignored in the jungle of the modern proliferation of more accessible literature, passed over by critics on their way to other game. It argues that dramatic literature (Aristotle and his defenders notwithstanding) is dangerously close to a contradiction in terms, and that the textual encoding of a dramatic piece is inexpungibly married to its stage life. It reminds us all that works of art from other times are meant to be tasted, savored, examined, dissected, reassembled, re-enjoyed at least every twenty years or so, like a wonderful collection of heirlooms re-appreciated at every dusting.

What Is Restoration Drama?

What do we mean by "Restoration" drama? The history books tell all there is to know about the return of Charles II to the throne of England, on an exact date in 1660. Did Restoration drama start the same day, or was it lurking in the interregnum theatre banned by the Puritans but floating like a movable feast from space to space? Or had the late Carolinian dramatists already moved uneasily toward the "comedy of manners," the "heroic tragedy," and the other play forms normally attributed to a new age, a new kind of thinking? What about the age's revivals and adaptations of plays by William Shakespeare, Ben Jonson, James Shirley, Philip Massinger—are they to be considered Restoration drama on the grounds that the changes in the original texts were so specifically pointed toward a changed audience, a changed texture in the sensibilities of the London theatregoer (and how does one city claim to dictate the tastes of a whole country)? No single theatrical event can have the same abrupt world-changing force as Charles II's regal disembarkation, but theatre and drama made a quantum leap in the next months and years, as Thomas Killigrew and William Davenant solidified their positions as the official patent holders, "by appointment to his Majesty the King."

And when did Restoration drama end? Technically, on the day Charles died in 1685. Or perhaps in 1700, when John Dryden died and William Congreve's last great work, *The Way of the World*, was performed. Or was it in 1707, as George Farquhar lay dying in the shadow of his masterpiece, *The Beaux' Stratagem*, the last play, in the consensus of subsequent critics, to contain all the necessary ingredients to qualify as a "comedy of manners"? What about Colley Cibber, who found himself a struggling actor and playwright, contemporary with the greatest Restoration dramatists—Congreve, Etherege, Wycherley, Dryden—at the turn of the century, but who outlived them all to make the transition to the sentimentality of the mid-eighteenth century? Did Jeremy Collier's scathing attack on the theatre in 1697 suddenly give London a conscience, ringing the death knell for whatever combination of social conditions allowed the putative immoral, obscene, irresponsible plays to find their audience (and an enthusiastic one)? Surely, by the time the Licensing Act of 1737 re-established the principle of "permission to perform," Restoration drama, however defined, had succumbed to the sobriety of the Augustan Age and the middle-class left-brained mediocrity of the Age of Reason, where the novel saw its opportunity and flourished.

For the purposes of the project at hand, then, Restoration drama means the theatrical food that fed the affluent, gossipy, class conscious, self-important, periwigged and pomandered society of late seventeenth century London, a growing giant making the lumbering, destructive, noisy adjustments of any great beast awakening to a new day. Sometimes that food is in the form of dramatic texts left behind in printed form, but seldom with a literary response as their reason for existing (although such an argument can be made for some of the plays of Dryden, for example). More often, that food is theatrical presence: the Aristotelian "imitation of an action in the form of action"; the vast architecturally innovative theatre structures, almost cathedrals, but designed specifically for the decidedly secular, even damnable, art of performance; the financial potential of a newly emerging and self-designing entertainment industry, along with a rapacious middle class ready to exploit the colony-generated power of the English pound; the new occupations— actor and manager (often in the same talented person)—especially attractive to the misfits and outcasts, the handsome but irresponsible rogues, the impoverished but beautiful girls, the black sheep of otherwise respectable families; and the visual excitement of the new Italianate scenography, whose possibilities had barely been tasted before Oliver Cromwell slammed the doors on English theatre. In short, the food of the living stage, consumed with an energy that drives *theatre* history straight through *social* history like a great binding spike.

An Overview of the Period and Its Drama

The period of English history known as the Restoration takes its name from the return of Charles II to the throne of England in 1660, after twelve years of exile at the French court of Louis XIV. The abrupt break in the long reign of monarchies had come when the extremely conservative Puritan faction of Parliament managed to hound Charles I from his throne, eventually beheading him in 1649. Only after this faction was weakened by the less fanatical middle class, who sought the stability of political and economic conditions that the titular monarchy represented, could Charles return to England.

The Restoration period was one of adjustment. The role of the monarchy in the day-to-day affairs of the country was reduced to figurehead status, with only occasional interference in Parliamentary procedure, and then for personal rather than political favors. Throughout Europe the dynamics of power shifted from Church to State, from royalty to the bourgeoisie, from superstition to science, from faith to reason. England was completing its overdue transition from medieval feudalism to international commerce.

London became, more than ever before, the center of all cultural activity, expanding past its original boundaries into "suburbs" and new housing arrangements. The Great London Fire of 1666 encouraged a "new broom" policy; many of the landmarks of previous years burned and were swept aside in the wake of progress. A new bourgeoisie, fueled by riches from the New World and the East, began to make its presence known, not only in political arenas but in the cultural profile of the country as well.

At first, the theatre of the Restoration was extremely elitist, perhaps more so than at any other time in dramatic history. The "court" (by which was meant the hangers-on, the minor nobility, the young, titled but often penniless "cavaliers," the king's favorites and their relatives, the ladies, mistresses, courtiers, and favor-mongers who formed Charles's retinue) came to the theatre as part of its social circuit, more to be seen by others than to see the play. Quickly, however, many of the middle class began to attend the theatre as well, drawn by the sense of current "news" the theatre seemed to generate, and anxious to advance their financial prospects by being seen with "the right people" (Samuel Pepys is an excellent example—he left a diary of his experiences, from which much Restoration theatre history has been gleaned).

Playwrights, some seeing opportunities for quick profit and others merely dabbling in the gossip of the stage, knew what their new audience wanted, and supplied it in a prolific outpouring of dramatic fare, most of it lacking literary merit but supplying an ever-changing source of sexual titillation, farcical condemnation of "outsiders," *bons mots*, and character assassination, as well as providing a showcase for the latest fashions in dress, speech, and manner. The kinds of plays most popular during this period were sufficiently different from the drama before the interregnum that contemporary critics coined such phrases as "comedy of manners" and "heroic tragedy" to distinguish them from the outmoded earlier forms. While the influence of Ben Jonson (especially his "humours" theories), Philip Massinger, John Ford, and James Shirley can be seen in Restoration drama, the only playwright whose plays regained some of their former popularity was William Shakespeare, but at considerable cost to the plays' original structural integrity. Two cases in point: John Dryden reworked the story of Antony and Cleopatra into *All for Love*, and Nahum Tate devised a happy ending for his version of *King Lear*.

But among the pedestrian playwrights turning out ready-to-wear dramas fitting safe formulas were several fresh theatrical voices, rescuing this period from a more universally endorsed literary obscurity. Notable among them were Sir George Etherege, William Congreve, and William Wycherley, who collectively invented the comedy of manners, perhaps the most distinctive genre of the Restoration. John Dryden led the way in serious drama, with his intensely poetical imagery accompanied by prose critical theory; his plays answer more successfully to literary analysis than most plays of the period.

The changing audience required a changing theatrical format: Theatrical events moved indoors with the licensing of performances, at first in makeshift and altered quarters, later in new buildings designed by the same notables who were designing cathedrals, public buildings, and multiple dwellings in response to London's exploding population. The raked stage and the horseshoe-shaped stage house were introduced as solutions to box-office demands. The acting profession, always perilous and of questionable social value, was further complicated by the introduction of females onto the stage (one example of the influence of French theatre practices). The Italianate scenic practices that had captured the rest of Europe fully fifty years before finally became standard in London as well. The scurry for commercial success was responsible for the proliferation of stage entertainments, including opera, pantomime, drolleries, raree-shows, even "coffee house entertainments" that dodged the letter of the licensing laws while violating the spirit with impunity.

Plays had very short runs compared to today's theatre, and theatergoers hurried from product to product with the impatience of their own cultural adolescence. The positive result of this artistic consumerism was a lively arena for the farcical reporting of current affairs, battles among actors tinging their fictive characterizations, and private matters publicly acted to great applause. Favorite targets included the fop, the country bumpkin, the innocent girl, the aging rake, the small-minded, the thrifty, the zealous, and the ordinary—in short, everyone except the gifted, handsome, favored, witty fellow traveler, whose lifework was to set an example for others to emulate without success.

If Restoration drama was a reaction to the constraints of Puritanism on a booming economy, the cause of its demise, other than its own self-destructing metabolism, was the counterreaction of the saner population to the moral bankruptcy the stage presumed to announce. Charles II died in 1685; his successors to the throne did not approach their royal obligations with the same theatrical flair. Jeremy Collier's tract on the immorality of the stage in 1698, *A Short View of the Immorality and Profaneness of the English Stage*, was a "majority opinion," in its own right a centerpiece for an emerging alternative: sentimental drama. All the forces of social change were gathering to move England into the Age of Reason, where the stage became either a pulpit for the dissemination of universally accepted moral principles or a variety entertainment package cashing in on the short attention span of the idle.

In retrospect, the Restoration period's gifts to theatre history were substantial: actresses, comedy of wit, indoor theatre, wing-and-drop scenery, the actor/manager configuration which was to drive theatre well into the twentieth century, and, most important, a sense of the relationship of theatre to society, reflected in the birth of theatre criticism. The superficially objectionable moral assumptions of Restoration theatre almost prevented its rediscovery between the world wars, but its undeniable liveliness, its verbal wizardry, its healthy sense of self-mockery, and the stunning accuracy of its human portraiture have ensured its survival for at least another generation.

A Working Definition of Restoration Drama

The criteria for insertion in this bibliography are simple: Playwrights are included whose dramatic output begins between 1660 and 1700 and responds to the changed social and political atmosphere of London; if their work continued into the eighteenth century, it is included so long as it directly reflects the Restoration genres of comedy of manners or heroic tragedy, even if traits of sentimentality have encroached on the pure forms. Furthermore, the playwrights included here have continued to be studied and produced to the present day, and scholarship on them has mounted to the point where an annotated guide may help to sort out specific approaches; thus George Etherege, William Congreve, William Wycherley, and George Farquhar find themselves well represented, largely the result of their continued popularity on the modern stage. John Dryden's place in English literature is unassailable; only his dramatic work (including dramatic criticism) is dealt with here. Aphra Behn, possibly of the second water but clearly a Restoration voice, finds herself at the center of many modern studies of women's literature, and thus is included; Thomas D'Urfey, her contemporary, has become simply a historical footnote, and no great body of scholarly work on him has emerged to date. Several playwrights included serve as transitional figures into the eighteenth century sentimental drama (Colley Cibber and Thomas Otway are examples). Some plays and playwrights have a high "citation index," figuring into theatre history far out of proportion to their actual contribution; thus, George Villiers, second Duke of Buckingham, an amateur compared to many others not represented, is included by dint of the presence of *The Rehearsal* in so many subsequent anthologies. Finally, in order to be included in this list, editions of the plays under discussion should be available; some of the more obscure plays by lesser-known playwrights have generated neither critical discussion nor modern editions and have therefore not been listed.

Much has been said and recorded, by both "insiders" and "outsiders," on the subject of Restoration drama. In a field of this size, it is necessary for the bibliographer to select among the literally thousands of books and articles on the subject. The criteria here have taken into account the needs of the undergraduate student and layperson seeking general and introductory information about the period, as well as help in understanding the specific playwrights and plays.

The entries themselves have answered to this criterion of accessibility. Full-length studies, important chapters in more comprehensive studies, introductions to definitive editions, and a limited number of very carefully selected journal articles are cited and annotated. Where a book on a general Restoration subject or author gives chapter-long attention to a specific play or playwright, those chapters are listed and annotated in addition to the book itself. The journals cited are common and authoritative, and the chosen articles demonstrate some important insights into Restoration drama in general, or illustrate a cross-disciplinary approach valuable for expanding the reader's ways of thinking about Restoration drama. This bibliography is selective rather than exhaustive, designed to intrigue and invite new scholars to explore the territory in more detail at their own pace.

Suggestions for Using This Bibliography

In the process of gathering and listing entries, it has been a temptation to organize the general material around some taxonomy, or to list the entries in a way that confines each study to the company of others with the same central focus. (*The Revels History of Drama in English* contains an informal bibliography divided by such categories.) Much of the best scholarship, however, is conceived through a more serendipitous combination of ideas, and the chances of such combinations coming about are greater when opportunities to browse through the entries present themselves to the reader.

This bibliography comes with a warning. It is easy for certain opinions, certain habits of mind, to take root in textbooks, anthologies, lectures, and other forms of "received opinion," in such a way that fresh ideas are choked out by prevailing "axioms": "Restoration drama is bawdy and obscene"; "Restoration theatre is without artistic merit"; "There were only two decent plays written between 1660 and 1700"; "Charles II brought French plays with him from his exile"; even "There was no important English theatre from Shakespeare to Shaw."

These are complex issues, fascinating not so much in their eventual resolution (there is none) as in the varieties of attacks, approaches, interpretations, and selection of evidence (logical and passionate) brought to bear on one or another view. In fact, much of the value of the present bibliography is that it presents methodologies for dealing with historical and aesthetic evidence. While the particular scholarly detail may have no special importance, the way in which the critic examines the data toward a greater understanding of the subject is what makes the entry worthwhile and deserving of a place on the list. The following suggestions only begin to indicate the richness of the material for further study.

Themes and Genres
Some of the best studies listed here point to fresh thematic approaches to Restoration theatre: women's studies, marriage relationships, and the attitude of society toward language are among them. Another way to cut through the material is to examine the structure of genre: What makes a play fit into or stand outside the prevailing, but often unspoken, rules of stage form? While tragedy was treated seriously, and given its share of the repertory, the real voice of the age was comedy, especially in its ironic and satiric manifestations. It was an age that laughed at itself, or rather, an age in which one class laughed at another. Plays gave offense, to be sure, but to admit to having been insulted was to place oneself in the targeted group. A better tactic was to laugh along, an "insider" ridiculing the "outsiders."

Structure

How does a playwright structure a play, open it and move it forward and close it? What are the tools of the playwright for the assembly of moral prescripts? What are the presumptions of the chamber-isolated artist imagining his or her witty dialogue coming alive in the voices of Mrs. Bracegirdle and Mr. Betterton? Who decided the taste of London, a task never left to the hoi polloi? And when did the Restoration spirit submerge itself into the self-conscious, self-chastising, melancholy age of bourgeois sentimentality?

Character Studies

Another way into the period: The Restoration stage tended to categorize its characters fairly strictly; frequent visitors were the fops, deceiving wives, cuckolded husbands, unscrupulous rakes, innocent country girls, disguised priests, the truly witty and the merely clever, the silly and the false, the old pretending to be young and the young pretending to be wise—all the silhouettes on the stage taken from three-dimensional figures in the streets of London. But it is a reductive practice thus to identify them by their most prominent feature. Inside these categories are worlds of variety and combinations of traits, to say nothing of characters who change from one category to another during their brief time onstage (possibly the most interesting characters of all). The playwriting geniuses separate themselves here from the imitators: Their characters, however recognizable for their type, are full-figured, carefully observed and meticulously embodied in the actor's art, specific in every detail. It is from this attention to detail that their universality gets its undeniable force.

The History of Scholarship

A review of the bibliographical entries here reveals yet another interesting area of inquiry: the changing interests of the scholars themselves as the calendar removes the period further and further from their scrutiny. The history of critical scholarship goes back to the Greeks, but in the modern age its adolescence occurred in large part because of the controversy generated by Restoration drama. Jeremy Collier, in his rage to indict every perpetrator of London's most popular entertainment, tarred with the same brush those guilty of exploiting the human predilection for depravity (there is some evidence that Samuel Pepys was in this category) and those simply attending the theatre as one would read the daily news—not to approve of it but to observe it with discernment. Today, those angry opinions can be filtered through more recent developments such as democracy, freedom of speech, and religious tolerance; Collier no longer speaks clearheadedly on his subject.

The Genealogy of Opinion

One path to understanding the period and its critics is to follow an article's citations backward through the development of a debate around a central, unresolved issue. For example, the aftershocks of L. C. Knights' condemnation of Restoration theatre, first voiced in 1946, can still be felt in the most recent defenses of (or counterattacks on) the morality of the whole era. By such a system of reverse map-reading, one can discover the whole history of Restoration scholarship, at least to the major contributions between the world wars, or perhaps all the way back to the first critical assessments by the playwrights' own ruthless contemporaries. (Those who view as boring the prospects of actually reading seventeenth century nonfiction are invited to glance at Samuel Pepys' diary, the documents of Nell Gwyn's biography, or George Etherege's letters from Ratisbon.)

Finally, another invitation:

We may blithely wander among the documents of this quixotic era, but nothing will bring them to life without our first digging into the primary play texts themselves. Modern editions of Restoration plays are readily available, with all the glosses and endnotes that help make sense of the convoluted language and unfamiliar genre (one will find herein listed the introductions to the best editions). One need not know what scholars have "pronounced" about a piece before one reads it for oneself. The richest dialogue is not what someone else says about Horner or Sir Fopling Flutter or Sir Novelty Fashion or Aureng-Zebe or My Lady Wishfor't, but what these fascinating characters have to say for themselves, with wit, insight, and grace.

This invitation, then, is to a great ongoing party, guested with gaily costumed fictive creations from the playwrights' imaginations, decorated with the foibles of London society, catered by the eccentric tastes of a hedonistic court, and being held on the raked stage of England's greatest theatre, in the neighborhood of Lincoln's Inn Fields, corner of Haymarket Street and Drury Lane.

General Studies

Anthony, Rose. *The Jeremy Collier Stage Controversy, 1698-1726*. Milwaukee, Wis.: Marquette University Press, 1937. Reprint. New York: Benjamin Blom, 1966.
     As complete a recapitulation and analysis of the stage controversy as modern scholarship has seen. Anthony discusses Collier as a man (concentrating on his motives for the original attack), analyzes Collier's *A Short View of the Immorality and Profaneness of the English Stage* itself in careful detail, and summarizes with exhaustive comment the wave upon wave of aftershocks over the next twenty-eight years. Beyond its immediate subject, the controversy generated a prototype for the art of theatrical criticism, one to which such luminaries as Oliver Goldsmith, Charles Lamb, and George Bernard Shaw owe a debt. Contains a valuable chart of the controversy, along with bibliographies.

Archer, Stanley L. "The Epistle Dedicatory in Restoration Drama." *Restoration and Eighteenth Century Theatre Research* 10, no. 1 (May, 1971): 8-13.

The dedicatory epistle, often added to the published play, and usually addressed to the playwright's patron or benefactor, provides information on the period in great variety. Archer counts 258 dedications to 182 patrons (the Earl of Dorset received seventeen). While a "highly varied literary genre," the epistles follow a pattern, and stand by themselves as works of literature; at the same time they demonstrate a substantial but by no means presumptive support of literature by the nobility.

Archer, William. "Restoration Romance and Tragedy." Lecture 6 in his *The Old Drama and the New: An Essay in Re-valuation*. Boston: Small, Maynard, 1923.
Archer, a very highly regarded critic, translator, and man of the theatre, sees neither a debt to France nor a breach of continuity from the Jacobean and Carolinian stage, in his description of Restoration drama, but does mark 1660 as the beginning of the Modern Age, when "Society, in the drawing room sense of the word, attained self-consciousness." Reviews the tragedies of John Dryden, Nathaniel Lee, Thomas Otway, Nicholas Rowe, and Thomas Southerne and describes the Thomas Betterton school of acting as "what I have ventured to call Passion in contradistinction to Imitation." Knowledgeable, witty, and often acidic, his comments still penetrate to the core of the dramatic life of these plays.

_____ . "Restoration Comedy." Lecture 7 in his *The Old Drama and the New: An Essay in Re-valuation*. Boston: Small, Maynard, 1923.
This essay puts the question of morality versus artistic merit in the clear light of Archer's theatrical analysis, which comes down hard on the putative light-heartedness of the times: "The whole case for Restoration comedy as a purely non-moral product breaks down the moment we look into it. . . . It is constantly calling upon us for admiration" of a reprehensible line of conduct. By responding to Edmund Gosse's opinions, Archer points out that "over-emphasis, over-colouring, gross and palpable exaggeration was the law of its being," even in Millamant (in William Congreve's *The Way of the World*), its "masterpiece . . . a lyrical creation, by many degrees removed from reality."

_____ . "The *Short View* and After." Lecture 8 in his *The Old Drama and the New: An Essay in Re-valuation*. Boston: Small, Maynard, 1923.
Archer minces no words in his defense of Jeremy Collier's tract condemning the theatre: "Among sensible men . . . there never has been the slightest doubt that Collier was substantially in the right and did yeoman's service to good feeling and good manners." Moving to "a somewhat wholesomer state of things" (although admittedly of lesser literary power), Archer notes that the word "sentimental" is used quite loosely in all literary history. George Farquhar and Colley Cibber are dealt with at some length before Archer moves on to Richard Steele and the rest of the century. The lecturing tone reflects both

the source of Archer's published material and his strong opinion as he moves self-righteously through the age.

Armistead, J. M. *Four Restoration Playwrights: A Reference Guide to Thomas Shadwell, Aphra Behn, Nathaniel Lee, and Thomas Otway.* Boston: G. K. Hall, 1984.
A valuable annotated bibliography to four less frequently studied playwrights, although the introduction notes considerable interest, even trends of interest, since Gerard Langbaine's critical observations of 1691. Valuable for its thesaurus-like taxonomy of critical subjects for each playwright and for its division by the year in which the criticism appeared. The introduction under-lines the main purpose of the work: "Now that much of the groundwork has been laid, the prospect for future criticism about these four dramatists seems bright."

Avery, Emmett L. "A Poem on Dorset Garden Theatre." *Theatre Notebook* 18, no. 4 (Summer, 1964): 121-124.
Discovered in a rare collection of broadsides and other ephemera gathered by Narcissus Luttrell during the Restoration, this little poem in rhymed couplets, entitled "A Description of a Play-House in Dorset-Garden," is neither com-mendatory nor venomously critical of the theatre world. A softer version of the popular satiric verses of the time, it possibly foreshadows Alexander Pope's famous description of Belinda at her dressing table in *The Rape of the Lock.* *Theatre Notebook* fills its pages with fascinatingly detailed information of this nature.

_____ . "The Restoration Audience." *Philological Quarterly* 45, no. 1 (January, 1966): 54-61.
Given the paucity of records on the tastes and inclinations of Restoration audiences, it takes inspired inference by someone intimately familiar with the period to assess the audience, especially in the face of previously published remarks that it should be easy to analyze (because of its basis in court pa-tronage). Avery notes the change in constituency from 1660 to 1700, and attempts to examine some generalizations commonly accepted but brought into question by his own research. Some important influences were men in posi-tions of political power, "men of distinction in public affairs" (especially, Avery points out, Samuel Pepys's associates in the Navy Office), the beaux and wits (and their female companions), and even families.

Barlow, Graham. "A First-Night Prologue for the New Theatre, Lincoln's Inn Fields." *Theatre Notebook* 38, no. 2 (1984): 51-53.
Barlow found this prologue tucked in a miscellaneous collection of such verses at the University of Nottingham and noted its significance for theatre history: It was written for Thomas Otway's *The Orphan* in commemoration of the open-

ing of an important new theatre on December 18, 1714. It seems to have been spoken by John Rich, possibly in mourning for his father, Christopher Rich, who died the month before. This sort of sleuthing among forgotten manuscripts transforms literary and theatrical scholarship into something of an adventure. A brief but fascinating excursion.

Barnard, John. "Drama from the Restoration till 1710." In *English Drama to 1710*, edited by Christopher Ricks. London: Sphere Books, 1971.
Barnard sorts out the generic impulses, the sources and social influences, the great from the merely professional writers of this "schizophrenic" age, in a smooth and readable review of the topic. While on the one hand "the extremities of heroic tragedy" are explained by the events of the Civil War and interregnum, the comic genres owe their birth to the fact that, after Charles II's return, "an established social order, based on degree and obligation, had been ousted by a permissive society." A brief but clearheaded review of the major playwrights, from George Etherege to George Farquhar. Richard Steele begins another era. Strong bibliography.

Bax, Clifford. *Pretty Witty Nell: An Account of Nell Gwyn and Her Environment.* New York: Benjamin Blom, 1932, reprint 1969.
A colorful account of the life of Nell Gwyn, Restoration actress, comedienne, and mistress to royalty. Her adventures are described year by year, from her barefoot days to her heyday as "the life and soul of the party" to her death, possibly from complications of syphilis. Bax's treatment, part scholarly biography and part gossip novel, is accompanied by thirteen illustrations, notes, appendices, bibliography, index, and (lest Bax be taken too seriously) Nell's horoscope (rising sign: Capricorn). An excellent way to be introduced to the theatre world of Charles II.

Bernbaum, Ernest. *The Drama of Sensibility: A Sketch of the History of English Sentimental Comedy and Domestic Tragedy, 1696-1780.* Boston: Ginn, 1915.
On the border of the period under consideration, this study is a refreshing defense of sentimental drama, otherwise maligned by Restoration critics as a bastardization and dilution of the high-spirited comedy of manners. Bernbaum even goes so far as to accuse dramatists of intentionally inhibiting the incipient sentimentalism in pre-interregnum plays revived and revised for Restoration audiences; only Aphra Behn is praised for retaining the sentimental elements in her raids on earlier English dramas. Bernbaum admits to the occasional presence of "figures that are amiable" (Fidelia in *The Plain Dealer*, and Alithea in *The Country Wife* are examples) among the otherwise vicious, odious, foolish, and affected cast of characters in the plays of George Etherege, William Wycherley, and William Congreve. Contains "an imaginary conversation between Master Softheart and Sir Hardhead," debating "the strength and the weakness of the drama of sensibility." Index.

Birdsall, Virginia Ogden. *Wild Civility: The English Comic Spirit on the Restoration Stage*. Bloomington: Indiana University Press, 1970.
Bracketed by Prologue and Epilogue and introduced by "Dramatis Personae" are eight chapters identifying and distinguishing the features of the Restoration rake-hero. Dealing with the three least prolific playwrights of the earliest period (George Etherege, William Wycherley and William Congreve), Birdsall keeps to literary analysis, virtually ignoring the stage, the audience, the actor, the event. She is more than a little psychological in her approach, and more concerned with characters as profiles of real behavior than as fictive constructions. Notes after each chapter act as bibliography; index.

Black, James. "An Augustan Stage-History: Nahum Tate's *King Lear*." *Restoration and Eighteenth Century Theatre Research* 6, no. 1 (May, 1967): 36-54.
Nahum Tate has gone down in the history books as the man who gave *King Lear* a happy ending. This article describes the history of Tate's version through the eighteenth century, in the process giving important information concerning the reception of this sentimental version as audience tastes changed from the time of its composition in 1681, when Restoration audiences apparently approved of it. Production histories of single plays are valuable for discerning the structure of theatrical changes taking place around the fixed center of the text.

Boas, Frederick S. *An Introduction to Eighteenth-Century Drama, 1700-1780*. Oxford, England: Clarendon Press, 1953.
Slightly to one side of the present study, this volume helps the transition from Restoration drama (always a vague term) to the sentimental and bourgeois drama of the eighteenth century. Chapters on George Farquhar and Colley Cibber, for example, show how the transition was gradual and the change in sensibilities almost seamless. Boas divides his sixteen chapters by playwrights, citing Nicholas Rowe as "a natural stepping-stone from Elizabethan and Restoration drama to that of the eighteenth century." Index.

Booth, Michael R. "Theatre History and the Literary Critic." *The Yearbook of English Studies* 9 (1979): 15-27.
This Theatrical Literature Special Number offers the clearest explanation of the problems of studying theatre history along with dramatic literature, the most active modern critical approach to Restoration drama. Starting with Charles Lamb's essay stating his preference for Shakespeare as literature rather than theatre, Booth pinpoints the central controversy: the literary critic's distrust of popular culture and entertainments, "rightly presuming a lack of intellectuality and the absence of the sort of standards to which he subscribes." Booth is referring to nineteenth century theatre/drama, but his observations apply equally well to the Restoration. Cited scholarship serves as a list for further reading.

Boswell, Eleanore. *The Restoration Court Stage, with a Particular Account of the Production of "Calisto."* Cambridge, Mass.: Harvard University Press, 1932.
An exquisitely valuable description of the playing areas at court, in private halls and stages. The difficulties of visualizing the stage treatments of Restoration plays are ameliorated here by copious illustrations from period engravings, with special attention to descriptions of physical space, maintenance and management, and stage personnel. Removes the play from its literary boundaries and reveals it as a recipe for performance. The student of Restoration staging must begin here.

Bowyer, John Wilson. *The Celebrated Mrs. Centlivre*. Durham, N.C.: Duke University Press, 1952.
Besides being an appreciative biography of one of the Augustan Age's bright lights, this book supplies a colorful and readable picture of the theatre world of Restoration drama on the decline. Susanna Centlivre satirized the Restoration rakes' and ladies' widely acknowledged passion for gaming during these years, in *The Gamester* and its sequel, *The Basset Table*. Illustrations throughout, with index and bibliography of her work.

Braunmuller, A. R., and J. C. Bulman, eds. *Comedy from Shakespeare to Sheridan: Change and Continuity in the English and European Dramatic Tradition.* Newark: University of Delaware Press, 1986.
A series of essays tracing comedy in its various manifestations from the English Renaissance to the nineteenth century. A section on Restoration and eighteenth century comedy includes articles on Shakespeare, the popularity of the Don Juan character, the finance-based marriages in the plays of William Congreve, and Richard Sheridan's comic language. Also valuable are three overviews attempting to explain the gradual proliferation of generic variations on the basic Aristotelian comic type.

Brooke, Iris. *Dress and Undress: The Restoration and Eighteenth Century*. Westport, Conn.: Greenwood Press, 1958, reprint 1976.
An illustrated survey of male and female wardrobe style changes from 1660 to 1800, with special emphasis not so much on stage costuming as on actual dress fashions in the period (much the same apparel until the first antiquarian actress dared to discard her pannier to appear "Roman"). By finding her references among personal letters, gossip columns, poetry, and other contemporary writings, Brooke draws an accurate sketch of English life, endorsed by the London stage. Sixty-nine figures, index, and an appendix on cleaning taken from a 1758 document.

Brown, John Russell, and Bernard Harris, eds. *Restoration Theatre*. Stratford-upon-Avon Studies 6. London: Edward Arnold, 1965.

Ten essays on various subjects of the Restoration, including an introduction to
the topic by Bernard Harris. In addition to separate articles on the four major
Restoration playwrights (George Etherege, William Wycherley, John Dryden,
and William Congreve), the collection contains a discussion of modes of
satire, a definition of heroic tragedy, and a study of acting during the period.
One interesting feature of each article is a prefatory note citing major sources
used by the author, inviting further study. Index.

Brown, Laura. "The Defenseless Woman and the Development of English Tragedy."
Studies in English Literature 1500-1900 22, no. 3 (Summer, 1982): 429-443.
An excellent example of the fruitful possibilities of Restoration scholarship
applied to modern views, this time on the role of women in literature. Nicholas
Rowe, in what Brown terms "the late Restoration" (1714), introduced the
"she-tragedy," in which "a new kind of heroine, whose victimization provides
the essential material of the plot," emerges, in contrast to "the passionate and
ambitious female characters" in previous tragedies. The phenomenon is part
of a larger development of tragedy, away from the heroic drama of the "aristo-
crat" toward a "bourgeois tragedy," whose most successful proponent was
George Lillo, in such plays as *The London Merchant*. The study closes with a
very interesting paragraph on the interrelation of social and aesthetic change.

——————— . "The Divided Plot: Tragicomic Form in the Restoration." *ELH* 47,
no. 1 (Spring, 1980): 67-79.
Far from lamenting the "apparently chaotic, contradictory form" of tragicomedy in the early Restoration, Brown argues that "sustained disjunction is a
primary end of this drama, and the best divided plays are those which seem to
strive for formal collision." Borrowing from the Spanish "intrigue" form, on
whose surface the contradictions ride, the divided tragicomedy "generates its
diversity" from its inherent strength as "a coherent form of its own, with its
own distinctive relationship to the drama that precedes and follows it."

——————— . *English Dramatic Form, 1660-1760: An Essay in Generic History*.
New Haven, Conn.: Yale University Press, 1981.
A full-length study of the drama of the period, based on classification by
genre; argues against the notion that it is too diversified; her study is "a
designation of formal categories based upon the local definition of individual
actions." Separates by form, "moral action," "structure"; defines merit in
terms of inner moral worth in later drama. A final chapter deals with the rise
of the novel and its own moral action. Notes and index.

Bruce, Donald. *Topics of Restoration Comedy*. New York: St. Martin's Press, 1974.
A defense of Restoration comedy "as a debating comedy, and as morally
purposeful within its debates." An introductory chapter and brief biographies

of seven major Restoration dramatists (George Etherege, Thomas Shadwell, Aphra Behn, William Wycherley, William Congreve, John Vanburgh, and George Farquhar) are followed by three essays in the manner of New Criticism (a subjective interpretation of random samples without recourse to critical apparatus outside the text), on the topics of Reason and Impulse, Epicureanism, and female characters (referred to as "bright nymphs of Britain"). Notes, bibliography, chronology, and index.

Burner, Sandra A. "A Provincial Strolling Company of the 1670's." *Theatre Notebook* 20, no. 1 (Autumn, 1965): 74-78.
To understand fully the established and patented theatre of London, one must also understand the less easily identified companies: roving players working their meager way through the provinces. One such troupe, "possibly the Duke of Monmouth's Company," run by one John Coysh, is described, offering its relatively old-fashioned repertory (not the new comedies of George Etherege, William Wycherley or William Congreve) in such places as the Red Lion in Norwich. A surviving promptbook gives a few clues regarding the special revisions for touring, and actors' names in the margins help flesh out the casts.

Burns, Edward. *Restoration Comedy: Crises of Desire and Identity.* New York: St. Martin's Press, 1987.
"A narrative of its development," considering Restoration Comedy critically and historically. The Restoration culture treats as literary form (rather than theatrical) "the prose comedy of London life [in which] Wit overrides decorum"; a series of readings of plays and playwrights, including evolution by wits, adaption by professional writers (and its place in the Royalist crisis of the 1680's), and revival after William and Mary. Offers a brief chronological checklist of plays.

Burns, Landon C. *Pity and Tears: The Tragedies of Nicholas Rowe.* Salzburg, Austria: Institut für Englische Sprache und Literatur, 1974.
Defends Rowe's importance in the study of Restoration drama. Serves as a valuable source for Rowe scholarship, and illuminates some methods for appreciating tragedy, often difficult for undergraduate readers. Rowe's "place" in English drama resides in his value for historical reasons, plus some artistic merit.

Cameron, Kenneth M. "Duffett's *New Poems* and Vacation Plays." *Theatre Survey* 5, no. 1 (May, 1964): 64-70.
"Hardly one of the shining lights of the Restoration drama," Thomas Duffett (not to be confused with Thomas D'Urfey) contributed to theatre history in his prologues and epilogues for "vacation performances," plays given during the summer by young Theatre Royal hirelings in the absence of the main season repertory (fall through spring). Little is known about the practices, repertories,

and casting of these apprentice groups, but Cameron finds, in Duffett's light-hearted additions to the classical fare, considerable information concerning the "little fifth rates, whom they all despise."

—————— . "The Edinburgh Theatre, 1668-1682." *Theatre Notebook* 18, no. 1 (1963): 18-25.
Not all Restoration theatre took place in London. This Scottish cultural center provided a favorable environment for "renegades" from the Theatre Royal, as well as considerable native talent. An expense account of an avid theatergoer (John Foulis of Ravelstoun), and some pictorial evidence from the mid-seventeenth century provide a portrait of theatre life in Edinburgh that is more robust than previously assumed. The theatre buildings themselves may have been better than the converted tennis courts of London.

Canfield, J. Douglas. *Nicholas Rowe and Christian Tragedy.* Gainesville: University Presses of Florida, 1977.
Examines Rowe's work for themes of trust in providential justice, suffering innocence, and sin and repentance. Trial is a Christian notion, and the greatest trial is temptation to despair. Provides a list of books in Rowe's library, a twentieth century bibliography on Rowe's tragedies, and a list of works cited. Scholarly and complete.

—————— . "The Significance of the Restoration Rhymed Heroic Play." *Eighteenth-Century Studies* 13, no. 1 (Fall, 1979): 49-62.
A discussion of the importance of this genre, often dismissed "as an outrageous experiment that failed," sometimes justified as satirical, but mostly ignored, adumbrated by the more accessible comic genre of the same period. Trials of faith, the "reaffirmation of the binding force of words in the face of the omnipresent threat of betrayal," and "anti-Republican, anti-Puritan" sentiments are detailed, toward the thesis that "the Restoration rhymed heroic play is an attempt to reinscribe across the pages of a disintegrating cultural scripture the chivalric code which had underwritten aristocratic society for centuries." The "tentative" bibliography of the Restoration rhymed heroic play in an appendix makes an excellent reading list of the primary texts.

Cecil, C. D. "Libertine and *Précieux* Elements in Restoration Comedy." *Essays in Criticism* 9, no. 3 (July, 1959): 239-253.
Although concentrating on a specific element in the drama, this essay is part of a general debate conducted in journals of this kind regarding the merits of Restoration drama as an object of literary study, usually contrasted with similar opportunities in "Elizabethan richness or high Augustan simplicity." Cecil takes an anti-New Critical view, arguing that the plays must be studied "contextually": "We can never know enough about the idiom of an age, nor can we draw a line at which we may legitimately stop trying to acquire its associa-

tions." His defense of contextual criticism leads eventually to the best current studies of the drama in performance, where they originally lived their lives, before descending to mere literature.

Chisman, Isabel, and Hester Emilie Raven-Hart. *Manners and Movements in Costume Plays*. Boston: The Walter H. Baker Co., n.d.
An indispensable little book for costumers and actors of period styles, detailing the effect of costume on "deportment" of body and limb. Approaches men's and ladies' fashion chronologically, dealing with the Restoration and eighteenth century in six exquisite pages: "The movement and gesture in this period should be that of a trained dancer, but in any case remember to hold your head beautifully, to take small steps and never to cross the legs."

Collier, Jeremy. *A Defence of The Short View of the Profaneness and Immorality of the English Stage*. New York: Garland, 1972 [1699].
This reprint of the 1699 continuation of the great debate is briefly prefaced by Arthur Freeman, who notes that the controversial first attack had been soundly answered in print by William Congreve, John Dennis, Thomas D'Urfey, and Charles Gildon, among others. Valuable for readers following the rhetorical styles that move the argument forward; Garland has published a whole series of reprinted tracts on this and other stage controversies, numbering some fifty volumes, making available the original texts otherwise lost to the general reader.

Cope, Kevin L. "The Conquest of Truth: Wycherley, Rochester, Butler, and Dryden and the Restoration Critique of Satire." *Restoration* 10, no. 1 (Spring, 1986): 19-40.
This substantial essay reexamines the definition of satire and its bases in social attitudes of confidence versus philosophical doubt. Through a careful review of William Wycherley's *The Plain Dealer*, along with several nondramatic pieces of the same period, Cope argues that "the Restoration and early eighteenth century revered satire as the weapon of order and elegance against too literal an idea of truth." A strong example of critical theory founded in genre study.

Corman, Brian. "Restoration Drama: Directions of Pursuit." *Restoration* 5, no. 1 (Spring, 1981): 38-42.
A sort of post-face to a compilation of the semiannual drama bibliography this journal offers, Corman's essay is a wish-list for future scholarship and, at the same time, a road map for fieldwork in Restoration theatre studies. Among his remarks are his approval of renewed interest in less-known texts and playwrights, his delight at continued scholarship in the social and intellectual contexts of Restoration drama, and his agreement with others in the field that the most fruitful approach to Restoration drama is "study of the relationship

between text and performance in Restoration drama." Recommended as an informal checklist of research possibilities.

Cox, James E. *The Rise of Sentimental Comedy*. Privately printed, 1926. Reprint. Springfield, Mo.(?): Folcroft Press, 1969.
Where Restoration drama became sentimental drama is difficult to pinpoint, but this study traces the gradual growth of the form through the transitional stages to Richard Steele, "the founder of sentimental comedy." Cox points at the early signs, credits Jeremy Collier as "central in the Moral Revolution," denies Colley Cibber as founder (despite his contributions, he was of the "old school"), and lists the distinctions between comedy of manners and sentimental comedy, a list that clarifies the distinction very well. Index.

Crawford, Bartholow V. "High Comedy in Terms of Restoration Practice." *Philological Quarterly* 8, no. 4 (October, 1929): 339-347.
A generally accepted but seldom defined term, "high comedy" is something more than simply the opposite of "low comedy." Crawford sorts out its features toward a definition, offering along the way a brief history of the relation of court patronage to comedy. Nine fairly specific observations bracketing the "standards" are eventually defined; at the center of high comedy is its marriage of artificiality with ideal social imitation.

Cunningham, John E. *Restoration Drama*. London: Evans Brothers, 1966.
The introductory and concluding chapters in this study of five playwrights provide a clear summary of central issues: origins and continuity in the dramatic literature; a description of theatres, audiences, actors, and repertoire; heroic tragedy; and comparisons of comedy of manners with similar forms. A very short bibliography and an index follow chapters on George Etherege, John Dryden, William Wycherley, Thomas Otway, and William Congreve.

Cunningham, Peter. *The Story of Nell Gwyn and the Sayings of Charles the Second.* Edited by John Drinkwater. New York: Benjamin Blom, 1927, reprint 1969.
Originally written in 1852, beginning with Nell's horoscope, which Cunningham confesses is an enigma to him, and ending with Nell's modest burial ("surely with much that was good in her," adds Cunningham), this study in the life and times of England's most notorious actress is embellished by thirty-nine illustrations, many of them portraits of Nell's contemporaries, but including views of London, Whitehall, and Nell's residence. In her story reside the charms and the evils of her time, presented here in a style that discloses the biographer's real affection for his subject.

Davison, Peter. "The Muse's Looking-Glass." In his *Popular Appeal in English Drama to 1850*. Totowa, N.J.: Barnes & Noble Books, 1982.

This chapter demonstrates the Restoration justification of Davison's thesis, that the stage has always aimed at popular acceptance rather than the approbation of the elite and the learned. "The awareness of the theatrical art, consciously made manifest, was extra-ordinarily pervasive in this period." Satire and burlesque were the forms that drew the Restoration audience to the stage. The entire study is indexed; select bibliography supplied.

Deane, Cecil V. *Dramatic Theory and the Rhymed Heroic Play*. New York: Barnes & Noble Books, 1968.
The spirit of exploration in dramatic theory was matched by the readiness to "graft on to the old stock" the new material of the Restoration. Seeing heroic drama as a combination of old and new forms, Deane traces French neoclassical influences (especially the theory of the unities), contemporary thought, and the Elizabethan legacy in this study of seven selected plays: "It was the synthesis of these elements which captivated and held spellbound a cultivated portion of seventeenth-century society." Bibliography and index.

Dobrée, Bonamy. *Restoration Comedy 1660-1720*. London: Oxford University Press, 1924. Reprint. Westport, Conn.: Greenwood Press, 1981.
Dobrée claims that tragedy thrives during periods of great national expansion and power, when there is a general "acceptation" of what is good and evil; comedy thrives during periods of readjustment and general instability, when policy is insecure and morality is in chaos. Thus Restoration comedy (divided into critical comedy, free comedy, and great comedy), which expressed a deep curiosity, not just licentiousness, about the new ways, did not give us masterpieces because of the "want of an inspiring, comprehensive philosophy." Instead, it "gave a brilliant picture of its time rather than a new insight into man." Separate discussions of George Etherege, William Wycherley, John Dryden, Thomas Shadwell, William Congreve, John Vanbrugh, and George Farquhar.

_____ . *Restoration Tragedy 1660-1720*. Oxford, England: Clarendon Press, 1929.
Beginning with the thesis that "tragedy, from the spectator's point of view, is the most personal of the literary forms," Dobrée moves through the subject, treating heroism, blank verse, John Dryden, Nathaniel Lee, Thomas Otway, and Nicholas Rowe in detail, with a separate chapter on *The Mourning Bride* and *Cato*, concluding that, at least in tragedy, "character is only the secondary symbol, meant to give life to the poet's main symbol, which is the plot." Bibliography and index.

Dobrée, Bonamy, ed. *Five Heroic Plays*. London: Oxford University Press, 1960.
With an introduction that differentiates between heroic and tragic drama,

Dobrée offers Roger Boyle's *The Tragedy of Mustapha*, Elkanah Settle's *The Empress of Morocco*, John Crowne's *The Destruction of Jerusalem, Part II*, Nathaniel Lee's *Sophonisba*, and John Dryden's *Aureng-Zebe*, in a popular edition but without separate introductory material. Explaining that dramatists wrote according to theory, Dobrée encourages modern readers to overcome resistance to heightened emotions and difficult rhymes, to enjoy these plays that "celebrate the heroic virtues, especially of valour and love."

Doran, Dr. [John]. *Annals of the English Stage from Thomas Betterton to Edmund Kean*. 3 vols. London: John C. Nimmo, 1888. Reprint. New York: AMS Press, 1968.
Recognized since its original publication as "the standard popular history of the English stage." Chapters on every aspect of theatre life, but not always arranged for easy reference. A full index in each volume helps the reader find information. The first volume, in eighteen chapters, gets up to 1730, with forty illustrations. The second volume overlaps the first slightly, in the biography of Mrs. Oldfield.

Downes, John. *Roscius Anglicanus*. Edited by Judith Milhous and Robert D. Hume. London: Society for Theatre Research, 1987 [1708].
In 1708, John Downes published what might be considered the first review of theatre history. An invaluable document for modern scholars, it is written almost entirely from his own experiences and contains lists of casts, repertory seasons, and other theatre material indispensable to an understanding of how the theatre world worked in the Restoration. Milhous and Hume provide an introductory essay on the substance and importance of the work, elaborate footnotes and endnotes, and a strong index.

——————— . *Roscius Anglicanus*. Edited by Montague Summers. New York: Benjamin Blom, 1929.
The original document really serves as an introduction to Summers' elaborate explanatory notes that accompany this edition. Corrects, emends, and comments on virtually every entry, since Downes was relying on memory as much as theatre records to write his unique chronicle. The fifty-two-page original is annotated with about 220 pages of Summers' conjectures and comments; together they serve not only as a portrait of the age but also as a record of changing scholarly attitudes in the intervening two hundred years.

Ellenhauge, Martin. *English Restoration Drama: Its Relation to Past English and Past and Contemporary French Drama*. Copenhagen: Levin & Munksgaard, 1933, reprint 1970.
A slightly overorganized attempt to discuss every possible subject embedded in both English pre-Restoration and Restoration drama, and in European counter-

parts, especially French. From "illustrations and criticism of the current code of conduct" to "useless knowledge," this attempt at cataloging the variations in the period often confuses rather than clarifies. An interesting but rambling discussion among the less familiar plays. Provides a summary and a bibliography.

Elwin, Malcolm. *The Playgoer's Handbook to Restoration Drama*. New York: Macmillan, 1928.

One of the earliest appreciations of Restoration drama to follow Allardyce Nicoll's comprehensive history, this study describes itself as "a bastard imbroglio of biography, history, criticism, and commentary . . . designed merely to remind its readers of the existence of an extraordinary epoch in theatrical and dramatic development . . . not to expand new theories, to explode moribund ideas, or to express dogmatic dictums, but to assist lovers of the theatre . . . in acquiring an intimate acquaintance with the drama of the Restoration." An excellent overview, with three valuable appendices: a diary of the Restoration period, brief biographical notes on actors and actresses of the period, and a reader's guide to Restoration drama. Bibliography and index.

Fairholt, F. W. *Costume in England: A History of Dress to the End of the Eighteenth Century*. 2 vols. London: Bell & Sons, 1885. Reprint. Detroit: Singing Tree Press, 1968.

In the section of the book dealing with Stuart customs ("the ladies of the court are . . . well known by the painting of Lely") through George I's reign, the peerless figure of Nell Gwyn and Pepys's diaries are cited, as are the numerous mentions of dress in plays of the period. Three hundred figures illustrate the first volume (on the history of dress); volume 2 is a glossary of terms with hundreds more illustrations of headdresses, gambesons (worn under the habergeon), accessories, laces, and even pomander balls. Delightfully detailed and informative, with an index at the end of the first volume.

Fink, Laurie A. "The Satire of Women Writers in *The Female Wits*." *Restoration* 8, no. 2 (Fall, 1984): 64-71.

Written anonymously around 1697, this unusual piece is a "rehearsal" play, in which three poetesses prepare a play very much like *The Royal Mischief*, by Mary De La Rivière Manley, a playwright and contemporary of Aphra Behn (the latter the first woman to make her living by her pen). Fink's article describes the play in some detail, noting that the goal of this and other satires on female artists is "laughing women from the stage . . . by reasserting the essential masculinity of art and of language." The play differs from the model for all "rehearsal" plays, *The Rehearsal* by George Villiers, Duke of Buckingham; it offends modern feminists because "the dramatist implies that female writing must fail because language, as a social construct and an artistic form, is foreign to women."

Five Restoration Comedies. Introduction by Brian Gibbons. London: A. & C. Black, 1984.
Includes *The Man of Mode*, *The Plain Dealer*, *Love for Love*, *The Provok'd Wife*, and *The Recruiting Officer*. Elaborate footnotes make this a valuable edition. Despite the absence of individual introductions, this work makes available the five most popular Restoration comedies of their time. A further reading list is also helpful.

Four Great Comedies of the Restoration and Eighteenth Century. Introduction by Brooks Atkinson. New York: Bantam Books, 1958.
William Wycherley's *The Country Wife* and William Congreve's *The Way of the World* are contrasted to the "sentimental, mawkish drama" of Oliver Goldsmith, and Richard Sheridan's *The School for Scandal* is described as "one more day of brilliance before an eclipse" of English comedy, in Atkinson's readable but biased introduction. The notes to these plays, at the end of the volume, make this a worthwhile pocket edition.

Freehafer, John. "The Formation of the London Patent Companies in 1660." *Theatre Notebook* 20, no. 1 (Autumn, 1965): 6-30.
What takes one or two sentences in theatre history textbooks is recounted here with exhausting detail: the initial formation of Thomas Killigrew's and William Davenant's companies, the King's Men and the Duke's Men respectively. The comprehensive history of those four months (July to November, 1660) is described here in what for this journal is a long article, offering names of original actors, legal and legislative actions surrounding the formation of the companies, the brief claim of the Rhodes company based on its activities during the interregnum, and myriad other pieces to a marvelously complex puzzle. A model of theatre scholarship.

Fujimura, Thomas H. *The Restoration Comedy of Wit*. New York: Barnes & Noble Books, 1952.
The first four chapters of this study are devoted to presenting a theory of wit: its nature, its intellectual background, its aesthetics. Fujimura discovers and identifies the Witless, the Witwoud, and the hero of Restoration comedy, the Truewit: "libertine, skeptical, naturalistic, more concerned with wit than with morality or 'manners.' " The final chapters apply the carefully wrought definition to three major playwrights, in an attempt to differentiate them through close reading. Very good bibliography (to 1951); index.

Gosse, Edmund, ed. *Restoration Plays from Dryden to Farquhar*. London: J. M. Dent & Sons, 1912, reprint 1922.

This assortment—one tragedy each by Dryden and Otway, and one seldom published comedy (Vanbrugh's *The Provok'd Wife*) with three others—is introduced by an essay summing up the opinions that the Restoration was an age less sober and more colorful than Gosse's own, and that the literature "is not lightly to be dismissed as in its nature absurd" because current audiences or readers are no longer morally in tune with it. The plays are modern, in that they were true, and "increased naturalness in writing or performing is always bitterly resisted at first."

Granville-Barker, Harley. "Wycherley and Dryden." In his *On Dramatic Method*. New York: Hill & Wang, 1956.
Noting the recent reediting and revaluing of Restoration drama, Granville-Barker applies his acerbic wit and cynical disposition to damning everything about the age: "I . . . make bold to say that this talk about the moral purpose of Restoration comedy is all stuff and nonsense, and the present claims made for the 'art' of it are not much better." Tragedy, wit, originality, plot, and character fare no better under Granville-Barker's gaze. Only *Aureng-Zebe* is spared, "a kind of play with a certain integrity of its own." An amazing example of negative criticism; as the author admits, "much in this chapter savours more of a speech for the prosecution than a judgment."

Harbage, Alfred. *Thomas Killigrew: Cavalier Dramatist*. Philadelphia: University of Pennsylvania Press, 1930.
Touching on Restoration drama's origins in the two-patent arrangement put in place by Charles II, this scholarly biography helps explain how the transition from the interregnum to the Restoration took place. As playwright in exile, Killigrew bridged the gap from Carolinian practices to the new professionalism of London's theatre scene under the new monarchy. Harbage defends Killigrew from charges that he used his playwriting to draw attention to his political accomplishments. Bibliography and index.

Harwood, John T. *Critics, Values, and Restoration Comedy*. Carbondale: Southern Illinois University Press, 1982.
By examining the critical biases of Restoration comedy's detractors and defenders, Harwood neutralizes with reason the often heated debate about the moral reprehensibility of the genre. Since the critical presuppositions of major Restoration critics color their observations, one can perceive the genre in its proper light only by noting the moral judgments inextricably embedded in the critical commentary. Criticism of criticism, its value lies in tempering the reader's admiration of others' arguments. Notes, selected bibliography, and index.

Hawkins, Harriett. *Likenesses of Truth in Elizabethan and Restoration Drama*. Oxford, England: Clarendon Press, 1972.

A primary dramatic concern is the degree to which the stage emulates and records life, and in this study "the presentation of self in everyday social life" is compared with its equivalent dramatic character depiction. *Love for Love*, *The Man of Mode*, and *The Way of the World* are discussed as models of the playwrights' ability to confront "our own illusions with their more accurate images of the tragic and comic ways of this world." Valuable for comparisons of Elizabethan with Restoration life. Index.

Heilman, Robert B. "Some Fops and Some Versions of Foppery." *ELH* 49, no. 2 (Summer, 1982): 363-395.
Beginning with a remarkable list of characters from 1660-1700 saddled with the term "fop" or "coxcomb," along with a brief description of their infinite variety, Heilman immediately makes his point: "Virtually anybody, it is clear, could be called fop or coxcomb" because the term is not a definition but an invective hurled almost at random, to mean "he is inferior to me, the speaker." From a central section dividing fops into types, the essay proceeds to display variations on the theme, concluding that "the fop is a quite unusual version of the outsider in whom some kind of truth or value not operative in the system is lodged." A remarkable study, wittily presented, full of insight and suggestion.

Holland, Norman N. *The First Modern Comedies: The Significance of Etherege, Wycherley, and Congreve.* Cambridge, Mass.: Harvard University Press, 1959.
A personal, well-conceived, and smoothly written discussion of Restoration comedy, starting with the ground rules and ending with a linguistic study of the conceits. Holland's inventive style of literary criticism is basically dialectic, comparing and contrasting pairs of characters, themes, images, and motives, toward a separation of "appearances" and "natural understanding." Very readable, on the subject of Restoration man's "new philosophy," the freedom it brought and the price paid for it.

Holland, Peter. *The Ornament of Action: Text and Performance in Restoration Comedy.* Cambridge, England: Cambridge University Press, 1979.
In the continuing defense of the dramatic text as performance recipe, Holland points to Restoration comedy as fertile ground for exploring the relation of the conventional form of play publication to the manner of performance. Beginning with the nature of performance in the Restoration and proceeding to the study of acting and staging, Holland concludes with specific readings of several plays, including William Wycherley's *The Plain Dealer*. Select bibliography, index, illustrations and three important appendices: thirty extant restoration promptbooks; casts for comedies, 1691-1693; and William Congreve's casts.

Hook, Lucyle. "Portraits of Elizabeth Barry and Anne Bracegirdle." *Theatre Notebook* 15, no. 4 (Summer, 1961): 129-137.

This article is valuable especially for its four plates: Sir Godfrey Kneller's portrait of William III, a detail of that portrait showing two women in the lower right-hand corner, a mezzotint of Anne Bracegirdle, and a portrait of Elizabeth Barry. Hook's article announces the discovery of the original paintings from which some unflattering copies were published in *The Biographical Mirrour*, heretofore the most widely known versions of these famous actresses. The tone of this piece demonstrates the affection that Restoration scholars have for their subject.

Hotson, Leslie. *The Commonwealth and Restoration Stage*. Cambridge, Mass.: Harvard University Press, 1928. Reprint. New York: Russell & Russell, 1968.
Presenting much new material from meticulous examination of obscure records, Hotson first argues for considerable theatre activity during the Commonwealth period, previously thought "a homogenous blank"; chapters on the Duke's Company, King's Company, United Company, and rivals take up the second half of this astute and scholarly detective work of five years' study. Provides an appendix of previously unexamined documents from the Public Record Office, an index, and sixteen illustrations.

Hume, Robert D. *The Development of English Drama in the Late Seventeenth Century*. Oxford, England: Clarendon Press, 1976.
Brings a new perspective to dramatic literary criticism. Lacking in previous studies, says Hume, is "any real sense of what defines this period . . . and how plays change over a span of nearly two generations. . . . My hope is to define these changes more precisely by examining a large number of plays with special attention to chronological sequence." This study requires a thorough knowledge of the plays from the reader. Indexes.

_____ . "The Nature of the Dorset Garden Theatre." *Theatre Notebook* 36, no. 3 (1982): 99-109.
An interesting debate regarding this theatre, built in 1671, about which very little is known. Hume is responding to several other scholars, who contend that it was built as an opera house and that it was essentially like the Drury Lane Theatre. Hume's approach is that of a scholar/detective, following the theatre's fortunes through its various periods—the formation of the United Company, Christopher Rich's management, even a period when the theatre was the home of weightlifters and lotteries—and gathering detailed evidence of stage size, repertory, and other data. Through Hume's endnotes, a student could retrace the steps of the argument back to its origins, with Edward A. Langhans' reconstruction in 1972.

_____ . *The Rakish Stage: Studies in English Drama, 1600-1800*. Carbondale: Southern Illinois University Press, 1983.

Largely a collection of essays published in journals over a ten-year period, some generic studies, some critical analysis, others contextual studies. The opening essay, "Content and Meaning in the Drama," outlines three kinds of content in drama of this period: commonplace, general ideology, and real-life specifics. Topics range from far-reaching "ideas" to close readings of Nathaniel Lee's *The Princess of Cleves*; a detailed appendix helps access the work.

——————— . "The Sponsorship of Opera in London, 1704-1720." *Modern Philology* 85, no. 4 (May, 1988): 420-432.
Slightly to one side of the present bibliography but justified by the free exchange of theatrical innovation in this period, and by Hume's preliminary review of the 1660-1704 opera practices of the patent theater companies. An information-packed piece, with an analysis of John Vanbrugh's motives in "intriguing to negotiate a separation of genres," a tactic Hume considers to have been "folly": "Separating opera from the theater that had sponsored it so well made no sense." Reason enough for joining them again here.

Hume, Robert D., ed. *The London Theatre World, 1660-1800*. Carbondale: Southern Illinois University Press, 1980.
A collection of essays in honor of A. H. Scouten by his colleagues in English theatre history, discussing in considerable detail the features of company management, scenery, promptbooks, performers, repertory, music, audience, politics, censorship, and publication during the 120-year period during and after the Restoration. The thirty-seven illustrations demonstrate the range and detail of the book's scope, including four views of the Drury Lane Theatre from 1674 to 1795 and the elaborate machinery for the operation of a drop curtain and descending clouds. This work is central to the study of Restoration theatre and drama. Edward A. Langhans contributes a bibliography on theatre architecture. Index.

Jackson, Allan S. "Restoration Scenery, 1656-1680." *Restoration and Eighteenth Century Theatre Research* 3, no. 2 (November, 1964): 25-38.
A more detailed look at the introduction into England of Italianate scene design, with five interesting illustrations accompanying this "study of the 'look' of stage scenery in the English Restoration." Divides scenery into *practicals*, *profile pieces*, *set props* (heavy and light), and *relieve scenes*, with examples of each; contrary to popular assumption, the actors used, climbed upon, and otherwise manipulated the scenery. Jackson also lists sources of information on scenic design, such as printed plays, promptbook material, diaries, and travelers' accounts. Full of fascinating information; a must for students of the design/technology history of the theatre and for period directors.

James, E. Nelson. " 'Drums and Trumpets.' " *Restoration and Eighteenth Century Theatre Research* 9, no. 2 (November, 1970): 46-55. Continued in 10, no. 1 (May, 1971): 54-57.

By listing and examining the battle scenes in heroic plays, often set off by stage directions to the prompter for battle effects, Nelson supports some previous notions that the heroic plays are not really centered on the military combat but on the love-combats precipitating and precipitated by the battles themselves. Moreover, some heroic plays have no battles whatsoever, others merely report offstage skirmishes, and still others limit battle action to one scene or act (particularly valuable is James's list of Restoration plays with exciting onstage swordplay, many of them obscure and forgotten). Seven remaining plays, however, call for "spectacular battle scenes." Of interest to film producers, as well as students of Restoration theatre.

Jantz, Ursula. *Targets of Satire in the Comedies of Etherege, Wycherley, and Congreve*. Salzburg, Austria: Institut für Englische Sprache und Literatur, 1978.

A methodical extraction of the subjects of satire in three major playwrights, the study finds that Hyprocrisy (in at least five manifestations), Affectation, and Materialism were most often attacked. More specifically, marriage, women, religiosity, literary pretenders, country manners, and the court shared the criticism of the wits on stage and off. Unlike most scholars of Restoration satire, Jantz examines as well the theoretical stance as mirrored in the poetry of the age. A thorough bibliography accompanies this published dissertation.

Jenkins, Annibel. *Nicholas Rowe*. Boston: Twayne, 1977.

There is much good to be said of the Twayne critical biographies, which bring facts to hand and offer clear analysis of each work in context. Information is organized in the form of chronologies, bibliographies, and index. There are chapters on seven of Rowe's works, and Jenkins concludes that he was "a man and writer of his time [who] did not require that the theatre be separated from the political and moral issues of their day." Emphasis is on the roles of women and their participation in government, society, and the family. Important for a comparison of changing ideas about women in the twentieth century.

Jordan, R. "Observations on the Backstage Area in the Restoration Theatre." *Theatre Notebook* 38, no. 2 (1984): 66-68.

A quarrel in the playhouse backstage area, which resulted in the death of a Captain Goring, serves modern scholars with some clues to the arrangements of stairs, dressing rooms, and wings of the typical Restoration theatre (no one is even sure in which theatre the sword fight took place). Most remarkable is the limited information available to modern scholars that would allow them to piece together the puzzle of theatre architecture, a puzzle destroyed by fire, neglect, and time itself.

Kenny, Shirley Strum. "Perennial Favorites: Congreve, Vanbrugh, Cibber, Farquhar, and Steele." *Modern Philology*, supp. 73, no. 4, part 2 (May, 1976): S4-S11.
A checklist of the most popular playwrights of the Restoration, as they continued to be produced and appreciated into the last quarter of the eighteenth century. The statistics, which reveal such facts as "twenty of the twenty-eight comedies were performed virtually by one company of actors," also become important "when one evaluates the plays' influence on later writers." Finally, this study tells more about the century of their revivals than about the century in which they were generated: They became "so much a part of the cultural milieu that they became embedded in the memories of educated men."

_____ . "The Play House and the Printing Shop: Editing Restoration and Eighteenth-Century Plays." *Modern Philology* 85, no. 4 (May, 1988): 408-419.
This article asks a series of questions about printing practices in this period, especially as applied to the common transformation of stage material into the printed page: What was the original function? Why were they republished? What were the common practices of author, printer, bookseller? What are some common assumptions of modern readers? Clearly in the camp of scholars insisting on contextual examination, not isolated literary analysis, Kenny believes readers of the original printed versions were trying to recapture the stage experience, not reading the texts as pure literature. Some interesting opinions on modern pedagogy for this period as well.

Kronenberger, Louis. *The Thread of Laughter: Chapters on English Stage Comedy from Jonson to Maugham*. New York: Alfred A. Knopf, 1952.
Heavily evaluative, with a personable style, steeped in erudition but without the burden of scholarly apparatus and citation, this survey (rather than a synthesis) of comedy was generated from courses taught at Columbia and Brandeis; eight chapters deal with Restoration plays and playwrights. Kronenberger treats Aphra Behn ("the first Englishwoman to earn a living by her pen") and Colley Cibber (who "found a way to reconcile virtue with spice"), along with other bright lights of the age. The writing style reflects the text's classroom origins, with entertaining, cleverly worded anecdotes throughout. Includes a brief "index of persons."

Krutch, Joseph Wood. *Comedy and Conscience After the Restoration*. New York: Columbia University Press, 1924, reprint 1949.
While the genius of the writers gets the credit for the brilliance of the plays of the Restoration, "the perversity of their tone must be charged to the spirit of the age." More than a literary evolution, the stage changes during this period reflect a change in social consciousness from Charles II down. Nine chapters combine scholarship in the plays with social criticism of the age. A new index joins an old bibliography in the reprint, but Professor G. S. Alleman adds a list of more modern works in an appendix.

Langbaine, Gerard. *An Account of the English Dramatick Poets*. Preface by Arthur Freeman. New York: Garland, 1973 [1691].

An excellent example from the invaluable Garland series, *The English Stage: Attack and Defense, 1577-1730*, "a collection of ninety important works reprinted in photo-facsimile in fifty volumes." This biographical dictionary lists in alphabetical order virtually every dramatic figure of the period, and served as the basis for a whole new area of study, English theatre history. Freeman cites its value "as a source for otherwise lost traditional information, and as a classic of seventeenth-century literary criticism."

Langhans, Edward A. "The Dorset Garden Theatre in Pictures." *Theatre Survey* 6, no. 2 (November, 1965): 134-146.

Collected here are twenty illustrations of the Dorset Garden Theatre from many sources, with Langhans' notes and observations on what the pictures reveal about the theatre. From sketchy plans to elaborate engravings, the illustrations show the interior (with settings from Elkanah Settle's *The Empress of Morocco*, 1673) and the exterior, with two conjectural rear and aerial views. A companion piece to the Langhans' article in the November, 1966, issue of *Theatre Survey* (see below), on the Bridges Street and Drury Lane theatres.

_____ . "New Restoration Theatre Accounts, 1682-1692." *Theatre Notebook* 17, no. 4 (Summer, 1963): 118-134.

The amount of information a theatre scholar can glean from payment lists, warrants, and similar bookkeeping records is astounding, and no better example can be found than this meticulous rendering of theatre fact from column after column of pounds and pence. From the payment sheets to Thomas Betterton, Langhans derives information about playing dates and theatre occupancies that take up more than half of this remarkable report. Students of Restoration theatre can learn much about scholarly methods from this example.

_____ . "Pictorial Material on the Bridges Street and Drury Lane Theatres." *Theatre Survey* 7, no. 2 (November, 1966): 80-100.

Reproduced here in eighteen illustrations is all the visual evidence available to reconstruct the architectural features of this famous theatre (the Bridges Street Theatre, destroyed by fire in 1672, stood on the same plot as the Drury Lane Theatre). Drawings by Christopher Wren, the architect, along with London maps showing the area and a famous illustration of an actor on a donkey on the Drury Lane stage, are reexamined for new discoveries, reported in this companion article to the Dorset Garden Theatre article listed above. From this meager collection, Langhans draws several conclusions, bringing Restoration theatre history scholars one step closer to understanding this difficult period.

_____ . *Restoration Promptbooks*. Carbondale: Southern Illinois University Press, 1981.

These unique documents, like clues to a detective, offer tantalizing glimpses of what the theatrical experience might have been backstage. Facsimiles of twelve promptbooks plus fragments of others (unfortunately none from famous productions) are accompanied by twenty illustrations; the introductory material includes lists of acting companies and discussion of playhouse, prompter, actors, and promptbook symbols and signals. Six appendices, bibliography, and index.

Langhans, Edward A., ed. *Five Restoration Theatrical Adaptations.* New York: Garland, 1980.

The flavor of the original quartos, as well as the sense of freedom with which writers adapted earlier work, can be enjoyed in this facsimile reproduction of five texts from the last quarter of the seventeenth century. A brief introduction by Langhans details some of the borrowings; his final remark sums up the age itself: "There is not much literary merit in these five works, perhaps, but they may well give us a more accurate picture of Restoration taste" than do the era's masterpieces.

Le Gallienne, Richard, ed. *Passages from the Diary of Samuel Pepys.* New York: Modern Library, n.d.

A lay reader's sampling of Pepys's diaries, from which much modern knowledge about Restoration theatre has been gleaned. Pepys's subjective sense of theatre and his personal acquaintance with the courtiers and actors keep his entries from being dull. Le Gallienne's introduction cites Pepys's "interest in himself" and his childlike interest in "the people about him and the things that are happening to everybody, all the time, to his nation as well as to his acquaintance." Unfortunately without notes or index.

Loftis, John. "Background: The Political Themes of Restoration Drama." In his *The Politics of Drama in Augustan England.* Oxford, England: Clarendon Press, 1963.

A preparatory chapter on a study of eighteenth century politics and drama, this overview divides the Tory and Whig factions, and their not-always-comparable Royalist and Parliamentarian counterparts, into a fairly understandable group of combatants. More valuably, the divisive nature of the theatre houses at the time is explained partly by the political climate. The upheavals from Charles II's death to the accession of William III saw John Dryden's important dramas on the stage, as well as the series of unions, separations, complaints, and repatenting of the theatre houses that mark this chaotic but interesting period of adjustment.

Loftis, John, ed. *Restoration Drama: Modern Essays in Criticism.* New York: Oxford University Press, 1966.

By collecting these essays under one cover, Loftis provides a chronological overview of the revival of interest in Restoration drama, beginning with L. C. Knights's attack on Restoration comedy: "The criticism that defenders of Restoration comedy need to answer is not that the comedies are 'immoral' but that they are trivial, gross and dull." Moving through the Restoration period from George Etherege to Thomas Shadwell, the essays also chronicle the period's growth, maturation, and old age.

Loftis, John, Richard Southern, Marion Jones, and A. H. Scouten. *The Revels History of Drama in English*. Vol. 5, *1660-1750*. London: Methuen, 1976.
A chronological table lists dates, historical events, theatrical events, nondramatic literary events, birth and death dates of nondramatic writers, dates of notable plays, birth and death dates of playwrights, and theatrical events on the Continent. The text is divided into social and literary context, theatres and actors, plays and playwrights. Part 3 is further divided into the emergence and development of Restoration comedy, the later comic dramatists, comic dramatists of the Augustan Age, farce and burlesque traditions, and tragedy. An essential and comprehensive survey of all British theatre, volume 5 helps explain the almost seamless joining of Restoration to sentimental drama. Illustrated with thirty-five plates.

The London Stage, 1660-1800. Edited by William Van Lennep, Emmett L. Avery, Arthur H. Scouten, George Winchester Stone, Jr., and Charles Beecher Hogan. Carbondale: Southern Illinois University Press, 1965.
A massive, eleven-volume calendar of performances. It took thirty-five years to assemble these 8,026 pages of information, with an extensive introduction and twenty-five illustrations. The first two parts (1660-1729) deal with the Restoration, listing every performance of every play by date, with cast (where known), theatre, and other pertinent information. Central to all subsequent Restoration scholarship. Index, but see Ben Ross Schneider's *Index to "The London Stage*," cited below.

Lynch, Kathleen M. *Jacob Tonson, Kit-Cat Publisher*. Knoxville: University of Tennessee Press, 1971.
A biography of the "Prince of Publishers," who, as a friend to John Dryden and the other wits and authors of the period, published many of the dramatic and literary works of the Restoration and early eighteenth century, notably those of Dryden, and William Congreve, and Alexander Pope. A valuable study for linking the stage with the publishing craft and for understanding how the circle of intellectuals at the Kit-Cat Club influenced literary and theatrical history. Lynch refers to Tonson's association with Dryden as "the bedrock of Tonson's publishing career," and also notes that Jeremy Collier's wrath extended to Congreve's publisher. Notes, bibliography, and index.

_____ . *The Social Mode of Restoration Comedy*. New York: Macmillan, 1926.

An introductory chapter outlines the main forces engaged in the battle of Restoration origins (Molière versus pre-interregnum English comedy); Lynch argues for the latter, citing among her arguments the strong *précieuse* tradition, which, "in the reign of Charles I, denied a favorable expression in dramatic literature, was diffused through other channels." After "a few years of transitional experiment," the tradition returned to the stage in the form of the comedy of manners. George Etherege and William Congreve are treated in separate chapters. Bibliography and index.

_____ . "Thomas D'Urfey's Contribution to Sentimental Comedy." *Philological Quarterly* 9, no. 3 (July, 1930): 249-259.

A fairly early study of one of the lesser lights of the Restoration period, important for its observations regarding the sentimental aspects in his twenty comedies, anticipating Colley Cibber and Richard Steele. D'Urfey, as early as 1679 (in *The Virtuous Wife*), inserted into his work "the sentimental heroine in some of her most characteristic poses," one of which is expressing "the gravity of her predicament, which she can never afford to laugh over." An interesting article, somewhat before the unfortunate reduction of the number of "important" playwrights of the period to merely three or four.

McAfee, Helen. *Pepys on the Restoration Stage*. New York: Benjamin Blom, 1916.

Samuel Pepys was a prolific journal writer and an inveterate theatergoer in the late seventeenth century; this volume separates his observations on Restoration theatre from the clutter of general observations. An index of names and titles brings the reader straight to Pepys's comments on specific productions. A long chapter on Pepys's relation to Restoration theatre and an introductory review of critical responses to Pepys help make this edition valuable.

McCollum, John I., ed. *The Restoration Stage*. Boston: Houghton Mifflin, 1961.

A collection of central documentary material for the study of Restoration drama, gathered under one cover for convenience and efficiency. Part of a series of such documentary collections, this guide makes selections on the basis of most frequently cited material and includes Jeremy Collier's famous *A Short View of the Immorality and Profaneness of the English Stage*, several letters and prefaces of John Dryden, and the Shadwell prefaces, prologues, and epilogues that continued the moral debate onto the pages of the published plays themselves. Valuable in assessing the contemporary attitudes of the educated toward the stage literature. McCollum supplies the original pagination for accurate citation and reference. Provides a preface and a handlist of Restoration plays and playwrights.

McDonald, Margaret Lamb. *The Independent Woman in the Restoration Comedy of Manners.* Salzburg, Austria: Institut für Englische Sprache und Literatur, 1976.
One of the most fruitful areas of inquiry in Restoration drama is the emergence of new attitudes toward femininity and the status of women in society. McDonald outlines the evolution of the comic heroine, who becomes more complex in her motivations and personality, demonstrating more "will" and less subservience to men; the witty heroine, a learned lady, who emerged after 1670; the emancipated woman, possibly a positive result of the dark-willed and aggressive ladies of Jacobean tragedy; and the sentimental woman, ruled by heart and not head, who lost some of the perspicuity and intelligence of earlier heroines. The best kind of feminist criticism, it offers many possibilities for comparisons with contemporary attitudes.

MacMillan, Dougald, and Howard Mumford Jones, eds. *Plays of the Restoration and Eighteenth Century*. New York: Holt, Rinehart and Winston, 1931, reprint 1959.
An anthology of plays, thirteen of which fall into the Restoration period, modernized for the lay reader. No introduction to the general subject, but a short commentary accompanies each play. This edition is valuable for the variety of plays offered and for the occasional footnotes.

McMillin, Scott, ed. *Restoration and Eighteenth-Century Comedy*. New York: W. W. Norton, 1973.
Besides the five play texts (*The Country Wife*, *The Man of Mode*, *The Way of the World*, *The Conscious Lovers*, and *The School for Scandal*), all well glossed, this edition offers background material on wit, the Collier controversy, the debate of Richard Steele and John Dennis on *The Man of Mode*, stages, actors, and audiences. A section on critical approaches from Charles Lamb to Louis Kronenberger completes this excellent volume, a strong introductory survey of the major themes and ideas of critical scholarship in this period. Selected bibliography.

Markley, Robert. *Two-Edg'd Weapons: Style and Ideology in the Comedies of Etherege, Wycherley, and Congreve*. Oxford, England: Clarendon Press, 1988.
In an attempt to define and describe the interaction of the admittedly problematic terms "style" and "ideology," as applied to specific Restoration plays and playwrights, Markley introduces the idea of "a *dialogics* of style, a cultural poetics of theatrical representation." Two chapters introducing the terms are followed by a chapter each on John Dryden (and "the Comick stile"), George Etherege (on ironies of wit), William Wycherley (a study of his language), and William Congreve (and *his* comic style). A complex study requiring familiarity with stylistic approaches to dramatic analysis. Bibliography and index.

Marshall, Geoffrey. *Restoration Serious Drama.* Norman: University of Oklahoma
Press, 1975.
Tackling the more difficult areas of Restoration drama, in which "laughter and
amusement are not their primary aim," Marshall argues that the playwrights
were no less sensitive than their modern critics but were writing plays the way
"all who understand poetry" would write them. Marshall returns scholarship
to the century where the works were created, removing as best he can the
prejudices of critics who are "patronizing, impatient and judgmental." While
the *manner* seems alien because of the distance between Restoration standards
of decorum and those of the modern age, the matter of serious drama has
always been substantial and universal. Marshall attempts a diagram of "stress"
in the drama to show "neatness" or symmetry and thereby craft, but he admits
his inability to reveal the true artistry of the plays by this method.

Martin, Lee J. "From Forestage to Proscenium: A Study of Restoration Staging
Techniques." *Theatre Survey* 4 (1963): 3-28.
This journal, published by the American Society for Theatre Research, special-
izes in theatrical scholarship as opposed to scholarship in dramatic literature:
the physical space, actors' lives, technical innovations, managerial and budge-
tary information, and the like. Martin's article, for example, discusses how new
understandings of the forestage and its eventual retreat inside the proscenium
arch can be gleaned from a scrutiny of script stage directions, lists of settings,
sequence of acts, and other internal clues. In return, the critic of the drama can
better comprehend the dramatic structure of Restoration plays by seeing how
the machinery worked to the playwright's advantage. An excellent study, with
considerable application for anticipated revivals.

Mignon, Elisabeth. *Crabbed Age and Youth: The Old Men and Women in the
Restoration Comedy of Manners*. Durham, N.C.: Duke University Press, 1947.
Mignon's purpose is "to trace the conventions of a dramatic form, as they are
reflected through a single and highly important group." Characters in advanced
years often represent a discarded set of beliefs, but the rigid structure of
comedy also dictates an attitude of youthful exclusivity in the circle of wit. The
interfering "would-be's," servants, and country fools are "consistently the
target for verbal and physical abuse." Six chapters on eight playwrights, with a
postscript on sentimental comedy. Index.

Miles, Dudley Howe. *The Influence of Molière on Restoration Comedy*. New York:
Columbia University Press, 1909.
Originally a doctoral dissertation, this study reviews Molière's accomplishment
in France, then looks into the borrowings of Restoration comedy in a series of
chapters using Aristotle's categories (plot, character, dialogue) as an ordering
device. Concludes that the spirit of the age determined Restoration comedy's

form, "but the fact remains that the peculiar variety . . . owed a good deal to Molière." Appendix of specific indebtedness; two bibliographies and an index.

Milhous, Judith. *Thomas Betterton and the Management of Lincoln's Inn Fields, 1695-1708*. Carbondale: Southern Illinois University Press, 1979.
A complete and scholarly (but readable) "biography" of a theatre, a company, and a vitally active manager/artist, whose contributions to Restoration theatre include the first successful rebellion by actors against exploitive producers. From the explanation of the patent situation in 1660, through the description of the controversial years at the rival theatre, to the summary of the Union of 1708 (which, Milhous warns, "by no means should . . . be considered a parallel to that of 1682"), this study calmly and thoroughly unravels the complexities of the age. Appendices, notes, and index.

Milhous, Judith, and Robert D. Hume. "Manuscript Casts for Revivals of Three Plays by Shirley in the 1660s." *Theatre Notebook* 39, no. 1 (1985): 32-36.
One of the most persistent misunderstandings regarding Restoration theatre is the degree of borrowing from pre-interregnum sources. Here, three James Shirley plays revived by the King's Company are found to have been cast oddly, possibly due to the murder of one of the actors in 1664. Hidden among the small details of this short piece are several clues to how theatre worked during the period: Casting preferences, available performance dates, alterations to accommodate unexpected departures, and other practicalities are considered. An excellent example of theatre-history detective work by two acknowledged masters.

_____ . *Producible Interpretation: Eight English Plays, 1675-1707*. Carbondale: Southern Illinois University Press, 1985.
A curative for the purely literary approaches of most Restoration dramatic criticism, this is a study of how the plays "play." The concept of "producible interpretation" is simply explained, in part 1, as "a critical reading that a director could communicate to an audience in performance." The methodology outlined is clear, intelligent, and adaptable, presented through tables and charts and demonstrated with William Wycherley's *The Plain Dealer* as a model. Part 2 gives applied analysis to eight plays, three of them (*The Spanish Friar*, *Amphitryon*, and *The Wives Excuse*) rarely given critical attention. A model for all subsequent scholarship. Illustrations, index, and an appendix outlining the use of music in the plays.

Miner, Earl, ed. *Restoration Dramatists: A Collection of Critical Essays*. Englewood Cliffs, N.J.: Prentice-Hall, 1966.
Collected from literary journals from 1940 through 1965, this work gives ready-to-hand some more specific examinations of diverse Restoration work.

From Arthur Kirsch's essay on *Aureng-Zebe* to Thomas Fujimura's study of William Congreve, these essays demonstrate the care and attention to detail required to extract the qualities of these dramas from their superficially complex and prolix texts. An introductory essay reminds the reader that theatre is "a representation of reality to be judged by the shared experiences of normal human beings."

Moore, Cecil A. Introduction to *Twelve Famous Plays of the Restoration and Eighteenth Century*. New York: Modern Library, 1933.
Seven of these plays are Restoration dramas and required a peculiar set of social circumstances in order to exist. The moral questions and their contemporary debate in pamphlets and on the stage, during a time "when wit was its own apology for being," are reviewed briefly. George Etherege and William Wycherley were at work at the right time, but William Congreve and John Vanbrugh "had the misfortune to be born an age too late. When called to account, they had no choice of weapon."

Mudrick, Marvin. "Restoration Comedy and Later." In *English Stage Comedy*, edited by W. K. Wimsatt, Jr. New York: Columbia University Press, 1955.
Defends Restoration comedy against its detractors, noting that Restoration drama shares with Elizabethan drama the distinction of dominating its own age. The superiority of one comic form over the other is entirely arguable, with William Wycherley and William Congreve holding their own against Ben Jonson and John Fletcher. In the "frank age" of Nell Gwyn and the Duchess of Cleveland, the "last English audience," an accomplished one "for whom manners were graces, and wit an exercise of the mind upon things in the world," was very well entertained by its dramatic poets.

Muir, Kenneth. *The Comedy of Manners*. London: Hutchinson University Library, 1970.
A chapter-by-chapter study of nine major Restoration comic dramatists is introduced by a substantive essay describing and defending the titular distinction, including "those plays written in the eighteenth century which were an attempt to capture something of its spirit" and a concluding essay that reminds the reader that "all comedy has a Saturnalian element." Contrasts pre-Restoration to Restoration conditions in London theatre, then chronicles the changes from Charles II to the public reaction against "indecency" in *The Spectator* of 1711, noting changes in moral tone "whether because of middle-class pressure, or exhaustion, or rationality." Heavily cited in subsequent scholarship. Bibliography and index.

Mullin, Donald C. "The Queen's Theatre, Haymarket: Vanbrugh's Opera House." *Theatre Survey* 8, no. 2 (November, 1967): 84-105.

A brief history of the design and construction of the Queen's Theatre, Haymarket (not the Haymarket Theatre made famous by Samuel Foote), a joint venture of William Congreve as manager, Sir John Vanbrugh as architect, and Thomas Betterton the actor. Built slightly past the height of Restoration drama (1704-1705) and designed for plays suited to the Society for the Reformation of Manners (Queen Anne), rather than the rakish tastes of Charles II, the Queen's Theatre flourished throughout the eighteenth century as an opera house, considered too big for legitimate theatrical fare. It burned in 1789. Four illustrations.

Nettleton, George H., and Arthur E. Case, eds. *British Dramatists from Dryden to Sheridan*. Revised by George Winchester Stone, Jr. Boston: Houghton Mifflin, 1969.
A collection of plays from several genres, from 1660 to 1780, ten of which can be classified as Restoration plays. In addition to a prefatory essay on each dramatic type (including heroic drama, Restoration tragedy, and the comedy of manners), each play receives a short but informative introduction; a brief review of the Restoration playhouse opens the volume. Textual notes and a select bibliography top off this valuable anthology.

Nicoll, Allardyce. *The Development of the Theatre: A Study of Theatrical Art from the Beginnings to the Present Day*. New York: Harcourt, Brace & Co., 1927.
Chapter 9 deals with the architecture and stage practices of the Restoration theatres, beginning with a recapitulation of available theatres on Charles II's return, from the Red Bull to the new Theatre Royal in Drury Lane opened in 1674. Excellent illustrations of plans for changing scenery, proscenium designs, graphic designs for shutters and backcloths, and section drawings of Whitehall. Christopher Wren's plans for Drury Lane and several settings for specific plays are reproduced here. An essential source for understanding the design of Restoration theatres.

——————— . *A History of Restoration Drama 1660-1700*. Cambridge, England: Cambridge University Press, 1923.
Part of a comprehensive study of English drama, this volume has become an indispensable source, demonstrating an impressive depth of understanding and a rich writing style in the text, unencumbered by apparatus but buttressed by the authority of the elaborate footnotes. The authoritative appendices serve as a checklist for studies of the playhouses, the documents of the history of the stage, and extant plays either published or in manuscript. The cutoff date of 1700 (Farquhar's early work is cited but not his post-1700 work) is disputable, but Nicoll's erudition is not. Provides a hand-list of Restoration plays and an index.

Orrell, John. "A New Witness of the Restoration Stage, 1660-1669." *Theatre Research International*, n.s. 2, no. 1 (October, 1976): 16-28.

Theatre historians are indebted to the diaries of Samuel Pepys and have drained all possible theatrical information from them. A welcome additional source is the diplomatic correspondence of Florentine agents in London from 1616 to 1680, notably from the Salvetti family, described and translated here for the first time. Genuinely interested in court theatre, the father and two sons noted plays, music, dances, and other entertainments, often providing details that help scholars reconstruct the theatrical practices of the Restoration. Orrell continues his report (1670-1680) in the next issue of the same journal, n.s. 2, no. 2 (February, 1977).

Oxenford, Lyn. *Playing Period Plays*. Illustrated by Bernice Carlill. London: J. Garnet Miller, 1958.

Part 3: "Restoration and Georgian Period," describes "the spirit of the plays" and outlines the silhouettes and movements of the costumes of the period; separate chapters on occupations, dances, and music are valuable to actors as well as costumers and historians. A final chapter offers practice scenes for the actor (one is Lord Foppington from *The Relapse*) and even a mime scene for learning Restoration movement with music and poetry. Forty-seven ink drawings (twelve in part 3) by Miller stress the silhouette and simple movements. Short index.

Palmer, John. *The Comedy of Manners*. London: G. Bell & Sons, 1913.

A pioneering attempt to fill what Palmer sees as a gap in English dramatic criticism. After briefly reviewing previous essays on disparate aspects of Restoration comedy, Palmer moves toward "an estimate of these men and their work, viewed in perspective with their period, measured by standards of morality and taste which they themselves would have accepted." Offers two chapters on George Etherege, one each on William Wycherley, William Congreve, John Vanbrugh, and George Farquhar, and a concluding chapter: "Responding to a genuine inspiration [the artist] will leave the moral result of his endeavours to look after itself." Illustrations, bibliography, and index. A major study, universally cited in subsequent scholarship.

Perry, Henry ten Eyck. *The Comic Spirit in Restoration Drama: Studies in the Comedy of Etherege, Wycherley, Congreve, Vanbrugh, and Farquhar*. New York: Russell & Russell, 1925, reprint 1962.

Because previous scholarship has been general, Perry analyzes "the comic theory and practice of the leading Restoration playwrights, with . . . a close study of the texts themselves." Five playwrights get a chapter each, bracketed by a chapter on dramatic comic theory and a chapter that places Restoration comedy in perspective relative to other literary times. Noting the Irish and

French influences, Perry wonders whether "the adroit touch of the Comic Spirit does not find itself at home in the theatre of tough-fibred Anglo-Saxons."

Persson, Agnes V. *Comic Character in Restoration Drama*. The Hague, Netherlands: Mouton, 1975.
The error of the ignorant is the "unexamined life." Comedy derived from the acting out of the consequences of deception, external or internal, and a "lack of awareness due to the inherent nature of the character" is at the base of Restoration comedy and a critical appreciation of it. This approach "enables the reader to explore the comic possibilities of ignorance in its endless variations." After her graceful discussion of the degrees and fields of Ignorance and Knowledge, Persson concludes that, since every literature is a product of its age, this approach "helps to illuminate the comic trends of a period, the comic style of a writer, and the make-up of a particular comedy."

Powell, Jocelyn. *Restoration Theatre Production*. London: Routledge & Kegan Paul, 1984.
Somewhere between literary criticism and theatre history, this is a study of the curious relationship between the staged play and its audience, producing "a kind of involved detachment that permeated the new dramatic forms the age created for itself." Moving through the subject in ten chapters (not always distinct in their topics), discussing the audience, the forms, the music, the characters, and the "changing times," Powell examines in detail four plays of the period. Extensive endnotes, select bibliography, and index; thirty-nine plates and twenty-two figures illustrate the text.

Pry, Kevin. "Theatrical Competition and the Rise of the Afterpiece Tradition, 1700-1724." *Theatre Notebook* 36, no. 1 (1982): 21-26.
The gradual development of the multiple theatrical experience, a notion assumed by earlier scholars, is called into question here, with a strong argument that afterpieces were the result of competition among the three theatres active in the first decade of the eighteenth century. This article is a good example of the use of statistics gathered from *The London Stage, 1660-1800* (see above) to revise previous impressions of the theatre scene. Pry concludes by listing the advantages of afterpieces, chief of which is that they could be produced by "in-house" talent, unlike outside expensive novelties.

Radaddi, Mongi. *Davenant's Adaptations of Shakespeare*. Uppsala, Sweden: Almqvist & Wiksell, 1979.
Slightly to one side of the mainstream study of Restoration drama, this essay demonstrates in scholarly detail the process whereby Shakespeare's work was adapted and redesigned to fit the Restoration stage and audience sensibilities.

William Davenant's work is journeyman-like at best, but the same principles prevailed when better poets, such as John Dryden, attempted to distribute the currency of Restoration life into the master's best-loved stories. Appendices list borrowings from Shakespeare's *The Tempest* for Davenant's *The Enchanted Island*. Bibliography and index.

Restoration and Eighteenth-Century Drama. Introduction by Arthur H. Scouten. New York: Macmillan, 1980.
In the series "Great Writers of the English Language," Scouten provides an introduction that sorts out the genres, influences, and transitional patterns of drama from 1660 to 1800, in three sections: 1660-1685 (the death of Charles II), 1685-1737 (the date of the Stage Licensing Act), and 1737-1800. Alphabetical by writer, the work consists of a brief biographical paragraph, a complete list of works (including poetry and prose), a bibliography, and a signed critical essay. Particularly valuable in tracing the gradual transition from Restoration to sentimental comedy, and as a quick reference for biographical information on each playwright.

Restoration Plays. Introduction by Brice Harris. New York: Modern Library, 1953.
An inexpensive sampler of the period's drama, offering eight plays, from George Villiers' *The Rehearsal* (1671) to George Farquhar's *The Beaux' Stratagem* (1707). While based on solid scholarship that returns to the original sources (excepting *The Rehearsal*), this edition does not include footnotes, glossary, or prefatory essays for each play and consequently requires support material. Harris' overview is helpful, organized around a description of genres, of which at least four are represented here.

Roper, Alan. "Language and Action in *The Way of the World*, *Love's Last Shift*, and *The Relapse.*" *ELH* 40, no. 1 (Spring, 1973): 44-69.
Speech discriminates and reconciles. Restoration plays are mostly talk, but talk filled with speech-acts, linguistic signatures, and "the congruence between the sayings and doings of characters," which Roper examines "to determine degrees of psychological probability, moral perception, and aesthetic wholeness" in the plays. Setting up a vocabulary for discussing such features as "language of virtue" (single) and "wit language" (double), the essay points to the best work of William Congreve, Colley Cibber, and John Vanbrugh to conclude that Cibber does not achieve the linguistic and aesthetic integrity, nor Vanbrugh the "wholeness of action and breadth of moral vision," of Congreve's winner and still champion.

Ross, Julian L. "Dramatist Versus Audience in the Early Eighteenth Century." *Philological Quarterly* 12, no. 1 (January, 1933): 73-81.
"Versus" is the operative word in the title of this study of the combative

relationship between the playwright and his or her public. The prologues and epilogues, ostensibly "to gain the favor of an audience," do not actually contain much "fulsome praise" of the recipients, or even "a sincere defense of the age." Rather, Ross finds the playwright criticizing the audience for poor taste, lamenting former times, when a more appreciative court attended the plays. The view is expressed fully in John Dennis' dedication to his play *The Comical Gallant*: A changing social and political world was to blame.

Salgado, Gamini. "The Restoration Theatre and Its Drama." In his *English Drama: A Critical Introduction.* New York: St. Martin's Press, 1980.
A general chapter introducing the topics of actors, audience, the nature of Restoration drama, and the genres of heroic drama ("Tragedy as Spectacle") and comedy. George Etherege, William Wycherley, and William Congreve get a closer look; John Vanbrugh and George Farquhar are in "the last phase." All portrayed "a world which is recognizably our own—sceptical, class-conscious, money-haunted, at once fascinated and repelled by the body's desires and imperfections." Valuable chronology, bibliography, and index.

Schlegel, Augustus William. Lecture 28 in *Courses of Lectures on Dramatic Art and Literature*. Translated by John Black. New York: AMS Press, 1965 [1846].
The famous German critic who lionized Shakespeare offered these lectures in Vienna; his analyses of tragedy and comedy have entered German letters as eloquent oration. This lecture treats the closing of the theatres, Charles II's revival of the stage, the depravity of the age, its best voices (John Dryden, Thomas Otway), and its transition into the period of Joseph Addison's *Cato*. "May Shakespeare find such worthy imitators as some of those whom Germany has to produce!"

Schneider, Ben Ross Jr. *The Ethos of Restoration Comedy*. Champaign: University of Illinois Press, 1971.
Schneider finds four pairs of elements in the ethical structures of Restoration plot and character: Generosity (defined as the quality of noble-mindedness appropriate to the high-born) rather than Meanness; Courage contrasted with Cowardice; Plain-Dealing versus Double-Dealing; and Love as opposed to Self-Love. The key to ethical evaluation, claims Schneider, is critical examination. His arguments explain the condemnation of Restoration drama based on superficial interpretation and its justification if the critic examines the ethical principles it really champions.

_____ . *Index to "The London Stage, 1660-1800."* Carbondale: Southern Illinois University Press, 1979.
This index to the comprehensive study *The London Stage, 1660-1800* (cited above) was computerized over a seven-year period. The effort (506,014 refer-

ences under 25,000 entries) gives future scholars access to all the data embedded in the massive calendar begun by William Van Lennep and completed by four others in 1965. Interpreting from these data, dozens of subsequent books and articles have examined even more closely the details of this busy theatrical period.

Scouten, A. H. "Notes Toward a History of Restoration Comedy." *Philological Quarterly* 45, no. 1 (January, 1966): 62-70.
One of the contributors to the Restoration volume of *The London Stage, 1660-1800* (see above), Scouten here rebuffs the notion that the comedy of manners appeared "all at once." He points out that there were at least two distinct periods to the genre, that it was by no means the only genre active in this period, and that it was not "the first new type of drama to appear upon the restoration of Charles II" (referring to topical political satire, musical drama, the Spanish romance, and the heroic play). While acknowledging the importance of George Etherege, Scouten also gives some credit for the development of the comedy of manners to Thomas Southerne (*The Wives Excuse*, 1691). The writer of the section on Restoration drama in the *Cambridge History of English Literature* "found . . . just what he was looking for—decadence."

Shafer, Yvonne Bonsall. "The Proviso Scene in Restoration Comedy." *Restoration and Eighteenth Century Theatre Research* 9, no. 1 (May, 1970): 1-10.
Separates out for close scrutiny the almost ubiquitous "proviso" scene, "a scene of wit combat between two lovers in which they establish conditions for marriage." Noting that these scenes take on a mock-legal structure (with major stipulations followed by minor articles), Shafer sees these scenes not only as cynicism but also "as a realistic appraisal of marriage and its pitfalls, and an attempt to establish conditions under which love might last." A dozen proviso scenes are identified, and the final scene from *The Way of the World* is held up as the pinnacle of excellence.

Shipley, John B. "The Authorship of *The Cornish Squire*." *Philological Quarterly* 47, no. 2 (April, 1968): 145-156.
The value of this article lies not so much in the details of the various claims to authorship of this play as in the illustration of the methodology for carrying out such inquiries, demonstrated here in a scholarly but creative fashion. Clearing a path through the jungle of pseudonyms, anonymity, false attributions, plagiarism, even signature forgeries, Shipley adds to his evaluation of the external evidence an examination of internal editing clues in the text itself. "Yet the very state of the . . . adaptation . . . would force anyone editing it to tinker, patch, improvise, and add." A model of scholarly detective work.

Silvette, Herbert. *The Doctor on Stage: Medicine and Medical Men in Seventeenth-Century England.* Edited by Francelia Butter. Knoxville: University of Tennessee Press, 1967.

By means of this cross-disciplinary comparison dealing with one character type and one occupation, Silvette draws a full picture of Restoration stage transformations of life into art, discussing how the stage reflects, distorts, exploits, and even instructs life. First published in short form in *Annals of Medical History*, the delightfully humorous but scholarly study argues that the playwright interprets science for the commoner: "It is chiefly in the dramatists' medical metaphors and allusions that the position of medicine in seventeenth century life may be sought and found." While more interested in what stage history can reveal about medicine than vice versa (chapters focus on uroscopy, phlebotomy, madness, ancient remedies and cures, physicians, and the pox), the study is a model of comparative literature. Thomas Shadwell's *The Virtuoso* (1676), on scientific quackery in the Royal Society, receives a close reading in a separate chapter.

Singh, Sarup. *Family Relationships in Shakespeare and the Restoration Comedy of Manners*. Delhi, India: Oxford University Press, 1983.
The massive topic is handled by dividing the family into three general chapters with two more chapters devoted to husband-wife relationships. The last chapter, on husband and wife matches and mismatches in Restoration comedies of manners, is particularly valuable, but Singh's remarks regarding the influence of Shakespeare's family units on William Congreve and others have some merit as well. The size of the subject overwhelms the scholar, whose attempts to say everything fall short but whose contribution is nevertheless considerable. Bibliography and index.

_____ . *The Theory of Drama in the Restoration Period*. Foreword by James Sutherland. Bombay, India: Orient Longmans, 1963.
With the exception of John Dryden's prefaces, modern scholars examining and evaluating Restoration drama seldom refer to the playwrights' own stated and deducible intentions. Using this deficiency as a focus, Singh examines the genres (tragedy, opera, tragicomedy, farce, and the comedy of manners), along with contemporary notions of poetic justice, rhyme, and the unities. Singh sees these theatre artists as the first generation who dared to examine their own achievements, a self-consciousness that paved the way for the Frenchification of dramatic form in the eighteenth century. Index.

Smith, John Harrington. *The Gay Couple in Restoration Comedy*. Cambridge, Mass.: Harvard University Press, 1948.
Despite all the critical attention to Restoration comedy, "the hero and heroine who manage their courtship action as if it were an amusing game . . . had not received the attention and the credit they deserved." Taking a chronological view of the changing forms of the gay couple—sometimes the gallants in the ascendant, sometimes the ladies, sometimes the couples united against their

detractors—Smith laments their decline after 1700 to make way for "the man and woman of sense." A healthy mix of scholarship and strong opinion.

Sorelius, Gunnar. *"The Giant Race Before the Flood": Pre-Restoration Drama on the Stage and in the Criticism of the Restoration.* Uppsala, Sweden: Almqvist & Wiksell, 1966.
By studying the drama that moved across the interregnum to fill the stages of the Restoration, Sorelius reveals the lasting theatrical qualities that can transfer from one age to another. A section on how repertories were constructed after 1660 is followed by chapters on comedy and tragedy, and a general chapter summarizing the evidence of the adaptations and what they can reveal about the age that successfully extracted "gold from oar [*sic*]." Bibliography and index.

Staves, Susan. "A Few Kind Words for the Fop." *Studies in English Literature 1500-1900* 22, no. 3 (Summer, 1982): 413-428.
Examines the historical phenomenon of the fop, not a theatrical invention but a constantly shifting attitude toward masculinity and its behaviors. As important as their dress is their sensibility— "Fops are delicate"—and it is a mistake to equate foppishness with homosexuality. Foppery came under attack in non-theatrical forms, such as pamphlets, as well, often "provoked by general moral considerations like disapprobation of vanity." Gradually transformed from the time of Charles II to William III, fops developed as "an early if imperfect attempt at the refinement, civility, and sensitivity most of us would now say are desirable masculine virtues." An interesting modern slant on a much maligned species.

_____ . *Players' Scepters: Fictions of Authority in the Restoration.* Lincoln: University of Nebraska Press, 1979.
Crimes against order, such as treason, heresy, blasphemy, bribery, and perjury, are crimes measured against a "fiction of authority." That authority can be based on religious and feudal myths (as in medieval times), secular democratic myths, words, or facts. By examining the Restoration stage's theatricalized attitude toward state, family, oaths/vows, and the laws of nature, the study follows the changes in the fiction of authority during the period as a whole.

Styan, J. L. *Restoration Comedy in Performance.* Cambridge, England: Cambridge University Press, 1986.
Part of a young breed of theatre criticism that treats the performance rather than merely the literature, this thorough and readable study addresses two questions: What properties made the comedy of the Restoration successful in its own day? and Why do we find it difficult to recapture those properties in ours? By dealing with each text and author as unique rather than derivative,

Styan shows how performances of Restoration comedy from its own time up to the present day are legitimate interpretations of the "celebration" of the age, but emphasizes that the simulated reconstruction of period comedy in its original playhouse, however difficult, must be attempted "if its demise is to be prevented." Fifty-two excellent illustrations, a selected bibliography, and an index.

Summers, Montague. *The Playhouse of Pepys*. New York: Macmillan, 1935.
The second volume (but independent of the first) of a long study of the period, this one concentrating on the years from Charles II's return to the combining of the two patents into the United Company in 1682 (Samuel Pepys actually abandoned his journal in 1669). In his typically thorough style, Summers presents exhausting details of the most minor playwrights, after a full chapter on such notables as Robert Stapylton, Richard Flecknoe, John Wilson, Abraham Cowley, and Thomas Porter. A general index and an index of plays help get into the difficult material. Twenty-four illustrations, many of them engravings of scenes from plays of the period.

_____ . *The Restoration Theatre*. London: Kegan Paul, Trench, Trübner, & Co., 1934.
The first of a two-volume study of the period (the second is listed above), this volume describes the details of theatre life, including practices of announcement and advertisement of plays, systems of admission, the nature of the audience, how the scenes changed, the degree of realism in design, and costume acquisition and practice. An appendix reprints a fascinating chapter from a deportment book (1674): "Instructions for a Young Gallant how to behave himself in the Play-house." As in the other volume, there are twenty-four illustrations, many representing scenes from the plays of the period. General and play indexes.

Taney, Retta M. *Restoration Revivals on the British Stage, 1944-1979: A Critical Survey*. Lanham, Md.: University Press of America, 1985.
A marvelous accompaniment to historical studies, this book describes modern adaptations of Restoration plays and enlightens the reader as to their topicality now. This is where production-oriented scholarship, such as the "producible interpretation" approach of Judith Milhous and Robert D. Hume (see above), finds its most fruitful application. In lieu of illustrations, careful descriptions of staging, cuts, and transitions of texts are noted. Each play's plot and background are described; then as many as five versions since 1944 are discussed. Several appendices, including cast lists.

Taylor, Ivan E. *Samuel Pepys*. New York: Twayne, 1967.
An informal report of the goings-on of the Restoration's great Puritan diarist,

Navy commissioner, bribe taker, womanizer, and theatergoer. Taylor attempts to "show the man in action as he lives his average days," careful to refer to the date of each activity for easy reference to Pepys's diary itself. The study is divided not chronologically but by special interest—family life, musical interests, theatre observations, reports of the coronation, and so forth—and is bracketed by a brief biography and an account of Pepys's life after abandoning his diary. Notes, bibliography, and index.

Thompson, James. "Lying and Dissembling in the Restoration." *Restoration* 6, no. 1 (Spring, 1982): 11-19.
An exploration of the changing definition of lying, particularly important in understanding this period "because role playing, disguise, dissimulation, and deceit are such important elements in the ethically muddy world of Restoration drama." The theory behind "the abuses of speech" comes from the courtesy literature of the seventeenth century, and Lying and Dissembling find themselves in company with Swearing, Blaspheming, Backbiting, Slandering, Mocking, Flattering, and several other faults in "a direction for the Government of the Tongue." Richard Steele's opinions on dissimulation (in *The Tatler*) and John Tillotson's view of "the value of closeness" join other documents in Thompson's interesting discussion.

Thorndike, Ashley H. "Manners and Wit, 1680-1700." In his *English Comedy*. New York: Macmillan, 1929.
As dependence on the Elizabethans decreased, new playwrights found their voices and their audiences. "The superiority of the English drama to the French was freely boasted by the very authors who filched from Molière." William Congreve, especially his *The Way of the World*, is dealt with at length, and John Vanbrugh is compared unfavorably to him. George Farquhar's *The Beaux' Stratagem* is outside these decades but brings the age to a close. Thorndike says of his characters: "All are gay and debonair, clever and witty, even the highwaymen and Scrub. No wonder they give Squire Sullen a headache, their Lichfield was no place for the spleen or the sullens."

――――――― . "The Restoration." In his *Tragedy*. Boston: Houghton Mifflin, 1908.
As Thorndike moves through the history of serious drama, the "sixteen years of closed theatres" is reported as unique in theatre history. Italian opera's influence was theatrical, not literary; France contributed "innovation in the poetry and art of the drama." Notes Elizabethan revivals, and briefly acknowledges the work of John Dryden, Nathaniel Lee, Thomas Otway, and others. A short but valuable bibliography of sources supplies a checklist of pre-twentieth century criticism.

_____ . "The Restoration, 1660-1680." In his *English Comedy*. New York: Macmillan, 1929.

A fairly early twentieth century view of the Restoration, warning against a hasty overemphasis on the hiatus of the Commonwealth. Grounded in a solid understanding of the audiences, the stages, and the *mise en scène* of Restoration London and filled with entertaining anecdotes of the court and the street, the overview puts Thomas Shadwell, George Etherege, John Dryden, and William Wycherley in focus but anticipates the next decades as bringing the early promises to fruition.

_____ . "The Return of Sentiment, 1700-1730." In his *English Comedy*. New York: Macmillan, 1929.

Not strictly Restoration comedy in Thorndike's view, the plays of this period turned on the sentiment called for by the change of heart in the audience. Richard Steele was a "leader in the effort for morality on the stage and one of the creators of sentimental comedy." Colley Cibber's contribution to the same causes was the "less ardent but scarcely less effective service of an astute playwright who understood his audience and his actors." Thorndike gives him more favorable critical attention (a full ten pages) than he receives at the hands of subsequent appraisers of Restoration and eighteenth century dramatic talent, as he does Susanna Centlivre, comparing her with Aphra Behn: "She is nearly as immoral, even less sentimental, and even more skilful in theatrical contrivance."

Traugott, John. "The Rake's Progress from Court to Comedy: A Study in Comic Form." *Studies in English Literature 1500-1900* 6, no. 3 (Summer, 1966): 381-407.

There is a dramaturgical problem with the rake: how to accommodate to the comic form the very "glass of fashion and mold of form" who is "handed all the rewards because he breaks all the moral codes." This study examines the problem and along the way treats the general written and unwritten rules of conduct for comic characters from Aristophanes' Pisthetaerus (in *The Birds*) to Charlie Chaplin. A strong example of using the Restoration traditions as a springboard for discussion of more universal areas of inquiry, here the nature of comedy itself.

Van Lennep, William. "The Death of the Red Bull." *Theatre Notebook* 16, no. 4 (Summer, 1962): 126-134.

The Red Bull was one of the last outdoor theatres to survive the Puritan ban on stage acting; round and open-topped, it resembled Shakespeare's Globe, long since destroyed. It had been occupied sporadically by "The Gentlemen Actors of the Red Bull, usually called the Old Actors or the Mohun Company after their leading actor at the Restoration." By 1662 it was mostly used for bear-baiting, bull-baiting, and fencing matches. London maps of 1665 no longer show the Red Bull; it "had enjoyed a few months of glory at the Restoration . . . but it was doomed to die. Its audiences . . . wanted new theatres, built very differently." A graceful obituary by a dear friend.

——————— . "Plays on the English Stage, 1669-1672." *Theatre Notebook* 16, no. 1 (Autumn, 1961): 12-20.
Working from previously unpublished, even uncataloged, documents in the Harvard Theatre Collection, Van Lennep offers this addendum to Allardyce Nicoll's 1952 publication of his Restoration play lists. The primary documents are warrants by the Lord Chamberlain, authorizing payment to the Duke of York's players for plays enacted during the period. Two reproductions of the warrants themselves accompany the article; taken together with the carefully worded article, they offer a rare insight into the methodical mind of this eminent scholar of primary theatre research.

Vernon, P. F. "Marriage of Convenience and the Moral Code of Restoration Comedy." *Essays in Criticism* 12, no. 4 (October, 1962): 370-387.
A further defense of Restoration comedy (against the accusations of L. C. Knights), this essay finds that Restoration comedy refuses "to settle down into [Knights's] categories of trivial, gross . . . and dull." Specifically, the Restoration period's increased attention to property ownership caused an unhappy acceleration of marriages of convenience, causing in turn the legitimate attacks from the stage against such unnatural liaisons. What appears to the superficial reader as disdain for the institution of marriage was in fact a strong statement of support for marriage based on true love rather than economic expediency: "Money came first in real life; love always triumphed on the stage."

Visser, Colin. "The Killigrew Folio: Private Playhouses and the Restoration Stage." *Theatre Survey* 19, no. 2 (November, 1978): 119-138.
One surviving copy of Thomas Killigrew's folio of plays (1664) contains his own emendations for adaptation from private playhouses (pre-Restoration) to the Restoration stage. Previous scholars assumed that the new scenographic elements—proscenium, Italianate scene changes, and the like—demanded considerable alteration, but Visser details an opposing argument, that the plays transformed quite easily to the new stage format and that "the Restoration stage . . . was greatly indebted to the stage of the earlier Caroline private playhouse." Evidence for a more gradual, less revolutionary transition from Caroline to Restoration theatre, this article is a model of scholarly deduction.

Wain, John. "Restoration Comedy and Its Modern Critics." *Essays in Criticism* 6, no. 4 (October, 1956): 367-385.
A kind of counterattack aimed at the first defenders of Restoration comedy

(see, for example, Thomas Fujimura's work, cited above), this heavily rhetorical article generated great waves of response in subsequent journal issues. It made no attempts at sober neutrality ("I say 'immoral' because this comedy is one of the symptoms of a sick society, and one of the things that society was sick of, naturally, was too much morality"), but rather threw down the gauntlet to young scholars who dared to find something of value in the plays, other than as documents for understanding a diseased age. The last sections of the essay are not printed here ("owing to pressure of space"), a testament to the long-windedness of Wain's very subjective opinions. This essay is not to be missed by anyone delighting in such displays of critical self-importance.

Walsh, Martin W. "Killigrew's Cap and Bells." *Theatre Notebook* 38, no. 3 (1984): 99-105.
A favorite of Charles II in exile and holder of one of the two coveted theatre patents during Charles's reign, Thomas Killigrew was also a sort of buffoon or court fool to the king, at least according to this interpretation of Samuel Pepys's diary entry of February 13, 1667. Whether his reference to "cap and bells" was metaphorical or literal is the subject of this short but enlightening review of Killigrew's place in court. It is a valuable addendum to his biography, at once pathetic and noble, that he may actually have held the office of jester.

Weber, Harold. *The Restoration Rake-Hero: Transformations in Sexual Understanding in Seventeenth-Century England*. Madison: University of Wisconsin Press, 1986.
Far from dodging the central issue of Restoration drama, Weber offers a book-length examination of the sexuality of the rake-hero in this close study of the changing attitudes toward "the rhythms of courtship and seduction, pursuit and conquest, foreplay and release." Contains five chapters, moving from demonic sexuality through the Hobbesian libertine-rake to the female libertine on the Restoration stage. An example of modern scholarship unencumbered by Puritan restraint. Notes and index.

White, Eric Walter. "Early Theatrical Performances of Purcell's Operas with a Calendar of Recorded Performances, 1690-1710." *Theatre Notebook* 13, no. 1 (Autumn, 1958): 43-65.
Because the patents of the active theatres were so explicit about the kinds of theatre allowed, the presence of opera (or plays with music), especially at the Theatre Royal at Drury Lane, is integral to the understanding of how the spaces were used for theatrical repertories. In addition, the playwrights of the period often wrote librettos—Thomas Shadwell, for example, wrote (with Matthew Locke) the libretto for *Psyche*, performed in Dorset Garden in 1675. This study concentrates on this opera/theatre partnership, discussing scene

designers, calendars, and other items of mutual concern to the composer and the Restoration theatre itself. The accompanying list attests to Henry Purcell's prolific talent.

Wickham, Glynne. "The Restoration Theatre." In *English Drama to 1710*, edited by Christopher Ricks. London: Sphere Books, 1971.
A brief introduction to John Barnard's more protracted essay on Restoration drama in the same volume. Wickham discusses the continuity of the period with the rest of British dramatic history, noting that the age nevertheless had "aspirations to move in new directions of its own." Stage improvements, via Thomas Killigrew, William Davenant and especially Christopher Wren, are discussed, with an outline of the financial and repertory considerations that changed the profession of acting during the period.

Wilcox, John. *The Relation of Molière to Restoration Comedy*. New York: Columbia University Press, 1938.
The influence of Molière, "plundered on every hand" by Restoration playwrights, is traced here in detail and may have been confined to plot adaptations only, not style. This exhaustive study fleshes out Langbaine's observations of 1691, moving playwright-by-playwright through the fifty years before 1710 and concluding that Restoration playwrights borrowed almost nothing of Molière's dramatic form. Provides a Molière chronology, Restoration comedy chronology, bibliography, and index.

Wilkinson, D. R. M. *The Comedy of Habit: An Essay on the Use of Courtesy Literature in a Study of Restoration Comic Drama*. Leiden, The Netherlands: Universitaire Pers, 1964.
A study of the "literary merits" of Restoration comedy, this work removes the play from its original *raison d'être* to examine its poetic components, its indebtedness to "courtesy writing," and its relationship to the literary world surrounding Charles II's restoration to the monarchy. By reducing the text to its Aristotelian origins as one type of poetic expression, this essay is directly antithetical to the "producible interpretation" approach of Judith Milhous and Robert D. Hume (see above). Wilkinson's strongest argument is that, balanced at they are on verbal pivots, the comedies of the period owe as much to a literary protocol as they do to an anticipated theatrical realization. Contains an index of proper names, and a bibliography of courtesy books from the period.

Wilson, John Harold. *All the King's Ladies: Actresses of the Restoration*. Chicago: University of Chicago Press, 1958.
A new phenomenon of the English Restoration stage, but a common practice on the Continent, women actors added considerably to the pleasures of playgoing (as Samuel Pepys's diary attests on almost every page). Wilson de-

scribes the actresses' life on stage and behind the scenes, in daily contact with the "drinking, quarreling, swaggering, wenching crew" of actors, and reports on the changes in the stage literature brought about by the presence of women. An extended appendix introduces the actresses from 1660 to 1689, with brief biographies and lists of roles played. Index.

——————— . *The Court Wits of the Restoration: An Introduction*. Princeton, N.J.: Princeton University Press, 1948.

An overview of the age and its attitudes toward "wit," as manifested in writers, actresses, and courtiers. Considerable discussion of George Villiers, Nell Gwyn, Sir George Etherege, William Wycherley, John Dryden, and other dramatic figures, as well as poets and statesmen. Brief biographies, bibliography, and valuable index.

——————— . *Mr. Goodman the Player*. Pittsburgh: University of Pittsburgh Press, 1964.

This account of the actor Cardell Goodman, "the antithesis of respectability," a comedian with the King's Company from 1673 to 1682, is at the same time a chronicle of the fortunes of a typical stage company of the Restoration. Especially valuable in relating stage events to political persuasions—Goodman was a Jacobite supporting the Stuart line and was once imprisoned for conspiracy—and in revealing how the business of theatre affected the art of the theatre. Index and three illustrations.

——————— . *Nell Gwyn: Royal Mistress*. New York: Pellegrini & Cudahy, 1952.

Wilson made his reputation partly from these popularizations of historical facts, and with this study he brings into focus England's most famous Restoration actress and mistress, mother to one of Charles II's illegitimate sons. The book does not concentrate on her theatre career, but is valuable for putting the period in perspective; much of the stage immorality condemned by Jeremy Collier was purely representative of the age itself, as this study demonstrates. Reprints Nell's letters; Sir Peter Lely's portrait of Nell is the frontispiece. Bibliographical notes and index.

——————— . *A Preface to Restoration Drama*. Boston: Houghton Mifflin, 1965.

Introduces the dramatic period to the general reader, admittedly advocating for it, but attempting to "define and describe the varieties of Restoration drama and to analyze outstanding examples of each kind objectively." Offers brief overviews of nine types, from "Villain Tragedy" to "The Comedy of Tears." Wilson's strength is his graceful and readable condensation of plot and character in each example, stemming from his lifelong scholarship on the subject. In the absence of scholarly footnotes, Wilson supplies a bibliography for further reading, and an index.

Wimsatt, W. K., Jr., ed. *The Idea of Comedy: Essays in Prose and Verse.* Englewood
Cliffs, N.J.: Prentice-Hall, 1969.
A useful anthology of comments on comedy as a structure and genre, begin-
ning with Ben Jonson's prologues to his "humour" plays (around 1600) and
ending with George Meredith's essay on the uses of the comic spirit (1877),
with a postscript by James Thurber. Several entries are valuable to the student
of Restoration drama: John Dryden's preface to *An Evening's Love: Or, The
Mock Astrologer* and his epilogue to *The Conquest of Granada, Part II*;
Thomas Shadwell's preface to *The Sullen Lovers*; William Congreve's letter to
John Dennis "concerning humour in comedy," as well as his prologue to *The
Way of the World*; several essays from *The Spectator* by Joseph Addison and
Richard Steele; and John Dennis' defense of *Sir Fopling Flutter* (that is,
George Etherege's *The Man of Mode*).

Zimbardo, Rose A. "Imitation to Emulation: 'Imitation of Nature' from the Restoration to the Eighteenth Century." *Restoration* 2, no. 2 (Fall, 1978): 2-9.
This essay lays the groundwork for a more complete analysis of the changing
perspectives of "imitation of nature" found in Zimbardo's book (see below).
Recognizes four stages in the change of forms, 1660 to 1730. The most remarkable of her observations is that "the change which occurs in the conception [of
imitation of nature] results in the novel's replacing the drama as the primary
popular mode in England"—a large idea, which, in combination with the full-
length study below, demonstrates how the keen scholarly mind works toward
its solutions through detailed examination, detective work, and imaginative
speculation.

——————— . *A Mirror to Nature: Transformations in Drama and Aesthetics,
1660-1732.* Lexington: University Press of Kentucky, 1986.
A carefully constructed essay on the changing focus of aesthetic principles as
reflected in the drama, which, while it "cannot altogether soar into the realm
of abstract idea, neither can it, as the novel does, enable us completely to
inhabit a fictional experience—in drama a character is what he does." The
history of dramatic characterization in the Restoration moved from imitation
of the Ideal to extremes of feeling and affective response, and eventually to
close the distance between ideal and experiential reality. As in George Lillo's
The London Merchant, sentimental drama comes full round, from external
criticism of man's actions against a social idea to an "inner arena" against
which public actions are weighed.

APHRA BEHN

Armistead, J. M. "Writings About Aphra Behn, 1675-1980." In his *Four Restoration Playwrights*. Boston: G. K. Hall, 1984.

From Edward Phillips' mention of "Astrea Behn" in 1675 to the social biography by Angeline Goreau, this annotated list of critical comments on Behn reflects a revival of interest in her work, generated not only by women's studies but also by new scholarly techniques for reconstructing scant biographies from social contexts. Several annotations speak to the question of whether the personality of the playwright can be easily separated from the characters and the subject matter, and the danger of making biographical assumptions from the fictive construction. The exhaustive nature of the bibliography lets no discussion of Behn fall through the cracks, even the brief mention in John E. Cunningham's 1966 study.

Balch, Marston Stevens. *Thomas Middleton's "A Trick to Catch the Old One," "A Mad World, My Masters," and Aphra Behn's "City Heiress."* Salzburg, Austria: Universität Salzburg, 1981.

The claims that Behn borrowed from two plays by Thomas Middleton (and one by Philip Massinger into the bargain) are supported by parallel readings, leaving the original Behn material fairly naked: "Mrs Behn's chief originality, aside from her own large portion of the repartee, lies not so much in her combination of the borrowed plots . . . as in the matching of borrowed characters." Because Restoration comedy is light on plot and heavy on repartee, Behn can be forgiven for a "sympathy" toward Middleton that prompted her drawing on his account. The study demonstrates an interesting kind of comparative scholarship, particularly useful in detecting such thefts.

Blashfield, Evangeline Wilbour. "Aphra Behn." In her *Portraits and Backgrounds*. New York: Charles Scribner's Sons, 1917.

This attempt to strengthen the "faint outlines" of Behn's contemporary biographer ("One of the Fair Sex") claims a scientific rigor not always demonstrated in the deed. An anecdotal style coupled with a distaste for close reading moves the narrative through Behn's life at a gallop, dismissing her dramatic work as a pantry for theatre gossip, noting her poetry and novels and concluding that "she died in harness, pen in hand." Her black marble tombstone in Westminster Abbey, and the lady herself, deserved better than the "wretched verses engraved on it."

Burns, Edward. "Aphra Behn." In his *Restoration Comedy: Crises of Desire and Identity*. New York: St. Martin's Press, 1987.

Restoration women dramatists, notably Behn and Susanna Centlivre, attempted to redefine "what drama *is*, what its proper language is . . . [in] the presentation of sexual differences and social relations." Behn finds the Neapolitan carnival an appropriate setting for *The Rover*, the story of banished cavaliers and disguised women, whose disguises "serve to generalize the women's experience." *Sir Patient Fancy* and *The City Heiress* are discussed in some detail, toward a conclusion that "Behn's muse luxuriates in the last glow of the Stuart myth."

Crawford, Patricia. "Women's Published Writings, 1600-1700." In her *Women in English Society, 1500-1800*, edited by Mary Prior. London: Methuen, 1985.
  Although Behn is mentioned only briefly, this article puts into perspective the remarkable accomplishments of this writer and the kinds of obstacles in the way of her success. Accompanying graphs tabulate the rarity of any women's writing during this century, drawing statistics and inferences that invite further study of Behn and her contemporaries. Other articles in this collection fill out the social setting in which women struggled for a sense of self-worth away from the spinning wheel and cradle.

DeRitter, Jones. "The Gypsy, *The Rover*, and the Wanderer: Aphra Behn's Revision of Thomas Killigrew." *Restoration* 10, no. 2 (Fall, 1986): 82-92.
  A close look at the common practice of borrowing from contemporary material for dramatic content, this study demonstrates Behn's dramaturgy by detailing the transformations from source to commercially successful play. Some of the changes were Behn's "conscious attempt to subvert the prejudices displayed in *Thomaso*," which DeRitter sees as Thomas Killigrew's "misogynistic joke." The long stage life of Behn's adaptation is evidence that its issues were popular "long after the cavaliers themselves had ceased to dominate the nation's political and social life."

Goreau, Angeline. *Reconstructing Aphra: A Social Biography of Aphra Behn*. New York: Dial Press, 1980.
  In the absence of satisfying biographical details that give Behn dimension, Goreau attempts to shape her out of the clay of the social milieu from which her plays emerged. What saves this study from mere feminist rhetoric is the legitimacy of her premise and the high quality of scholarship that articulates it. Behn is truly "reconstructed" from the portrait of women, especially literate and unprivileged women, painted with the brush of Goreau's convincing arguments. Thirty-seven illustrations, solid bibliography, and index.

Guffey, George. "Aphra Behn's *Oroonoko*: Occasion and Accomplishment." In his *Two English Novelists*. Los Angeles: William Andrews Clark Memorial Library, 1975.
  Although dealing with the novel as a political strategy, Guffey offers consider-

able biographical information about Behn's background, Surinam experiences, and political bias, information which can inform the Thomas Southerne dramatization of this novel, as well as Behn's comedies and literary life in general. (An accompanying list of other publications by the Clark Library leads to other Restoration subjects, but these volumes are relatively difficult to find.)

Kronenberger, Louis. "Aphra Behn." In his *The Thread of Laughter: Chapters on English Stage Comedy from Jonson to Maugham*. New York: Alfred A. Knopf, 1952.

The Town Fop represents the uninspired "dead level" of everyday Restoration comedy, but Behn is an effective social commentator, if guilty of "hack" work on occasion. Plot and character summary singles out Betty Flauntit, "with her mixture of something spirited and something shameful," and quotes her speech as of the kind that "got Mrs. Behn her bad name." In *The Lucky Chance* Kronenberger sees her warming to her subject (sex), but he treats her material somewhat cynically, damning with faint praise throughout. Kronenberger misses the period's theatrical point entirely with his opinion that *The City Heiress: Or, Sir Timothy Treat-All* still makes a good read; however, Behn can excel but "somehow not make the last and decisive leap, the leap into literature"—a leap she never even considered worth taking in the dramatic genre.

Link, Frederick M. *Aphra Behn*. New York: Twayne, 1968.

An opening chapter on the life and times of Behn summarizes the scarce details; subsequent chapters move through her dramatic canon in stages from early to posthumous work. The second half deals with Behn as poet, translator, and novelist, and closes with a recapitulation of critical opinions to date. While essentially a literary analysis, Link's critical examination takes the stage life into account where required and is particularly enlightening with regard to Behn's pairing of characters. Borrowings from other sources are natural and customary during the age and do not detract from her talent. Good selected bibliography of journal articles, but considerable scholarship has appeared since.

———. Introduction to *The Rover*, by Aphra Behn. London: Edward Arnold, 1967.

The Regents Restoration Drama series makes available this most famous play of the first woman to make her living with her pen. Emerging from the middle of her career (1677), it is based on a closet drama by Thomas Killigrew (such borrowings were standard practice in this age), from which Behn brings order out of chaos. Its success is easy to understand: "It had something for everyone." In addition, Link remarks, "the interest in spectacle is served by well-managed stage business, by the elaborate costuming required in the disguises and masquerades, by the fighting, and by Blunt's trap door." Chronology in appendix.

Mendelson, Sara Heller. "Aphra Behn." In her *The Mental World of Stuart Women: Three Studies*. Amherst: University of Massachusetts Press, 1987.
An impressive scholarly examination of Behn and her writing, inside a larger study of gender-specific occupational and social discrimination during the reign of the Stuart kings, based on sound sociological detective work. Intelligent deductions from scanty clues to Behn's mental world, with a self-governing clearheadedness against such leaps of hope as (referring to the absence of evidence surrounding her possible marriage): "It is tempting to infer from her silence that the match was not a happy one."

Mignon, Elisabeth. "Dryden, Shadwell, and Aphra Behn." Part 3, "Aphra Behn." In her *Crabbed Age and Youth: The Old Men and Women in the Restoration Comedy of Manners*. Durham, N.C.: Duke University Press, 1947.
Mignon sees Behn as less gifted than her contemporaries, reducing the form to "the level of intrigue and farce." Moving fairly rapidly through the canon, Mignon notes that Lord Desbro, the "decayed Puritan" of *The Round-Heads*, "is actually killed off before the end of a play which is given unqualified classification as a comedy." The "repulsive" and "unpopular" notions of old age and Puritanism are combined here, fused by Mrs. Behn "into unmistakable unity."

Musser, Joseph F., Jr. " 'Imposing Nought but Constancy in Love': Aphra Behn Snares *The Rover*." *Restoration* 3, no. 1 (Spring, 1979): 17-25.
In Behn's versions of the battle of the sexes, a struggle which informs all of her sexual characterizations is the struggle over "constancy: the man resents and fears it, the woman demands it." *The Rover* is part of a transition begun by George Etherege's *The Man of Mode*, from lover-centered to lady-centered; Behn "looks on marriage as the accommodating of male inconstancy to the natural feminine desire for stability." An interesting article for students of the Restoration attitude toward sex, as well as a strong argument for the value of feminist approaches to theatre history.

Sackville-West, V. *Aphra Behn: The Incomparable Astrea*. New York: Viking Press, 1928.
Both charmingly personal and hopelessly subjective, this appreciation of Behn is noteworthy for its early date and its haste to leap from conjecture to pronouncement. "The fact that she wrote is much more important than the quality of what she wrote," but the fact and the quality are both remarkable in this almost novelistic treatment of "unsparing, ardent Astrea" Behn, who "claimed equal rights with the men; she was a phenomenon never before seen, and, when seen, furiously resented."

Wilcox, John. "The Minor Borrowers." Part 7, "Mrs. Aphra Behn." In his *The Relation of Molière to Restoration Comedy*. New York: Columbia University Press, 1938.

Two of Behn's fourteen comedies make use of Molière material: *Sir Patient Fancy* used the "bare hint" of *The Imaginary Invalid* for Argan and his imaginary illness; in *The False Count: Or, A New Way to Play an Old Game*, Behn took Molière's pretentious young ladies and transformed them into Isabella, "a social snob, not a *précieuse*." Her work, in Wilcox's view, was "without artistic insight."

COLLEY CIBBER

Ashley, Leonard R. N. *Colley Cibber*. New York: Twayne, 1965.
Apologizing for another study of Cibber in the face of his own autobiography, Ashley offers to "present a unified, coherent, entertaining, and informative combination of critical biography and literary analysis." The arrangement of material is biographical, with play analysis confined to twenty-three subsections of varying length in a chapter on Cibber as playwright. Most interesting are chapters on his management of Drury Lane and on the nature of theatre companies, repertories, and acting styles during the period. Strong selected bibliography and index.

Barker, Richard Hindry. *Mr Cibber of Drury Lane*. New York: Columbia University Press, 1939.
A biography of Cibber's life, with emphasis on his business dealings among the theatre patent holders and power holders from the late Restoration to his death in 1757. His complex relationships with Christopher Rich, John Dennis, Alexander Pope, and Henry Fielding, his achieving the title of poet laureate, the rise of his son Theophilus, and his own autobiography all receive full chapter treatment. Bibliography and index.

Burns, Edward. "The Etheregean Revival." In his *Restoration Comedy: Crises of Desire and Identity*. New York: St. Martin's Press, 1987.
On Colley Cibber, John Vanbrugh, and Thomas Southerne. The split of the United Company caused a "Cibberian" style of comedy, "a frothier kind," to develop at Drury Lane, partly attributable to the limitations of the younger actors who stayed with Rich. The style, in reaching for modern propriety, actually became more immoral. Cibber's *Love's Last Shift* discussed at length (along with Vanbrugh's *The Provok'd Wife*) as a model of this new comic type, plays "with an easy construction and a lovely wit [that] enclose the people and subtly diminish them."

Cibber, Colley. *An Apology for the Life of Mr. Colley Cibber Written by Himself*. 2 vols. Edited by Robert W. Lowe. London: John C. Nimmo, 1886. Reprint. New York: AMS Press, 1966.
Lowe set about to correct the errors of fact that mar Cibber's otherwise magnificent account, with a protracted series of notes, emendations, glosses, and commentary accompanying this edition. The result is Cibber's lively recollections calmly clarified in footnote. Twenty-six messotint portraits are printed here, and eighteen etchings introduce separate chapters. Volume 2 contains a supplementary chapter by Lowe, a bibliography, memoirs of actors and actresses, and an index.

Fone, B. R. S. "Colley Cibber's *Love's Last Shift* and Sentimental Comedy." *Restoration and Eighteenth Century Theatre Research* 7, no. 1 (May, 1968): 33-43.

An actor of considerable merit but a playwright of the second water, Cibber offered this play in 1695 to a Restoration public already shifting away from the hard, cynical line of George Etherege, William Wycherley, and William Congreve, but before Jeremy Collier's vicious attack on the stage in general. Even his contemporaries saw his play as a new direction, and Thomas Southerne recommended it for a major production, advising the actor Cibber to stay out of it. Fone discusses the sources and composition, placing the play higher in the importance of theatre development than other scholars have been prone to do. Cibber "was not unaware of the value of lewdness . . . [but] he knew too, the power of tears."

Hamilton, Walter. "Colley Cibber." In his *The Poets Laureate of England*. London: Elliot Stock, 1879. Reprint. Detroit: Gale Research, 1968.

After a long life of mediocrity, Cibber achieved the office of poet laureate (1730-1757), and "never has any man of so little public importance been so bitterly, so perseveringly, and so unjustly satirized." Alexander Pope was probably the most adept of Cibber's critics; Hamilton reports the part of *The Dunciad* in which Cibber is ridiculed, and his own less-than-scathing response. Brief mention of Theophilus and Charlotte, his children.

Kalson, Albert E. "Colley Cibber Plays Richard III." *Theatre Survey* 16, no. 1 (May, 1975): 42-55.

A biographical study that concentrates on Cibber's image of himself as an actor. Around 1699, "the winter of his discontent," Cibber revised Shakespeare's great history play for his own purposes: to be acknowledged and recognized as a tragic actor in the title role. His portrayal was ludicrous ("because of his shrill voice, his comic facial expression, and his awkward movements"), but "his alteration was to be the most lasting of all the many revisions of the plays of Shakespeare and was to hold the stage in preference to the original for nearly two hundred years." An informative and oddly touching sketch of this typical, yet unique, Restoration theatrical personality.

Kronenberger, Louis. "Cibber and Vanbrugh." In his *The Thread of Laughter: Chapters on English Stage Comedy from Jonson to Maugham*. New York: Alfred A. Knopf, 1952.

By the time Restoration comedy comes to the eighteenth century, reactions generated from within have joined forces of repression from outside, to bring the stage around to respectability, at least in the final act. The sense of something illicit yet respectable—that is the tone of Colley Cibber and John Vanbrugh. The two are paired because Cibber's *Love's Last Shift* has Vanbrugh's *The Relapse* as its sequel. Because Kronenberger views all plays as literature, no mention is made of Cibber's intimate knowledge of the stage as actor and as manager.

Sullivan, Maureen. Introduction to *Colley Cibber: Three Sentimental Comedies*, edited by Sullivan. New Haven, Conn.: Yale University Press, 1973.
The editor of *Love's Last Shift*, *The Careless Husband*, and *The Lady's Last Stake* takes an opportunity to outline the important features of Cibber's contributions as a theatre person who implemented the transition from Restoration to sentimental comedy. An outline of the plays is followed by a review of the context in which they were received; Cibber's comedies adhere to the same Christian ethic as the heroic dramas of the Restoration. Contains thorough notes to each text and a facsimile of some of the music for *Love's Last Shift* and *The Careless Husband*.

Vance, John A. "Power and Conversion in Cibber's *The Careless Husband*." *Restoration* 7, no. 2 (Fall, 1983): 68-74.
A "rebuttal" to John Vanbrugh's *The Relapse*, this play (considered to be the best of some thirty by Cibber) supplies in its final "conversion" scene a focus for Vance's discussion of Cibber's abiding interest "in probing the innate desire for power which manifests itself in human relationships." By this light, the act 5 conversions of Sir Charles Easy and Lady Betty Modish are not so improbable, because "both changes of heart are precipitated by a loss of power."

WILLIAM CONGREVE

General Studies

Armstrong, Cecil Ferard. "William Congreve." In his *Shakespeare to Shaw: Studies in the Life's Work of Six Dramatists of the English Stage*. Freeport, N.Y.: Books for Libraries Press, 1913, reprint 1968.

A charming and personalized view of the gentleman turned dramatist, and the author of what Armstrong believes is called "a comedy of manners, though a comedy of the lack of them would be a better description, and a comedy of intrigue better still." Notes Congreve's distress at the aside and the soliloquy: "No better way has yet been invented for the communication of thought," according to Congreve. Armstrong points out the discovery in modern times, however, that "audiences are quite capable of gauging a character's thoughts by its actions."

Avery, Emmett L. *Congreve's Plays on the Eighteenth-Century Stage*. New York: Modern Language Association of America, 1951.

Congreve's last play, *The Way of the World* (1700), ushered in a century that found much to applaud in his whole canon, as Avery shows in this discussion of revivals. Culled from his larger study of the calendar of theatrical events of the period, it serves to illustrate as well the business and art of theatre during the age of John Gay, James Quin, David Garrick, Charles Macklin, and Richard Sheridan. Congreve's popularity reinforces his position as pivotal poet from the Restoration to the Augustan Age. Appendices cite revisions and list each performance by year. Index.

Birdsall, Virginia Ogden. "Congreve's Apprenticeship." In her *Wild Civility: The English Comic Spirit on the Restoration Stage*. Bloomington: Indiana University Press, 1970.

Congreve's early plays contain a thoughtfulness that marks the maturation of an age, not signaling a beginning but the end of the genre. He marks a decrease of libertine attitudes from George Etherege, but still insists on a sense of life as a "plaything" to be enjoyed fully. *The Old Bachelor* was a concession to audiences' delight in horseplay. *The Double-Dealer* can be seen as its sequel; the villain Maskwell is more interesting than the hero Bellmour. Villains and fools interest Congreve more than the "lifeless allegorical representations" of standard comic characters.

Burns, Edward. "Congreve." In his *Restoration Comedy: Crises of Desire and Identity*. New York: St. Martin's Press, 1987.

Employing "a classicism of an intensely personal kind," Congreve wrote to

please himself in his digressions, an indulgence he could afford. Close readings of all four comedies (his other works are outside Burns's study), leading
to the arguable but unorthodox conclusion that "Congreve invents nothing, his
plays are virtuosic rearrangements of received ideas. . . . Alone of any major
Restoration dramatist he bequeaths the form no new conventions or types."

Davis, Herbert. Introduction to *The Complete Plays of William Congreve*, edited by
　　Davis. Chicago: University of Chicago Press, 1967.
　　In addition to a short introductory note to each play in Congreve's canon,
　　Davis supplies an essay emphasizing his "taste and wide interests in litera-
　　ture," his education (in spite of his law school experiences), and the good use
　　of opportunities as he wrote. The serious play, *The Mourning Bride*, often
　　overlooked among his witty comedies, was dedicated to Princess Anne and
　　demonstrated considerable talent in the heroic tragedy verse genre.

Dobrée, Bonamy. "Congreve." In *Restoration Drama: Modern Essays in Criticism*,
　　edited by John Loftis. New York: Oxford University Press, 1966.
　　Culled from Dobrée's massive work on Restoration comedy in 1924 (from
　　which all subsequent critics draw), this essay reviews the nineteenth century
　　opinions of Congreve as a "constructive thinker," citing the opening lines of
　　The Old Bachelor in support. Congreve himself was modest regarding *The
　　Double-Dealer*, a comedy where emotions are unimportant. The Mellefont-
　　Maskwell intrigue is not comic at all. *Love for Love* "shows some careless-
　　ness" and the humours are treated with Jonsonian obviousness. The famous
　　bargaining scene between Mirabell and Millamant is quoted in its entirety.
　　Dobrée's style is not sedulous, as the absence of endnotes suggests.

――――――――― . *William Congreve*. London: Longmans, Green, 1963.
　　Number 164 of a series of bibliographical supplements to *British Book News* on
　　writers and their work (whose general editor is Dobrée himself), this mono-
　　graph presents an overview of Congreve's life, comedies, and other literary
　　work, in as succinct and readable a form as could be hoped. As in previous
　　scholarship on the same playwright, Dobrée asserts that *The Way of the World*
　　was Congreve's best answer to Jeremy Collier's assaults on the Restoration
　　stage. Dobrée concludes that Congreve was "a man who had a good deal
　　pondered, and experienced, the way of the world." Bibliography.

――――――――― . "William Congreve." In his *Variety of Ways: Discussions on Six
　　Authors*. Oxford, England: Clarendon Press, 1932. Reprint. Freeport, N.Y.:
　　Books for Libraries Press, 1967.
　　A two-part study ("His Life" and "His Works") of Congreve, who undertook
　　to defend the whole art against the "muscular onslaught" of Jeremy Collier's
　　A Short View of the Immorality and Profaneness of the English Stage, "reluc-

tantly, but by no means so ineffectually as is usually stated." Part 2 envelopes a summary of the plays in an essay on their combination of pleasure and instruction; Dobrée's praise of Congreve's accomplishments goes beyond sober criticism on occasion: "Then one awaits the delicious phrase, the thrilling movement, the breath-catching swerve of tempo. . . ."

Edgar, Irving I. "Restoration Comedy and William Congreve." In his *Essays in English Literature and History*. New York: Philosophical Library, 1972.
Congreve is treated here as a paradox, both the best spokesman for the high Restoration and a person born outside it. Edgar's explanation is that Congreve studied the literature before his time and wrote from outside the social world of his characters, but in the genre's style. In the process he reveals his own predilection for studying the "intimate relations between the sexes" and "also the matter of sex-antagonism so common in these plays." This collection of essays deals with "psychological sources of creative literature"; Congreve's reputation is built on artificial imitation and an intellectual distance from his subject.

Evans, Gareth Lloyd. "Congreve's Sense of Theatre." In *William Congreve*, edited by Brian Morris. Mermaid Critical Commentaries. London: Ernest Benn, 1972.
This professional theatre critic, concerned with the plays onstage, compares Congreve's potential excellence with the very real limitations of modern actors and audiences in understanding and enacting the texts. The sense of theatre cannot be replaced by mere "information" about the age but must come from the same acute attention to casting, language, and even the "gait" of the actor. Since Congreve so often used his actors (over and over) as "raw material" to invent the characters, one must credit the Bettertons and Bracegirdles. "The world of theatre had and has its own society, its own moral patterns, its own particular structure of behaviour."

Foakes, R. A. "Wit and Convention in Congreve's Comedies." In *William Congreve*, edited by Brian Morris. Mermaid Critical Commentaries. London: Ernest Benn, 1972.
Analyzes Congreve's notions of wit and convention, beginning with his dedicatory remarks in *The Way of the World*, showing a deliberateness and consciousness in following the heritage of dramatic wit in its second sense: "qualities of the mind . . . expressed in speech and behaviour." Full of the serious business of courtship and marriage, cautionary tales of fallen women, and the true wit's exercise of judgment, Congreve's plays were models of the "happiness of language."

Fujimura, Thomas H. "William Congreve." In his *The Restoration Comedy of Wit*. New York: Barnes & Noble Books, 1952.

Reviews the critical opinion of Congreve as a "soulless," artificial stylist, whose personal life was prudently free of scandal. A merciful disposition and an "inwardness and reserve born of good taste and judgment, which might have impressed strangers as a sign of coldness" inform Congreve's work; his place in Restoration history (*The Way of the World*, 1700) makes his contribution a culmination of the comedy of wit as well as a transition to the Age of Enlightenment. Despite the appearance of the illustrative "Truewit" in the canon, it is not a far step, according to Fujimura, from Congreve to Addison.

Gosse, Edmund. *Life of William Congreve*. London: Walter Scott, 1888. Rev. enlarged ed. London: Heinemann, 1924.
An authoritative and sober account in the nineteenth century biography tradition, from which all subsequent studies of Congreve begin. The table of contents is a valuable outline in itself but is excluded from the 1924 "enlargement." Each play's "characteristics and history" reported, as well as production revivals after his retirement from public life around the death of his friend and literary benefactor, John Dryden, in 1700. Appendix.

Henderson, Anthony G., ed. *The Comedies of William Congreve.* Cambridge, England: Cambridge University Press, 1982.
The biographical introduction reviews Congreve's Irish education, his coming to London, his early acquaintance with Dryden, his writing successes and retirement in tactful diplomacy. A good summary of his biographers' opinions up to L. C. Knights. Each play receives its own brief introduction along the same structural lines but with more stage history. All dedicatory epistles, prologues, and the like are intact. Good footnotes.

Hodges, John C. *William Congreve the Man: A Biography from New Sources*. New York: Modern Language Association of America, 1941.
Attempts a new reading of Congreve's life "from fresh sources," notably the genealogical tables reconstructed here in appendix, documents in the Public Record Office, and the *Buttery Book* of Trinity College, Dublin, in which Congreve's name is entered forty-one times. Answering Gosse's surmise that no new matter on the playwright was forthcoming, Hodges repairs Congreve's deteriorating reputation as he "became progressively more distasteful to his biographers" after contemporary eulogies praised him as a gentleman and artist.

_____ , ed. *William Congreve: Letters and Documents*. New York: Harcourt, Brace & World, 1964.
Gathered here are 157 letters and documents from, to, and about Congreve, including personal notes, business correspondence, literary dedicatory epistles,

and critical observations. Besides shedding light on Congreve, this collection illustrates the variety and stylistic grace of seventeenth and eighteenth century correspondence, an art lost to the present generation. An extremely valuable index to the pieces, a work of scholarship in its own right, helps locate specific topics and persons.

Kelsall, Malcolm. "Those Dying Generations." In *William Congreve*, edited by Brian Morris. Mermaid Critical Commentaries. London: Ernest Benn, 1972.
As Brian Morris summarizes in the introduction to this collection, Kelsall's essay "examines the theme of Age and Youth as it appears in all four plays, showing how Congreve uses his 'old' characters to make trenchant discoveries about the frailties of passion and the mysterious nature of energy." The transience of passion and beauty is emphasized in Lady Wishfort and her predecessors, deprived of those qualities which temporarily sustain the interest of others in exchange for the more lasting qualities of love and honesty.

Kronenberger, Louis. "Congreve." In his *The Thread of Laughter: Chapters on English Stage Comedy from Jonson to Maugham*. New York: Alfred A. Knopf, 1952.
Aphra Behn marks the end of the true Restoration, and Congreve begins the next period ("high Restoration" has been suggested as a term for this later period). Congreve is "so much finer an artist, and the stage so much less of a bear garden." From *The Old Bachelor*, written at age twenty-one (Kronenberger modernizes the spellings and approximates the dates), Congreve "is always a patrician, a master of the kind of writing that has breeding without stiffness, style and at the same time ease." Maskwell, in *The Double-Dealer*, is "all villain and only villain: it is his nature and it is his trade." *Love for Love* is the best theatre piece, and *The Way of The World* the "supreme example of high comedy . . . one does not know where to babble first."

Krutch, Joseph Wood. Introduction to *The Comedies of William Congreve*, edited by Krutch. New York: Macmillan, 1927.
"Completely a man of the world, free from all the irritating vagaries generally associated with 'artistic temperament,' " Congreve had a mind that "perfects rather than originates." His plays are briefly described and his affection for Anne Bracegirdle and Henrietta, Duchess of Marlborough, is noted. No gloss or critical apparatus with the text.

Leech, Clifford. "Congreve and the Century's End." In *Restoration Drama: Modern Essays in Criticism*, edited by John Loftis. New York: Oxford University Press, 1966.
Congreve, whose work blends the distinct genres of the earlier Restoration, has a *fin de siècle* flavor indicating the end of an era. Sobriety of tone, calm

appraisal, seriousness of purpose, and more ambitious intention—"a fusion of judgment and delight, with a greater range and a sharper sensitivity than English drama had known since the Civil War"—are the marks of the playwright. Leech sees Congreve as enlarging the Restoration world into a more universal image, in which characters become "aspects of a single humanity."

Lincoln, Stoddard. "Eccles and Congreve: Music and Drama on the Restoration Stage." *Theatre Notebook* 18, no. 1 (Autumn, 1963): 7-18.
A thorough discussion of the always close relationship between music and drama in this period ("at least one quarter of an evening at the theatre was devoted to music"), this essay differentiates between plays with incidental music and the more musically spectacular form, the masque. Lincoln chooses as examples the collaborations of William Congreve, John Eccles, and other members of the United Company (around 1692) and follows the complex theatre histories of this and Thomas Betterton's company, formed in 1695. Eccles' duties were to set lyrics to music, and his successes and failures are discussed here in some detail. An excellent reminder of the marriage of these two arts during this busy period of theatrical partnerships.

Love, Harold. *Congreve*. Oxford, England: Basil Blackwell, 1974.
Claims Congreve was interested in the literary value of his work as well as its stage life, but the texts cannot submit to the same scrutiny as a novel or poem, lacking "the voice and its utterance." Reviews the acting style of the period until David Garrick, and Anne Bracegirle's and Thomas Betterton's influence on his writing as well as his personal life. This study approaches the texts as recipes for performance, and as such joins the production analysis approach increasingly popular in Restoration scholarship. Introductory and concluding chapters bracket four chapters on the comedies (*The Mourning Bride* is not dealt with at any length here). Chronology, bibliography, and index.

Lynch, Kathleen M. "Congreve." In her *The Social Mode of Restoration Comedy*. New York: Macmillan, 1926.
Lynch summarizes her argument regarding the *précieuse* tradition in Restoration drama by a close look at its crowning genius. His plays are filled with "young people who wisely interpret the affectations of the age" contrasted with "false wits and with meddling fools." His major devices are "similitude debates and contests in raillery of the type popularized by [Sir John] Suckling," employed with "precision and graceful symmetry." Mirabell's and Millamant's proviso covenant is noteworthy because it "never violates the essential restrictions of the Restoration mode." Congreve's work is a "brief, authentic record of the *précieuse* movement in comedy."

——————. *A Congreve Gallery*. Cambridge, Mass.: Harvard University Press, 1951.

By presenting a gallery (including reproductions of their portraits) of Congreve's friends, social acquaintances, and literary compatriots, Lynch draws the playwright's own portrait more clearly. Congreve's relation with Joseph Keally (Kelly in the later correspondence), the Fitzgeralds, and Dr. Messenger Monsey are very informative, but the chapters on Mary, Duchess of Leeds, and especially Henrietta, Duchess of Marlborough, go beyond mere biographical data-gathering, toward a deeper understanding of Congreve's sense of life. Notes, bibliography, and index.

Mignon, Elisabeth. "Congreve." In her *Crabbed Age and Youth: The Old Men and Women in the Restoration Comedy of Manners*. Durham, N.C.: Duke University Press, 1947.
Heartwell, the "old batchelor" in the title of Congreve's first play, is the first old man (relative to the ages of Bellmour and Vainlove) to be "really conscious of his weakness, who has power to predict the results, the jeers of the younger generation," a self-awareness that does not prevent his falling into the trap. More clearly, Fondlewife is aware of his shortcomings as a husband, and as such is "on a somewhat higher level than his fellow-cuckolds," the result of Congreve's sensitivity to character. In Congreve's last play, Mirabell's forgiving attitude toward Sir Wilfull is not a clear sign of a changing attitude toward old age, still "a desert of charm."

Morris, Brian, ed. *William Congreve*. Mermaid Critical Commentaries. London: Ernest Benn, 1972.
Congreve has been relatively neglected in his native Yorkshire, with no "full-length critical assessment of Congreve's development and dramatic achievement" to date. This volume is a record of the third University of York Symposium, held in 1970; each paper, substantially as given, is printed here. The introduction reviews modern editions from Montague Summers (1923) to Herbert Davis (1967) and briefly summarizes the contents. The symposium concluded that "the plays have a contemporary relevance and a continuing life in the theatre which does not depend on any false, romantic evocation of the past. . . . The key word may be 'elegance.' " Combined index to all the essays at the end of the book.

Muir, Kenneth. "The Comedies of William Congreve." In *Restoration Theatre*, edited by John Russell Brown and Bernard Harris. Stratford-upon-Avon Studies 6. London: Edward Arnold, 1965.
A defense of Congreve's reputation as "incomparably the best writer of comedy between Shakespeare and Shaw," after a brief review of that reputation's ups and downs. What follows are declarations of genius, "advanced" dramaturgy, "carefully dovetailed" comic scenes, and other high praise, laced with examples from the texts. Muir's real argument is with critics who censure

Congreve for depicting adultery and unhappy marriages, "facts of life" in his time, and who do not see that he presented "at least, by implication, an ideal of marriage based on reason and respect."

—————————— . "Congreve on the Modern Stage." In *William Congreve*, edited by Brian Morris. Mermaid Critical Commentaries. London: Ernest Benn, 1972.
As part of a longer chronicle of Restoration's long shadow, and the changing fortunes of Congreve's plays through three full centuries of production and performance, this essay focuses on twentieth century productions, from the Stage Society's performance of *The Way of the World* through Dame Edith Evans' Millamant in several mountings (and her Lady Wishfort in 1948) to the National Theatre's *Love for Love* (1965), staged by Peter Wood, whose mixed reviews are quoted here at some length. For this publication, Muir adds cast lists from eleven productions.

—————————— . "William Congreve." In his *The Comedy of Manners*. London: Hutchinson University Library, 1970.
Lauded as the "heir to Dryden" in his own age after *The Old Bachelor*, Congreve never quite fulfilled that promise. Muir detects weaknesses in the play's structure, with little connection of sub- to main plots, and a tendency for the passions to override the comic moment. Later works, notably *Love for Love* and *The Way of the World*, were more successful and "beautifully varied in style"; they are treated at some length, with contemporary opinions weighed against Muir's own reassessment.

Myers, William. "Plot and Meaning in Congreve's Comedies." In *William Congreve*, edited by Brian Morris. Mermaid Critical Commentaries. London: Ernest Benn, 1972.
The political intrigues of Congreve's age were instrumental in changing the comic vision of the stage at the time. Standing "between these two Worlds of Etherege and Steele," Congreve the traditionalist carried his values into the next century. The proviso scene of *The Way of the World* is examined for signs of Congreve's probable convictions, and Congreve's work in general for its place in the literary mainstream.

Palmer, John. "William Congreve." In his *The Comedy of Manners*. London: G. Bell & Sons, 1913.
Thomas Babington Macaulay's condemnation of Congreve does not square with Congreve's reputation among his contemporaries. As a way into the playwright's biography, Palmer examines Congreve's responses to critics of his own time. Gives highest praise to *The Way of the World* and cites the Mirabel/Millamant agreement, declaring that the entire play "but rarely falls beneath the level of this passage. . . . Every sentence is replete with sense and satire, conveyed in the most polished and pointed terms."

Parfitt, George. "The Case Against Congreve." In *William Congreve*, edited by Brian Morris. Mermaid Critical Commentaries. London: Ernest Benn, 1972.
Not since L. C. Knights's attack on Restoration drama has so critical and unforgiving an essay examined the period. What Congreve's defenders have seen as passion and real feeling, Parfitt sees as mere "intensity," and, in *Love for Love*, Valentine's "generosity" after his earlier brutality cannot be explained away by his sudden reform. Ben's behavior "lacks social grace," but his blunt honesty may or may not be ironic. Congreve's vision is "neither large enough nor sufficiently clear to be really satisfying." Parfitt's final opinion is that Congreve's art ultimately fails.

Perry, Henry ten Eyck. "William Congreve." In *The Comic Spirit in Restoration Drama*. New York: Russell & Russell, 1925, reprint 1962.
There was a fifteen-year gap between Congreve and earlier Restoration dramatists of note. Dryden praises his "satire, wit and strength," a view "overstated" in Perry's opinion. The device of the gallant's clever lie of *The Old Bachelor* is used twice in *The Double-Dealer* "and consequently does not go so well." Soliloquies also hurt the structure of Congreve's early pieces. *The Way of the World* avoids previously overworked situations. This study is confusing to lay readers because Perry skips too familiarly from character to character in the canon without identifying the plays to which they belong.

Taylor, D. Crane. *William Congreve*. Oxford, England: Oxford University Press, 1931.
A critical biography more thorough than Gosse's, this study praises Congreve's "compactness and polish of phrase [and] his understanding of the rich quality of words." Besides introductory chapters and separate chapters on each of the five plays (including the seldom-analyzed tragedy *The Mourning Bride*), there is an extended discussion of the Collier controversy with an appendix listing the tracts. Long bibliography and index.

Wertheim, Albert. "Romance and Finance: The Comedies of William Congreve." In *Comedy from Shakespeare to Sheridan*, edited by A. R. Braunmuller and J. C. Bulman. Newark: University of Delaware Press, 1986.
"The conflict of marriage based on romantic feeling versus marriage based on a cash nexus" has driven many dramatic plots, sometimes bald and obvious, sometimes "recognizable but muted," as in Congreve's four great comedies. All the major characters in the plays are "directly affected by the financial state of affairs" surrounding the wooings, seductions, and assignations. The famous last act of *The Way of the World* hinges on the collision of "the avarice of Fainall and the generosity of Mirabell." Notes.

Wilcox, John. "Congreve, Vanbrugh, and Farquhar." Part 1, "William Congreve." In his *The Relation of Molière to Restoration Comedy*. New York: Columbia

University Press, 1938.
The character types found in Congreve are not found in Molière, but their
origins can be traced to pre-interregnum English drama and to the first generation of Restoration drama itself. Wilcox's argument is that some plots, but no
dramatic forms or styles, were borrowed from the French genius; Congreve,
one of the best of the Restoration dramatists, makes the point convincingly.

Williams, Aubrey L. *An Approach to Congreve*. New Haven, Conn.: Yale University
Press, 1979.
Arguing against critics who view Congreve as Epicurean and lacking "religious dimension," this study places him more comfortably inside the Christian ethic; it is "an approach that takes into account the essential com-
patibility . . . with traditional Christian 'explanations' and 'configurations' of
human life." Williams sees in *The Way of the World* a trace of Christian mercy
in the forgiving and forgetting of the central characters; Congreve, his audience
and his work are "of one faith." Notes and index.

_____ . "Poetic Justices, the Contrivances of Providence, and the Works of
William Congreve." *ELH* 35, no. 4 (December, 1968): 540-565.
An essay arguing that Congreve's works "are all, in their various ways, the
beautifully carved images of a Providential justice that governs all human
affairs, even those that occur in the most sophisticated and flirtatious drawing-
rooms." These are the terms of challenge in an attack by the Reverend John
Tillotson, the late seventeenth century Archbishop of Canterbury, on all wits
of the period. The argument works its way through contemporary references to
the subject, Congreve's canon (briefly), and some linguistic examinations of
terms like "contrivance" and "design," which place Congreve in the same line
of work as "God the Divine Playwright." Demonstrates "the close connection
of literary principle and religious persuasion."

The Double-Dealer

Barnard, John. "Passion, 'Poetical Justice,' and Dramatic Law in *The Double-
Dealer* and *The Way of the World*." In *William Congreve*, edited by Brian
Morris. Mermaid Critical Commentaries. London: Ernest Benn, 1972.
If Congreve owes a debt to Ben Jonson, he also owes a debt to Roman comedy
and the neoclassical literary theories of the French Academy. *The Double-
Dealer* tries to follow the neoclassical rules but is a "radical experiment" as
well, attempting to obtain a seriousness inside the comic framework. Thus the
"flaw" of sentimentality in these two works is actually Congreve's marriage of
classical dramaturgy with "real" concerns of the day.

Birdsall, Virginia Ogden. "Congreve's Apprenticeship." Part 2, *"The Double-Dealer."* In her *Wild Civility: The English Comic Spirit on the Restoration Stage*. Bloomington: Indiana University Press, 1970.

A different note is struck from Congreve's first work. The villain Maskwell is a kind of melodrama figure, but closer to the medieval vice character, the progenitor of Iago: a personification of a weakness in the main character. Maskwell often is called "devil" by the other characters. Goodness defeats the Iago-like Maskwell, because the villains are on the side of sterility and destructiveness.

Henderson, Anthony G. "Introduction to *The Double Dealer*." In *The Comedies of William Congreve*, edited by Henderson. Cambridge, England: Cambridge University Press, 1982.

Only eight months after the success of his first play, Congreve announced his second, dedicated to Charles Mountague in a long epistle printed here with the play and ushered into print with several commendatory verses by prominent men of letters (John Dryden's accompanies this edition). Congreve claimed it followed Aristotelian principles of unity, unusual for a comedy, and that Maskwell's character owed something to the Roman writer Terence. Queen Mary asked for a performance of this play one month after its first run.

Holland, Norman N. *"The Double-Dealer."* In his *The First Modern Comedies: The Significance of Etherege, Wycherley, and Congreve*. Cambridge, Mass.: Harvard University Press, 1959.

A "sophomore slump," in Holland's opinion, the play's two plots are used to reveal each other; the comic plot satirizes folly, but the serious plot takes a more critical view of villainy than previously experienced. "The forms of life equal the substance" for the fools; the paucity of metaphorical language in the serious plot, along with Maskwell's and Cynthia's use of soliloquy, are evidence for an interpretation of the play as the beginning of an eighteenth century sentimentality, "a faith in the 'natural goodness' of people." Foreshadows Congreve's emphasis in his later work, "the unwritten assumption that cleverness and morality are inconsistent, and therein lurks an awful solemnity."

Love, Harold. *"The Double Dealer."* In his *Congreve*. Oxford, England: Basil Blackwell, 1974.

John Dryden says the women think Congreve has "exposed their Bitchery too much" with his second comedy in 1693. Here, Love sees direct evidence that Congreve sought literary approbation as well as stage success, by observing the unities "to satisfy 'the dreadfull men of Learning.' " Some of the longer speeches serve a literary rather than a dramatic end, although it is possible someone could produce and act the play in a way that would complete it and hide its flaws. It is "a comedy about a dynasty and ultimately a class," toward which Congreve's attitude is complex and not always clear.

McCarthy, B. Eugene. "Providence in Congreve's *The Double-Dealer*." *Studies in English Literature 1500-1900* 19, no. 3 (Summer, 1979): 407-419.
Several critics have debated whether Congreve worked from a universally accepted social idea of "providence" in his plays. McCarthy, following John Barnard (see above), disagrees, finding little or no evidence in the texts for such an acknowledgment. Concentrating on *The Double-Dealer* (partly because it was the target for previous criticism), the article examines the structure of the play and the effects of Providence on its movement, coming to the conclusion that "if anything, [Mirabell, in *The Way of the World*] has demonstrated minimal trust in Providence and a great deal of faith in his own abilities to foresee eventualities and thus minimize the effects of chance upon his own goals."

Ross, J. C. Introduction to *The Double-Dealer*, by William Congreve. New York: W. W. Norton, 1981.
Ross's edition, full of valuable glosses and longer end notes, begins with a full forty-page recapitulation of the play's author, sources, and stage history, as well as a thorough prose summary of the plot and characters. Illuminating the play from every angle, he includes all dedicatory epistles, prologue, epilogue and even an appendix with the scores of the songs Congreve incorporates into the play.

Taylor, D. Crane. "*The Double Dealer*." In his *William Congreve*. Oxford, England: Oxford University Press, 1931.
More serious and ambitious than his first effort, Congreve's second play departed too drastically from the expectations of the audience and was not well received: "The audience did not know how to classify this play, they had never seen another like it" in its balance of power and playfulness. Colley Cibber, playing Lord Touchwood before Queen Mary in 1694, enjoyed a considerable rise in reputation from his performance. More a review of the play's reception than an analysis of its form.

Love for Love

Avery, Emmett L. Introduction to *Love for Love*, by William Congreve. London: Edward Arnold, 1966.
Part of the Regents Restoration Drama series, this edition is introduced by Avery's summary of the play's original reception in 1695, after two earlier successes; Thomas Betterton's new license and his remodeled theatre at Lin-

coln's Inn Fields were first employed in staging this work, "brilliantly cast" from actors previously known for originating other Congreve characterizations. Credits the simplicity of plot (and summarizes it) for the play's success through the eighteenth century, and notes the "natural" Ben in accompaniment with the "natural" but sophisticated Angelica. Chronology in appendix.

Birdsall, Virginia Ogden. *"Love for Love."* In her *Wild Civility: The English Comic Spirit on the Restoration Stage*. Bloomington: Indiana University Press, 1970. Although the plot lines are fairly simple, this is Congreve's most complex play, in that the patterns of the themes are contradictory and confusing. The comic characters have a philosophical side that adds dimension to the play's structure. No longer clear satire, this play presents real problems, with real danger of unhappy resolution. Threats and warnings take on a seriousness when relationships fail "in one way or another, to achieve a balanced unity based on mutual respect for individual right." Ben, the free sailor, speaks the play's themes clearly, although steeped in the salt-brine of sea jargon.

Hawkins, Harriett. " 'Diversity of Signification': Religious Imagery in Restoration Comedy and Secular Reality in *Love for Love*." In her *Likenesses of Truth in Elizabethan and Restoration Drama*. Oxford, England: Clarendon Press, 1972. By tracing the religious imagery in Congreve's third play, and through a careful reading of Congreve's response to Jeremy Collier, Hawkins argues that notions of a "providential justice," possibly represented by Angelica, are misleading and unfair to Congreve's insistence upon reflecting real life; *The Way of the World* is "even more explicitly insistent upon truth to its model."

Henderson, Anthony G. "Introduction to *Love for Love*." In *The Comedies of William Congreve*, edited by Henderson. Cambridge, England: Cambridge University Press, 1982. Congreve's third play opened the new Lincoln's Inn Fields theatre in 1695. The unusual circumstances, recorded in two prologues and an epilogue printed here with the play's text, brought an audience sympathetic to Thomas Betterton's new company, and one which reacted favorably to "the skill of the language, and the brilliance of the performance." This play continued its popularity well into the next century, sometimes in a shortened, purified format.

Holland, Norman N. *"Love for Love."* In his *The First Modern Comedies: The Significance of Etherege, Wycherley, and Congreve*. Cambridge, Mass.: Harvard University Press, 1959. Holland sees three kinds of knowledge in Congreve's most carefully crafted play— "presocial, social, suprasocial"—and builds his discussion around the proofs he perceives in the text. This is an "epistemological comedy," in that the way the characters know the truth of things determines their distribution among the three ways of life. Marking the influence of *The Plain Dealer* on Congreve, Holland notes that "the solitary [character] moves further and further out toward the periphery of the action" as Congreve perfects his craft.

Kelsall, M. M. Introduction to *Love for Love*, by William Congreve. London: Ernest Benn, 1969.
Gives a brief biographical sketch of Congreve and describes the play's reception in 1695. In summarizing the major themes, characters, and language of the play, Kelsall observes that "it is this low epicureanism which the high seriousness of Puritanical morality cannot stomach." Includes the prologue meant to be spoken by Anne Bracegirdle in men's clothes, and another by Thomas Betterton. Not as heavily footnoted as other editions.

Love, Harold. "*Love for Love*." In his *Congreve*. Oxford, England: Basil Blackwell, 1974.
A kinder, less threatening play than Congreve's earlier efforts. Not purely a social comedy, the structure works from the juxtaposition of three sets of teacher-pupil relationships. Mrs. Frail matches Ben sea-term for sea-term, until he retreats to his own element. The close reading of the text reveals a more complex social arrangement than critics have previously extracted, and "generous" Valentine's conversion is a "miracle" of understanding.

Milhous, Judith, and Robert D. Hume. "*Love for Love* (1695)." In their *Producible Interpretation: Eight English Plays, 1675-1707*. Carbondale: Southern Illinois University Press, 1985.
Congreve's most popular play, it has attracted less critical attention. In this "production analysis," it is more effective as a stage vehicle than *The Way of the World*. Should it be approached as a humorous comedy or as a romance? The questions are raised as to whether Valentine changes in the play, whether "the education of Valentine" (rather than a test) is a legitimate approach, or whether the play is a fairy tale. Milhous and Hume attempt an "ideal" casting of two approaches using actors from Congreve's time: humorous comedy versus romance. The play is "basically a ragout of popular devices from 1690s' comedies of all sorts."

Taylor, D. Crane. "*Love for Love*." In his *William Congreve*. Oxford, England: Oxford University Press, 1931.
The play's historical value comes from its place in the split of acting companies in 1695; Congreve may have been an original patentee in the new arrangement, or have gained his partnership from *Love for Love*'s success with the new company. Taylor takes more time discussing the plot and characters of this play than Congreve's earlier works ("because of the distinct contribution

which they make to English comedy") and concludes that "the wit is finer than in either [earlier] comedy, more subtle, pointed, deft, and graceful."

The Mourning Bride

Potter, Elmer B. "The Paradox of Congreve's *Mourning Bride.*" *PMLA: Publications of the Modern Language Association of America* 58, no. 4 (December, 1943): 977-1001.
The paradox is that this play (first produced in 1697) is Congreve's only serious play, a "melodrama" before its time, in the tragic genre perfected by John Dryden, Colley Cibber, and Thomas Otway. In its first reception, Congreve was praised (and rode his reputation into a distinguished if impoverished maturity), but later critics have been harsher. Jeremy Collier, in singling out this effort for his attack in the *Short View*, may have been right for once, but the paradox reconciles itself with a close look at the play's merits. Potter concludes with a review of subsequent productions and editions, some designed for specific actors and actresses.

The Old Bachelor

Birdsall, Virginia Ogden. "Congreve's Apprenticeship." Part 1, "*The Old Batchelor.*" In her *Wild Civility: The English Comic Spirit on the Restoration Stage.* Bloomington: Indiana University Press, 1970.
Congreve immediately takes a mental approach. Here is the thinking playwright with thematic ideas at the center of his plan. Bellmour is the sign of a philosophical streak new to Restoration comedy. His dedication to pleasure (quite different from Sir Jasper's in *The Country Wife*) is a philosophy of life, not just a concession to indolence. An Epicurean, he believes "being alive and living life well" is best. The metaphorical pattern of the play deepens in act 5, with mention of Aesop's *Fables*, and remonstrances against too literal an interpretation of carpe diem attitudes.

Gibbons, Brian. "Congreve's *The Old Batchelour* and Jonsonian Comedy." In *William Congreve*, edited by Brian Morris. Mermaid Critical Commentaries. London: Ernest Benn, 1972.
Gibbons takes a historical perspective concerning the influence on Congreve's first play from Ben Jonson's previous successes in the form before the interregnum. First considerations regarding Congreve's exposure to the stage prior to his London experiences, referring to Trinity College and to Smock Alley Theatre in Dublin. Structurally and stylistically Congreve's first work is "under

Jonson's guidance," and the debt is "in the essentials" of design and mood, analyzed here in traditional critical language.

Henderson, Anthony G. "Introduction to *The Old Batchelour*." In *The Comedies of William Congreve*, edited by Henderson. Cambridge, England: Cambridge University Press, 1982.
Congreve's "precocious" first play had been written four years earlier according to the published dedication; in its premiere (1693) it was well served by a prominent cast that included Thomas Betterton, who was to be connected with Congreve through both their careers. Also popular in published form, it borrowed from Congreve's classical education as well as from Jacobean, French, and Restoration predecessors; it is his least known comedy.

Hodges, John C. "The Composition of Congreve's First Play." *PMLA: Publications of the Modern Language Association of America* 58, no. 4 (December, 1943): 971-976.
The Old Bachelor (1692), generally acknowledged as a remarkable first play for a young man in his early twenties, may have been written even four years earlier, when Congreve was only nineteen. In fact, even the place of composition (before his London life) is not clear: in Dublin as a student, or sitting by the banks of a river near his family home in Derbyshire? This article brings together all the pertinent facts, sorting them out, adding a discovery by Hodges himself of a "recess . . . half way down a rocky, wooded hill that rises sharply from the banks of the Manifold River," which he claims could be exactly where the play was composed. The details are unimportant; Hodges' methodologies are interesting for their creative leaps from fact to fancy.

Holland, Norman N. "*The Old Batchelor*." In his *The First Modern Comedies: The Significance of Etherege, Wycherley and Congreve*. Cambridge, Mass.: Harvard University Press, 1959.
The almost twenty-year gap between William Wycherley and Congreve saw a shift in the relation of "right" and "wrong" ways of life as well, a schism rather than a reconciliation. Congreve's fools, heroes and heroines experience a tension in a "co-ordinate system" which Holland supplies in graph form, this time three-dimensional because "conversion up" and "conversion down" are added to the other polarities. Conversions "upward" are suggested in the heavenly images, for example, with which Vainlove describes the prospect of marriage to Araminta. Holland's schematic idea reveals the truth of conventional critical opinion of many of Congreve's characters: They are "isolated individuals surrounded by choices." One of the best applications of the imaginative tools Holland has devised for this study.

Love, Harold. "*The Old Batchelour*." In his *Congreve*. Oxford, England: Basil Blackwell, 1974.

The opening scene is a categorical dismissal of all such pretenses and "re-
• ceived values" as wisdom, learning and virtue, to be set aside at least during
the play's duration and replaced by wit and pleasure. This daring attitude was
an invitation of the drama itself to its audiences. In subsequent work Congreve
will try to "atone for his folly" in this first effort. Congreve's notion of the
function of wit "is in advance of Dryden's." Love makes the point that several
pages of analysis are required for a scene that passes the stage in brief minutes.

McComb, John King. "Congreve's *The Old Bachelour*: A Satiric Anatomy." *Studies
in English Literature 1500-1900* 17, no. 3 (Summer, 1977): 361-372.
This is the kind of essay that argues for increased attention to the early work of
a playwright whose eventual genius is universally acknowledged. McComb
sees in the collection of stock characters, the borrowed plot, and inherited
tradition the emergence of "satiric themes that will interest him in some of his
finest later work." By employing Restoration materials in "the form of a satiric
anatomy of the vice of unbridled lust," in the service of Augustan satire,
Congreve achieves the refinement of style culminating in *The Way of the
World*.

Taylor, D. Crane. "*The Old Batchelor.*" In his *William Congreve*. Oxford, England:
Oxford University Press, 1931.
The production of Congreve's first play in 1692(?) marks a new generation of
Restoration drama, in which "wit in English comedy had been raised to the
peerage." Discusses Congreve's technique, debts to John Dryden and Thomas
Southerne, relations with John Dennis and Henry Purcell, and the social accep-
tance of his work, but does not analyze the play's plot or characters in any
depth.

The Way of the World

Barnard, John. Critical introduction to *The Way of the World*, by William Congreve.
Edinburgh, Scotland: Oliver & Boyd, 1972.
"A mature and human exploration of the necessary artifices of feeling and
passion" which "rejects dissimulation in favor of lasting and reciprocal relations between man and woman" is Barnard's assessment, noting that "over-
emphasis in the structure and themes of comedy at the expense of its wit and
humour" can distort the play's real value. Reviews importance of "generosity"
(versus sentiment) in the play. An appendix clarifies the Wishfor't family tree;
a final glossary helps immensely, but might have been distributed as footnotes
on pertinent pages. Textual notes and commentary, and a good bibliography.

Birdsall, Virginia Ogden. "*Way of the World*." In her *Wild Civility: The English Comic Spirit on the Restoration Stage*. Bloomington: Indiana University Press, 1970.*
Restoration comedy has come a great distance from Sir Frederick Frollick (in George Etherege's *The Comical Revenge*) to Witwoud and Petulant. Mirabell and Millamant retain "that core of irrepressible naturalness and aggressive independence" recognizable in all Congreve's work. The play is the culmination of Congreve's genius, with Lady Wishfor't's portrait contrasted to that of Millamant, who does not allow passion or sentiment to tyrannize her. Mirabell and Millamant have "socialized" the passions: "After them, the comic spirit of Restoration drama could scarcely have aspired to any higher development."

Fujimura, Thomas H. "Congreve's Last Play." In *Restoration Dramatists: A Collection of Critical Essays*, edited by Earl Miner. Englewood Cliffs, N.J.: Prentice-Hall, 1966.
Extracted from a longer chapter on Congreve in Fujimura's book-length study of the Restoration wit. Mirabell is a character who, like the age, is being transformed from a pleasure-seeking wit into a simpler, more responsible wit of the "age of sense and sensibility"; it is an important point that the play opens with "sententious Mirabell" having already broken off relations with Marwood and concerning himself with the possibility of offspring. Fujimura follows his distinctions of the kinds of wit, identifying Mirabell as suffering from "sobriety."

Gagen, Jean. "Congreve's Mirabell and the Ideal of the Gentleman." *PMLA: Publications of the Modern Language Association of America* 79, no. 4 (September, 1964): 422-427.
A character study of Mirabell (*The Way of the World*, 1700) in the light of past critical opinions, but with a new consideration of the rules of gentlemanly behavior and reputation, this study treats the text as literature, without substantive reference to its life on the stage. In its treatment of affairs, illicit amours, scandals, unhappy marriages, and suitors in opposition, the analysis reads more like a gossip column than an essay, but makes several telling points about Mirabell's superficially villainous but ultimately gentlemanly behavior. The structure of the play "accurately reflects the standards which prevailed when Congreve penned his masterpiece," and "Mirabell is a gentleman beyond reproach."

Gibbons, Brian. Introduction to *The Way of the World*, by William Congreve. London: Ernest Benn, 1971.
A long and thorough introduction which includes biographical data, a summary of the play, and a review of sources for Congreve's last dramatic comedy. "A practical economy of stagecraft" and the consistent invention of Thomas Betterton and Anne Bracegirdle in creating central characters gave Congreve's

work a uniformity of quality of which this play is the culmination. Facsimile of title page of the 1700 publication.

Hawkins, Harriett. " 'Offending Against Decorums': The Reflection of Social Experience in *The Way of the World*." In her *Likenesses of Truth in Elizabethan and Restoration Drama*. Oxford, England: Clarendon Press, 1972.
Examines the structure of Congreve's last play, concluding "that we like it with its faults, nay, even like it for its faults," an observation logically extended to Congreve's world as well. In place of active plot, the "progressive revelations of character" move the play forward; genuine passion is what survives without illusion. The characters are finally as worthy of love in the Restoration world as *King Lear*'s characters are in his.

Henderson, Anthony G. "Introduction to *The Way of the World*." In *The Comedies of William Congreve*, edited by Henderson. Cambridge, England: Cambridge University Press, 1982.
Dedicating his work to the Earl of Mountague, Congreve returned to the comic genre after the success of his tragedy, *The Mourning Bride*, in 1697. Jeremy Collier's scathing condemnation of the stage had appeared in 1698, singling out Congreve's earlier work for its criticism. In many respects his last play is a dramatic response more effective than his prose defense, which was "scarcely more moderate in tone than the fulminations against him." The role of Millamant continues to be an enviable one, right up to Geraldine McEwan's portrayal in 1969.

Hinnant, Charles H. "Wit, Propriety, and Style in *The Way of the World*." *Studies in English Literature 1500-1900* 17, no. 3 (Summer, 1977): 373-386.
The concept of wit, almost a formal designation in the period, is examined to unravel the complex verbal gymnastics of Congreve's characters, possessed with a linguistic ingenuity even to the lowest figure. Equally complicated and formal is the notion of "propriety," a social distinction possibly lost to modern critics but clearly discernible to Restoration theatergoers. Thus the subtle differences among the rhetorical devices of the several characters were detected and appreciated by the sophisticated audience of this comedy, successful because of Congreve's "refusal to confine wit to mere wordplay, to separate language from serious social and moral concerns."

Holland, Norman N. "*The Way of the World*." In his *The First Modern Comedies: The Significance of Etherege, Wycherley, and Congreve*. Cambridge, Mass.: Harvard University Press, 1959.
Unsuccessful in its premiere, this last play may have suffered from Collier's "foolish tract." Congreve's language here is "champagne, with all the virtues and limitations of that singular beverage" (as is Holland's rhetoric as he nears

the end of his study). Holland diagrams the complicated family tree in order to launch into a comparison between "appearances (the overt family relations) and 'nature' (the hidden emotional facts)," and more important, "the true interaction between these two kinds of relationships." His last diagram, curving and flowing from erections to emancipations to unravelings, takes the play from opening to closing curtain with an intoxicating visual grace of its own.

Hopper, Vincent F., and Gerald B. Lahey, eds. (with George L. Hersey). *The Way of the World*, by William Congreve. Great Neck, N.Y.: Barron's Educational Series, 1958.
A singularly unremarkable edition, except for a long introductory essay on the playwright and play, with a "note" on Restoration staging contributed by George L. Hersey. Remarks on Congreve's highborn status, Irish upbringing, and the "notable social affliction" of membership in the Kit-Cat Club. The title refers to the "infidelities and deceptions of husbands, wives, and lovers . . . and the slightly cynical acceptance of the facts." An illustration of Drury Lane's wing-and-drop stage, with two pairs of proscenium doors, circa 1700.

Kroll, Richard W. "Discourse and Power in *The Way of the World*." *ELH* 53, no. 4 (Winter, 1986): 727-758.
A long and complicated essay, itself divided into four parts (plus five pages of notes, themselves continuations of the arguments), dealing with "the inescapable nature of memory (both individual and social) and the necessity of discourse," as they threaten freedom and align themselves with power. An application of theory of discourse (part of linguistic studies) applied to the specific text, whose language is examined in great detail, inside the context of Congreve's work, society, and philosophical predilections.

Love, Harold. "*The Way of the World*." In his *Congreve*. Oxford, England: Basil Blackwell, 1974.
An "infectiously enjoyable" play by the thirty-year-old Congreve, but Love senses a darkening of tone from *Love for Love*. Modern producers must deal with the indirectness of discourse in Congreve's world, in which "quite minor alterations to the elaborate formulae of compliment and civility could bear a heavy burden of implication." Comedy in general teaches us to resist the restrictions of human possibilities, a lesson this play in particular teaches at its center.

Lynch, Kathleen M. Introduction to *The Way of the World*, by William Congreve. London: Edward Arnold, 1965.
Reviews the original casting for the play and its place in popularity after Congreve's retirement from public life. Attention paid to the safeguards against

bad marriages and the prenuptial arrangements of Mrs. Fainall with Mirabell. The famous proviso scene is analyzed, with Millamant remaining "in control of the situation." Fair gloss, and appendixed chronology.

Powell, Jocelyn. "*The Way of the World.*" In her *Restoration Theatre Production.* London: Routledge & Kegan Paul, 1984.
After describing the methodology for studying production values in Restoration drama in the first half of the book, Powell examines several plays in detail; Congreve's last play, "an archetypal gallery of fools," works from the conventions of "humours" but inserts affected wit as a cause rather than "natural Folly." "Danger, viciousness, and absurdity" are blended in the finale, "by the continuous sense of inner action throughout the play." Select bibliography and index help put this play into the larger perspective of Powell's study.

Roberts, Philip. "Mirabell and Restoration Comedy." In *William Congreve*, edited by Brian Morris. Mermaid Critical Commentaries. London: Ernest Ben, 1972.
Examining *The Way of the World* as a play that "explodes the artifices of . . . 'the comic dance,' " this essay puts the play at the declining end of Restoration comedy, commenting on and repairing the genre's imperfections. Seeing the comic world suffering "from withdrawal symptoms," Roberts cites the shadowy decay of form in Witwoud and Petulant. Together with Congreve's lack of plot per se and his mention of the "Perfection of Dialogue" in the dedicatory epistle (seen here as an essay on the form itself), the evidence stacks up in favor of a dismantling of the "comic dance" of his predecessors.

Taylor, D. Crane. "*Way of the World.*" In his *William Congreve*. Oxford, England: Oxford University Press, 1931.
"With a fine disregard of the stupefying forces of conventional morality, Congreve has given in this comedy the mature and final expression of the Cavalier attitude," Taylor states in this discussion of how the play responds to Jeremy Collier's attacks by its mere existence. The plot, "wholly original," and the characters, "characters of humour raised to the realm of individuality," are examined at some length, with praise for every aspect of the masterpiece, especially language and style: "The closer one studies it the more its magic becomes apparent."

Weales, Gerald. Introduction to *The Way of the World*, by William Congreve. San Francisco: Chandler Publishing Co., 1966.
Accompanying a reprint of the text (Nettleton and Case, 1939), this essay concentrates on the distinctness of the characters compared with their universality: a "conventional hero-villain plot" that delighted its audiences, who believed themselves more discriminating. "A good-mannered satirist," however contradictory, is Congreve's description of himself. Lightly glossed text.

JOHN CROWNE

Burns, Edward. "Professional Dramatists: Shadwell and Crowne." Part 2, "John
Crowne." In his *Restoration Comedy: Crises of Desire and Identity*. New York:
St. Martin's Press, 1987.
In an exceedingly long career (1665 to 1698), Crowne tried to regain family
properties in Nova Scotia by endearing himself to the court. His first comedy,
The Country Wit, presents the eponymous character of Mannerly Shadow; *Sir
Courtly Nice*, from a Spanish source, "places the whole Whig/Tory contro-
versy within the family structure." His last comedy, *The Married Beau*, har-
nesses a "bitter moral energy" found more often in his dedications and fore-
words than in the plays themselves.

Hughes, Charlotte Bradford. *John Crowne's "Sir Courtly Nice" : A Critical Edition*.
The Hague, Netherlands: Mouton, 1966.
More than an edition of the play, this study outlines Crowne's life, his work,
and his contribution to the daily stage fare of the Restoration. His tragedies,
considered mediocre, were interspersed with more successful comedies, of
which this one was the most successful. Written to procure favor from Charles
II, it was just out of rehearsal when the king died, crushing Crowne's hopes for
preferment. Subsequent stage history, analysis of Spanish sources, a calendar
of performances, extended explanatory notes, and a bibliography.

Wilcox, John. "The Minor Borrowers." Part 4, "John Crowne." In his *The Relation
of Molière to Restoration Comedy*. New York: Columbia University Press,
1938.
One episode in *The Country Wit* is borrowed from Molière's *The Sicilian*; *The
English Friar* shares some of *Tartuffe*'s politico-religious ideas, but the relationship between the two plays is more complicated. Crowne is, according to
Wilcox, "third rate," and "his method and spirit did not reach England
through" Molière.

Wilson, John Harold, ed. *City Politiques*, by John Crowne. Lincoln: University of
Nebraska Press, 1967.
The Regents Restoration Drama series includes Crowne's pro-Tory comedy (his
second), possibly typical of the "professional" plays that held the stage between geniuses. Political in its implications and originally refused a license, it
was successful onstage because of its satirical references to real figures (at least
one was a lawyer); much of its bite is lost to history. The colloquial dialogue
does not rely on sexual overtones for its wit. Notes and chronology.

JOHN DRYDEN

General Studies

Arundell, D. D., ed. *Dryden and Howard 1664-1668*. Cambridge, England: Cambridge University Press, 1929.
The texts that trace the collaboration and controversy between Dryden and Sir Robert Howard, conducted in dedicatory epistles, letters, and essays. *The Indian Queen* was the collaboration (Dryden also married Howard's sister), and *An Essay of Dramatic Poesy* served as one side of the intellectual controversy centered on the value of rhyme in the drama; their differences and agreements are summarized in the introduction. Each entry is accompanied by editorial notes; an index gives access from essay to essay.

Attridge, Derek. "Dryden's Dilemma, or, Racine Refashioned: The Problem of the English Dramatic Couplet." *The Yearbook of English Studies* 9 (1979): 55-77.
A study in the couplet versification of Restoration heroic drama, influenced, by but by no means a direct transliteration of, the French practices admired and recommended by Charles II on his return to England. Carefully examining and comparing metrical constructions in both languages, Attridge asks larger questions about the history of rhyme in English literary tradition, and about the characteristic rhythmic organization in every language. "The failure of the English dramatic couplet" is seen as "the extinction in the evolutionary struggle of a species unfitted for its environment," with its formality "at odds with the colloquialism of much of the syntax." A valuable study for students of poetry as well as drama.

Barbeau, Anne T. *The Intellectual Design of John Dryden's Heroic Plays*. New Haven, Conn.: Yale University Press, 1970.
This study treats Dryden's work as plays of ideas "in which discourse and action stand in an almost mathematical relationship." Dryden's conservatism, his love of design, and his awesome classical education inform the heroic plays at every turn. Five plays get a close reading: *The Indian Queen*, *The Indian Emperour*, *Tyrannic Love*, *The Conquest of Granada*, and *Aureng-Zebe*. A chapter uniting the heroic drama with Dryden's narrative poems *Astraea Redux* and *Annus Mirabilis* is particularly valuable. Barbeau notes that "in all of the works analyzed, Dryden suggests that private conviction must in some way be balanced against the common good." List of works consulted; index.

Beaurline, L. A., and Fredson Bowers, eds. *John Dryden: Four Comedies*. Chicago: University of Chicago Press, 1967.
This and the companion volume on tragedy (listed below) are models of

modern textual scholarship, culling from the various extant manuscripts, quartos and publications of Dryden's lifetime the most authoritative text available to modern critics and readers. In addition to a protracted general introduction to the topic (working toward a sorting out of the genres from "high farce" to "romantic"), each play (*Secret Love*, *Sir Martin Mar-All*, *An Evening's Love*, and *Marriage à la Mode*) has its own introduction, summarizing major themes and structure, production history, and textual difficulties. Bibliography.

—————————. *John Dryden: Four Tragedies*. Chicago: University of Chicago Press, 1967.
A textually accurate edition of Dryden's major tragedies, with a general introduction comparing Dryden's "impassioned sense of design" with Edmund Spenser, William Shakespeare, and John Milton. Dryden's work, "replete with besieged cities, tyrannical monarchs, lecherous fathers, . . . generous rivals, discontented generals . . . and with grand opportunities for confrontation scenes and for debates of political policy," is represented here with *The Indian Emperour*, *Aureng-Zebe*, *All for Love*, and *Don Sebastian*, each play given its own introductory summary of themes, structure, and textual and stage history. Bibliography.

Dobrée, Bonamy. *John Dryden*. London: Longmans, Green, 1956.
A monograph in the bibliographical series of supplements to *British Book News* (number 70), this brief recapitulation of previous scholarship by the same author provides a convenient comparison of Dryden's poetry, criticism, and life to his dramatic output, especially in the chapter entitled "Finding the Way," an overview of young Dryden's experiments in the lyric and dramatic forms. In any study of Dryden's drama, it is important to realize the giant intellect of the man responsible for the relatively simple-minded popular stage writing. Dobrée shows where his attraction to a life of literature begins, "namely to improve, clarify and enrich the language," driven by his desire "to bring order, grace, expressiveness, into verse writing." A select bibliography.

—————————. "John Dryden." In his *Variety of Ways: Discussions on Six Authors*. Oxford, England: Clarendon Press, 1932. Reprint. Freeport, N.Y.: Books for Libraries Press, 1967.
In Dryden's age, "poetry must instruct as well as delight, though what themes exactly it was to instruct in was left conveniently vague." Without being pedantic ("because he does not have to be"), Dryden theorized and practiced dramatic art, not always in harmony with each other, constructing "distinctive, solid objects, which it is rash to despise if we do not wish to lose an opportunity for delight."

_____ . "John Dryden (1631-1700) and Artificial Tragedy." In his *Restoration Tragedy, 1660-1720*. Oxford, England: Clarendon Press, 1929.

Dobrée takes on the subject of reality versus artificiality in Restoration drama, in this study of Dryden's unsentimental tragedies, including *The Conquest of Granada* and *Aureng-Zebe*. The quality of "prettiness" is examined in a long passage from *Don Sebastian*; Dobrée claims that Dryden is the "purest artist of all the Restoration writers of tragedy, besides being the most accomplished craftsman."

Doyle, Anne. "Dryden's Authorship of *Notes and Observations on The Empress of Morocco* (1674)." *Studies in English Literature 1500-1900* 6, no. 3 (Summer, 1966): 421-445.

Here is a model of close critical work, presenting a methodology for research as well as the specific conclusions of the inquiry at hand. The central concern is a controversy surrounding a prose response to the dedicatory epistle accompanying a published play by Elkanah Settle in 1673, *The Empress of Morocco*, attacking various contemporaries. While the conclusion is undramatic (Dryden wrote alone), Doyle's argument, sophisticated in its attention to detail, is crisp and convincing and demonstrates the clearheadedness required for this kind of literary scholarship.

Grace, Joan C. "John Dryden's Theory of Tragedy: 'They, Who Have Best Succeeded on the Stage, Have Still Conform'd Their Genius to Their Age.' " In her *Tragic Theory in the Critical Works of Thomas Rymer, John Dennis, and John Dryden*. London: Associated University Presses, 1975.

In a larger study on tragedy, this essay examines Dryden's attention "to the demands of the work itself and to its effects upon the audience in terms of the age in which he lived." He seeks a compromise between the French constrictions and the "undisciplined irregularity of the English" in his versification; at the same time, he holds "conscious reasoning, clarity, and refinement" in the highest esteem. Some terms, such as "probability" and "imagination," are unclear in Dryden's work.

Guffey, George R. "Politics, Weather, and the Contemporary Reception of the Dryden-Davenant *Tempest*." *Restoration* 8, no. 1 (Spring, 1984): 1-9.

By examining at close range the various records of reception of this Shakespeare adaptation, Guffey reduces the force of modern criticisms of the play as "monstrous." Samuel Pepys liked the play at every viewing, and it was presented at court at least five times. The reason for the disparity between opinions rests in "layers of meaning and nodes of affect that have over the last two or three centuries gone unrecognized." Among them are the weather reports at the time ("tempestuous weather"), and the political parallels dis-

cerned by Dryden's audience but not by modern scholars. A strong defense of
theatre as a living art, not a literary scholar's dusty footnote.

Hamilton, Walter. "John Dryden." In his *The Poets Laureate of England*. London:
Elliot Stock, 1879. Reprint. Detroit: Gale Research, 1968.
In Hamilton's opinion (with which he makes free throughout), Dryden "holds
first place in the second rank of our classical poets." Hamilton presents a
biography of Dryden, whose life bridged the interregnum. He notes that Dryden's character was called into question on several occasions: "Surely it is
possible to admire the *poetry* of Dryden, without seeking to justify its licentiousness, or its sickening adulation of the predominant faction." Lists Dryden's dramatic works.

Hathaway, Baxter. "John Dryden and the Function of Tragedy." *PMLA: Publications of the Modern Language Association of America* 58, no. 3 (September,
1943): 665-673.
Bridging the transition "between the explanation of the function of tragedy
created by the Neo-Stoics . . . and the sentimental view . . . after the advent
of Shaftesbury," Dryden sought a reconciliation in such contemporary philosophical works as René Rapin's interpretation of Aristotle. In his essays,
"Dryden combines the functions of purgation from tragedy [while] resisting
the approaches of passion in his breast [and the] dangers resulting from action
based upon passion," with the sentimental attitude of tragic pity. He concludes
(in Hathaway's words): "Tragedy should remove pride and hardness of
heart . . . it should increase our fear to humble us to the will of God . . . it
should increase our disposition to pity the sufferings of our fellow men."

Hughes, Derek. *Dryden's Heroic Plays*. Lincoln: University of Nebraska Press, 1981.
Chapters on five of Dryden's heroic plays are bracketed by an essay on the
"idealisation of Man" in Dryden's work and a postscript on Dryden's work
after his great political and religious poems. Hughes sees "the quest for perma-
nence, and the limitations of heroism" as pervading themes, with the imperfect hero pitted against the Unregenerate Man. *The Indian Emperour* embodies
most of Dryden's principles; he is contrasted with his contemporary John
Milton, who "repudiates the epic celebration of fallen belligerence." Sources
and analogues provided in an appendix; notes and index.

Hume, Robert D. *Dryden's Criticism*. Ithaca, N.Y.: Cornell University Press, 1970.
In essays, prefaces, and dedicatory epistles, Dryden articulated the principles
of dramatic poetry in a series of statements rivaled only by Aristotle. Hume
examines the documents toward answering the question, "What does Dryden
set out to accomplish in his criticism?" Dryden's critical methods, his sense of
history, and his relation with Thomas Rymer and other critics of his day are

analyzed; a chapter on neoclassicism puts Dryden in perspective with French critics of his time. Makes some difficult material more accessible; valuable for rhetorical studies as well. Index.

Jalali, R. K. *John Dryden: An Essay of Dramatic Poesy*. New Delhi, India: Aarti Book Centre, 1974.
More than simply an edition of Dryden's tract, this study is an exhaustive review of virtually every critical aspect of his work. Fourteen chapters and a summing up (which succinctly summarizes the entire contents of Dryden's work), followed by the text itself. Elaborate annotations and glosses; selected literary observations about Dryden; even a series of examination questions with answers are supplied, ending with a chronology and selected bibliography.

Jefferson, D. W. " 'All, All of a Piece Throughout': Thoughts on Dryden's Dramatic Poetry." In *Restoration Theatre*, edited by John Russell Brown and Bernard Harris. Stratford-upon-Avon Studies 6. London: Edward Arnold, 1965.
A good general article on Dryden's consistent habits of poetic construction, particularly useful in tying in his dramatic work with his poetry. *Don Sebastian* is dealt with at length, compared both to other dramatic works such as *Aureng-Zebe*, *All for Love*, and *Tyrannic Love*, and to *The Hind and the Panther*, Dryden's allegorical Christian poem. A prefatory note gives a brief biography and a list of scholarship for future study.

───────── . "The Significance of Dryden's Heroic Plays." In *Restoration Drama: Modern Essays in Criticism*, edited by John Loftis. New York: Oxford University Press, 1966. (Also published in *Restoration Dramatists: A Collection of Critical Essays*, edited by Earl Miner. Englewood Cliffs, N.J.: Prentice-Hall, 1966.)
The rhymed heroic plays of Dryden are not well understood because, according to this essay, they are not always to be taken seriously; even the preface to *The Conquest of Granada* invites ironic reading. Dryden's conception of heroism—the irresistible conqueror with a dynamic personality—allows him "unlimited opportunities for exercising his gifts of rhetoric." Consequently, he endows his heroes with debating powers. Long passages from *Aureng-Zebe* demonstrate the striking imagery; the genre gives Dryden "more scope for free indulgence in fantasy" than the earlier satires.

Kirsch, Arthur C. *Dryden's Heroic Drama*. Princeton, N.J.: Princeton University Press, 1965.
Dryden's criticism of heroic drama can be misread; "he was inclined to emphasize his innovations and minimize his debts." Discussions of central ideas such as the epic analogy, structure and staging, rhyming, and the heroic hero lead to a two-part analysis of his career, concluding that his plays must be

understood "as a product of a theater which was poised between two dramatic traditions," the exhausted Elizabethan/Jacobean/Carolinian tradition and the modern dramatic tradition of the Age of Reason. Index.

Kronenberger, Louis. "Dryden." In his *The Thread of Laughter: Chapters on English Stage Comedy from Jonson to Maugham*. New York: Alfred A. Knopf, 1952.
Dealing only with Dryden's comedies, which are not comic in the same way as others, Kronenberger observes "the Restoration stage has a strikingly indoors quality, at odds with Dryden's own outdoor vigor." Reviews the plot of *The Spanish Friar*, questions characters' motives, and concludes that the play's energetic verse "has fire but no warmth." Remarking that these plays are still pleasant to read, Kronenberger moves through the two plots and reversals of *Marriage à la Mode*. "Lacking in salt" is his opinion—Dryden's "qualities have the drag of an anchor and chains."

Larson, Richard Leslie. *Studies in Dryden's Dramatic Technique: The Use of Scenes Depicting Persuasion and Accusation*. Salzburg, Austria: Institut für Englische Sprache und Literatur, 1975.
By concentrating on a relatively specific part of Dryden's dramaturgy and theory, this study of confrontations in the work illuminates Dryden's "single prominent dramatic technique" and speaks to important thematic issues emerging from such confrontations, whether resolved or not. Divides his discussion by genre and devotes separate chapters to *Aureng-Zebe*, *All for Love*, and *Don Sebastian*. Concludes that Dryden's techniques of accusation and persuasion "enabled him to achieve fullness, variety, and suspense." Bibliography.

Law, Richard. "The Heroic Ethos in John Dryden's Heroic Plays." *Studies in English Literature 1500-1900* 23, no. 3 (Summer, 1983): 389-398.
Law addresses the question of whether Dryden's plays are "dramatic counterparts of the epic poem" or separate creations answering to other (French romance) principles. The relationship between the heroic poem and the heroic play is examined from the standpoint of ethical theory prevalent in Dryden's time. Besides the primary documents (including Dryden's own extensive critical essays), Law cites Homer, Milton, and other great thinkers in the question of the heroic ethos. An important article for the continuing discussion of Dryden's critical theory in relation to its dramatic realization.

McHenry, Robert W., Jr. "Dryden's Architectural Metaphors and Restoration Architecture." *Restoration* 9, no. 2 (Fall, 1985): 61-74.
In an age when theatre architecture in particular, and London architecture in general, was so active (Christopher Wren, Sir John Vanbrugh), Dryden finds

all around him the metaphorical inspiration he employs in his poetry, even his prose criticism, but not, oddly, to any great degree in his plays; at least McHenry does not choose his examples from them, except for a prologue for an unnamed play to commemorate the opening of the King's Company's theatre in Drury Lane in 1674. If images of foundation, symmetry, fabric, and "a structure that unites two potentially contradictory values, strength and grace" can be found in the nondramatic material, perhaps a further study can illuminate the plays in this same regard.

Mignon, Elisabeth. "Dryden, Shadwell, and Aphra Behn." Part 1, "Dryden." In her *Crabbed Age and Youth: The Old Men and Women in the Restoration Comedy of Manners*. Durham, N.C.: Duke University Press, 1947.

Dryden's comedies cannot be easily compared with George Etherege and William Congreve for his use of age, where such characters significantly "appear when Dryden is writing in the strain of sentimental or intrigue comedy." Lord Nonsuch (in *The Wild Gallant*) shows Jonsonian influence, but "represents the new preoccupation of the comedy of manners with senility." Dryden's experiment with combining heroics and sentiment with comedy in *The Assignation* is an example of why "he remains in literary history the clearheaded theorist whose practice fell short of his critical principles."

Moore, Frank Harper. *The Nobler Pleasure: Dryden's Comedy in Theory and Practice*. Chapel Hill: University of North Carolina Press, 1963.

A chronological report of Dryden's apprenticeship, early formulation of his theory, and the application of that theory through several periods of success and adjustment. Citing the dual accusations of Gerard Langbaine (for wholesale plagiarism) and Jeremy Collier (for immorality and profaneness) for the critical disregard of Dryden's comedies to date, Moore attempts a neutral description of six periods but also defends the poet, noting that "he wrote for a cynical and obstreperous audience." Notes, bibliography, index.

Pendlebury, F. J. *Dryden's Heroic Plays: A Study of the Origins*. New York: Russell & Russell, 1923, reprint 1967.

By comparing the heroic traditions that Dryden inherited with his own theoretical and practical contributions to the genre, Pendlebury points out the inconsistencies in Dryden's work that place them outside "the compass of a rigid theory" but notes also that "the best and most original quality of Dryden's criticism, its suggestiveness, would be lost sight of in a summary." This study puts Dryden in perspective with the English heroic play and the companion influences of the personal tastes of Charles II and Restoration stage conventions. A final chapter concentrates on the success of Dryden's versification. Contains a list of books consulted and an index.

Reverand, Cedric D., II. "Dryden's 'Essay of Dramatick Poesie': The Poet and the
World of Affairs." *Studies in English Literature 1500-1900* 22, no. 3 (Summer,
1982): 375-393.
Far from the modern view that the poet is removed from his or her society by
the aesthetic distance of the art, Dryden and his contemporaries saw the poet
as possessing "a tie in nature betwixt those who are born for worthy actions
and those who can transmit them to posterity," as he expresses in the dedicatory epistle to *All for Love* (1678). Reverand cites the passage in full and
continues his investigation of the "relationship between the poet and the world
of affairs" into Dryden's most important prose work, "Essay of Dramatick
Poesie." The question is whether the poet can compose "away from the din of
society, unheard by the people on the shore, and at the same time be a
significant and effective voice in that world of action." Opens new avenues of
inquiry for poet and student alike.

Saintsbury, George, ed. *John Dryden: Three Plays*. New York: Hill & Wang, n.d.
A late nineteenth century edition often reprinted, with an introduction that
gives "some considerable room to a general account of the author and of his
works." *The Conquest of Granada* (both parts), *Marriage à la Mode*, and
Aureng-Zebe are printed, with full dedicatory epistles and essays attached, but
without individual introductions or substantial footnotes. While denying Dryden's theatre "action, character, and completeness of effect," Saintsbury still
justifies this edition from the "astonishing evidences of literary craftsmanship
and of its results in good literature," thus shelving Dryden among the poets
rather than the playwrights.

Sherwood, Margaret. *Dryden's Dramatic Theory and Practice*. New York: Russell
& Russell, 1898, reprint 1966.
"Few plays are more undramatic than those of Dryden," Sherwood begins, and
takes her argument through 104 pages to conclude: "Dryden's dramatic work
is imitation, not organic creation. It lacks vital centre, and it has not endured."
Luckily, it endured long enough for T. S. Eliot to defend it. This study is
valuable as negative criticism and as an example of how the sensibilities of an
age can thwart the pursuit of critical truth. In fairness to Sherwood, she does
credit Dryden's dramatic theory as showing "on Dryden's part wide reading,
careful reflection."

Summers, Montague, ed. *Dryden: The Dramatic Works*. New York: Nonesuch
Press, 1932. Reprint. New York: Gordini Press, 1968.
Concentrating on the dramatic output, Summers supplies an introductory essay
of more than one hundred pages, plus prefatory notes, chronology, and commentary. Because Dryden was master of more than one genre, he stands apart
from virtually all other dramatists of the Restoration. As poet laureate he

influenced the entire literary scene of Charles II's time. Much of what Summers has written has since been corrected and revised, but this edition would be consulted by all subsequent scholars of Dryden.

Waith, Eugene M. "Dryden." In his *The Herculean Hero in Marlowe, Chapman, Shakespeare, and Dryden*. New York: Columbia University Press, 1962.
Dryden uses the features of the heroes of his predecessors, but adds to them the distinct traits called for by "the ideals and the stage conventions of a new age." Waith analyzes *The Conquest of Granada*, *Aureng-Zebe* and *All for Love*. "Firmly based in a morality of its own" in an age "hostile to moral ambiguity," the Herculean hero was not very popular despite the respect for individuality at the time. "The growing sense of civic responsibility . . . demanded unequivocal self-sacrifice of the hero," a notion more palatable to Richard Steele's Cato than to Hercules.

Wilcox, John. "John Dryden and Thomas Shadwell." Part 1, "John Dryden." In his *The Relation of Molière to Restoration Comedy*. New York: Columbia University Press, 1938.
Neither "important" to Restoration comedy nor quite a "minor" writer, Dryden failed to acknowledge Molière's influence on *An Evening's Love: Or, The Mock Astrologer*, but Wilcox claims the borrowing was so slight that Dryden did not deserve Gerard Langbaine's attack on his honesty. In a clearer adaptation, *Amphitryon: Or, The Two Socias*, Dryden freely credits Molière (and Plautus) in the dedicatory letter. *Sir Martin Mar-All* and *Marriage à la Mode* contain borrowings as well, but otherwise Dryden's work is "far from the norm of Molière."

All for Love

Andrew, N. J., ed. *All for Love*, by John Dryden. London: Ernest Benn, 11975.
The full text, with epistle dedicatory, preface, prologue, and epilogue; Andrew supplies an introductory essay (analyzing important passages as illustrations of Dryden's theories) and a summary of the author's life, the play's sources, and its place in Dryden's canon. "The theatrical purity and structural beauty" of the play is noted, along with "its power to arouse strong emotional reactions even on a casual reading." Strong gloss and footnotes.

Beaurline, L. A., and Fredson Bowers. "*All for Love*." In *John Dryden: Four Tragedies*, edited by Beaurline and Bowers. Chicago: University of Chicago Press, 1967.
While "in imitation" of Shakespeare, Dryden's treatment of the historical event does not pretend to return to Elizabethan forms. "An act of imaginative transposition" is called for, "a conscious recreation, a witty attempt to adapt a

classic so that the audience may very well see the differences between the
original and the imitation." Antony's character, and the consistency of his
"inner force," is Dryden's best accomplishment here. The original reception is
discussed, with subsequent publication history.

King, Robert L. "*Res et Verba*: The Reform of Language in Dryden's *All for Love*."
ELH 54, no. 1 (Spring, 1987): 45-61.
From his position in the Royal Society, Dryden paid careful attention to language reforms in his time, addressing problems of language and demonstrating
its correct use in his essays. This article suggests that Dryden's plays may be
studied as well, as pertinent to language reforms and the communication of
meaning. For example, the shift from rhymed to blank verse in the later plays
may articulate discussions of "the value of abstractions as embodiments of
ideals." An overview of some linguistic approaches, inviting further inquiry in
the same discipline.

Kirsch, Arthur C. "*Aureng-Zebe* and Its Successors." Part 2, "*All for Love*." In his
Dryden's Heroic Drama. Princeton, N.J.: Princeton University Press, 1965.
"Subverted at every turn by sentimental effects which emphasize not the
heroic glory of love, but its domesticity and compassion," Dryden's first un-
rhymed play also introduced, according to Kirsch, a new kind of characterization. Antony would sacrifice everything yet is tossed from emotion to emotion
as each character offers pleas to him: "His ability to assume such postures
with extravagance and tears becomes the final measure of his heroism," rather
than his resistance to passionate argument. Dryden is indebted to Nathaniel
Lee for the idea of expanding Octavia's role.

Larson, Richard Leslie. "*All for Love*: The Hero as Listener." In his *Studies in
Dryden's Dramatic Technique: The Use of Scenes Depicting Persuasion and
Accusation*. Salzburg, Austria: Institut für Englische Sprache und Literatur,
1975.
Because the structure of this play is built on a series of confrontational scenes,
it demonstrates Larson's theory well. The ideas of free will versus the "uncon-
trollable forces operating from within themselves" elicit pity in readers, because "this self-destruction . . . has high moral as well as political significance." The cosmic imagery and the subtitle ("The World Well Lost") imply
"that all creation responds to the actions" of the lover/rulers.

Milhous, Judith, and Robert D. Hume. "*All for Love* (1677)." In their *Producible
Interpretation: Eight English Plays, 1675-1707*. Carbondale: Southern Illinois
University Press, 1985.
A "production analysis" of the Dryden play that begs comparison with
William Shakespeare's *Antony and Cleopatra*. *All for Love* held the stage

through the eighteenth century. This interpretation is based on critical analysis of major turning points: Dryden's concept of tragedy; character analysis (especially that of Antony and Cleopatra, but also Ventidius and Alexas); production choices of rhythm, with charts of "gloom to death"; Antony's vacillations; emotional polarity (explained with valuable visualization of the dramatic elements); and the sense of direction (four main locations). A history of casting, 1677-1718, suggests the separate approaches of three productions.

Vieth, David M., ed. *All for Love*, by John Dryden. London: Edward Arnold, 1972.
After reviewing the textual history (rather more complex than most from this period), Vieth summarizes past criticism of the play, "appealing to the Augustan taste for economy, propriety, and polish even while occasionally offending the Augustan moral sense." The unavoidable comparisons with William Shakespeare's *Antony and Cleopatra* form the basis for the introductory essay, in which Vieth concludes, "If tragedy is Man Suffering, Dryden is Man Thinking," and the "rational and the tragic may be radically incompatible." Chronology.

Waith, Eugene M. "*All for Love*." In *Restoration Dramatists: A Collection of Critical Essays*, edited by Earl Miner. Englewood Cliffs, N.J.: Prentice-Hall, 1966. (Originally published in *The Herculean Hero in Marlowe, Chapman, Shakespeare, and Dryden*. New York: Columbia University Press, 1962.)
Working from a thematic premise of the Herculean hero, Waith sets aside the romantic considerations demanded in the title and examines Antony for traits of "the warrior whose nobility and generosity are combined with strong passion and a contemptuous disregard for the mores of his society." His scenes with Ventidius dominating the first act are as important as the scenes with Cleopatra, who is herself "carried away by a passion of heroic proportions." The key trait is their "shocking" indifference to the code of decency subscribed to by the ordinary citizen; the profile of the Herculean hero will appear again in the German romantic drama and the nineteenth century novel.

Aureng-Zebe

Barbeau, Anne T. "A Reading of the Heroic Plays." Part 5, "*Aureng-Zebe*." In her *The Intellectual Design of John Dryden's Heroic Plays*. New Haven, Conn.: Yale University Press, 1970.
"Like the impulsive heroes of previous plays," the hero of Dryden's last heroic play must struggle "against his desire to restore justice around him by means of violence." Dryden's introduction of the theme of conversion or repentance is proper to a play "dealing with private, moral issues rather than political ones." Barbeau does not see love as the central theme of the play, despite Indamora's

attraction in the eyes of at least four of the play's characters. Dryden was "ready to abandon heroic drama for a different kind of play" and to write *All for Love.*

Beaurline, L. A., and Fredson Bowers. *"Aureng-Zebe."* In *John Dryden: Four Tragedies*, edited by Beaurline and Bowers. Chicago: University of Chicago Press, 1967.
Surpassing "any other drama of the Restoration in intricacy, tension, balance, contrast, and variety," Dryden's last heroic play is a complex dramatic and poetic accomplishment, with supple lines and diverse moods. A long dedication to the Earl of Mulgrave, originally printed in the first quarto of the play, is quoted here as evidence that Dryden was anxious to write a "Heroick Poem." The source from François Bernier is mentioned. Good footnotes throughout this edition.

Hughes, Derek. *"Aureng-Zebe."* In his *Dryden's Heroic Plays*. Lincoln: University of Nebraska Press, 1981.
Despite Dryden's innovations in dramaturgy, this work retains the same protagonist, according to Hughes, who claims that Aureng-Zebe is "still of the same genus, the differences between him and [predecessors] being no greater than those between the contrasting heroes of any single romance." After a subsection entitled "Rebellion Against Time and Slavery to Change," Hughes offers a very close reading of passages in which Indamora is *not* onstage with Aureng-Zebe, as well as a careful examination of their confrontations and private scenes.

Kirsch, Arthur C. *"Aureng-Zebe* and Its Successors." Part 1, *"Aureng-Zebe* and the Fall of Glory." In his *Dryden's Heroic Drama*. Princeton, N.J.: Princeton University Press, 1965.
Unlike other plays, *Aureng-Zebe* is pervaded by "domestic sentimentality," especially in the portrayal of Melisinda. Kirsch examines Aureng-Zebe, the only hero of this drama, as a "departure from [Dryden's] earlier conception of heroic drama," more temperate, lacking "the marks of heroic virtue," and thus undermining the ethical properties of the hero. Morat's death-bed conversion and Aureng-Zebe's rise are Dryden's recognition of "the exhaustion of the form of drama which only four years before he had acclaimed as the equal of the tragedies of the last age."

_____ . "The Significance of Dryden's *Aureng-Zebe.*" In *Restoration Drama: Modern Essays in Criticism*, edited by John Loftis. New York: Oxford University Press, 1966. (Also published in *Restoration Dramatists: A Collection of Critical Essays*, edited by Earl Miner. Englewood Cliffs, N.J.: Prentice-Hall, Inc., 1966.

The 1670's saw two changes in Dryden's serious drama: the advent of sentimental heroes and the abandonment of rhyme. After the "Fall of Glory" hero in the rhymed *The Conquest of Granada*, the title character is passionless, a departure from previous heroes in the genre. His love for Indamora is his only passion, so the prospect of his father as rival forges an intolerable conflict of loyalties. The compassion here, as in Indamora's praise of Aureng-Zebe's "capacity for pity," is fully realized in *All for Love*. Notes continue the argument in greater detail.

Larson, Richard Leslie. "*Aureng-Zebe*: Heroism Purified and Sentimentalized." In his *Studies in Dryden's Dramatic Technique: The Use of Scenes Depicting Persuasion and Accusation.* Salzburg, Austria: Institut für Englische Sprache und Literatur, 1975.
The hero of this title "is content to earn admiration in the form of unmixed approval and emulation of his loyalty and intuitive magnanimity," setting him apart from previous heroes. Confrontational scenes do not serve to delineate character and communicate moral themes, but to "inspire our more unqualified emulation" through a series of highly emotional and persuasive appeals. A close reading of such scenes among Morat, Indamora, and Aureng-Zebe; the form may signal a change "from the delineation of heroism to the cultivation of strong feelings . . . for their own sakes."

Link, Frederick M., ed. *Aureng-Zebe*, by John Dryden. London: Edward Arnold, 1971.
A modernized version that owes something to the Beaurline-Bowers edition, with some admittedly arbitrary changes to the punctuation. A strong discussion of the source of the play from François Bernier; *Aureng-Zebe*, however, "is not an exploration of character developing through inner conflict toward self-knowledge, but a play demonstrating the proper conduct of a prince." Link notes the "forensic" nature of much of the dialogue, demonstrating Dryden's "interest in complex design and his rhetorical intent" and counting 1,900 of the play's 2,869 lines as two-character confrontations. Footnotes and chronology.

Newman, Robert S. "Irony and the Problem of Tone in Dryden's *Aureng-Zebe*." *Studies in English Literature 1500-1900* 10, no. 3 (Summer, 1970): 439-458.
Irony is not always visible in the written text, but must be deduced from the overall structure of the dramatic work. Dryden's tone, especially in his heroic tragedies, suggests he may override the "uniformly heroic and solemn" reception of his play with a satiric intent. Methods which "reveal ironic plot structures, mixtures of mode, and contrasts, shifts, qualifications and progressions of tone" may inform the work more thoroughly than a sober interpretation of the "panegyric."

Waith, Eugene M. "*Aureng-Zebe*." Chapter 6, part 2, in his *The Herculean Hero in
    Marlowe, Chapman, Shakespeare, and Dryden*. New York: Columbia Univer-
    sity Press, 1962.
    Discusses whether Aureng-Zebe is a "stock type," like Almanzor or Max-
    imine, or his character is unique. Argues that the differences among the gen-
    eral types is what makes this character so interesting. Dryden here "presents
    something much closer to a 'pattern of exact virtue' than he had done in
    Almanzor." While Morat is important, the play never leaves the struggle of
    Aureng-Zebe, who presents a "golden possibility" of controlling the heroic
    energy that Dryden praises in all of his heroic tragedies.

The Conquest of Granada

Barbeau, Anne T. "A Reading of the Heroic Plays." Part 4, "*The Conquest of
    Granada*." In her *The Intellectual Design of John Dryden's Heroic Plays*. New
    Haven, Conn.: Yale University Press, 1970.
    Continuing his dramatization of the disintegration of the non-Christian world,
    Dryden uses this play to make "an argument for tolerance and freedom of
    conscience," through the betrayal by the Zegry faction. Dryden uses the typical
    debate form, this time between the Duke of Arcos and Boabdelin; the "correct
    hero and the passionate hero" are Ozmyn and Almanzor, respectively. The
    theme of the play is that "those who follow the dictates of conscience and who
    keep their peace of mind" are without guilt.

Hughes, Derek. "*The Conquest of Granada*." In his *Dryden's Heroic Plays*. Lin-
    coln: University of Nebraska Press, 1981.
    Dryden had a surer hand in writing this play (1670), no longer tentative but
    still preoccupied with the same themes: "The commingling of passion and
    death is for the first time derived from a profound and overmastering psycho-
    logical compulsion" in the character of Almahide. After examining the "hero/
    villain" pairs in parts 1 and 2 of the play, Hughes treats the subject of the
    failure of ideal love in the characters of Almahide and Lyndaraxa, through
    close readings of their confrontations. In the "heroic world" of the play,
    actually a series of prison-dreams, they are "inhabiting a world of fantasy, lost
    in dreams of omnipotence."

Kirsch, Arthur C. "The Rhymed Plays from *The Rival Ladies* to *The Conquest of
    Granada*." Part 6, "*The Conquest of Granada*." In his *Dryden's Heroic
    Drama*. Princeton, N.J.: Princeton University Press, 1965.
    Written in two parts, Dryden's most ambitious heroic drama features a com-
    posite of the heroes of the past in the character of Almanzor, but "unlike his

Cavalier predecessors . . . he does not welcome his martyrdom." In her "driving ambitions for a throne, an ambition to which they subordinate every sentiment and every natural inclination," Lyndaraxa resembles her counterparts in Pierre Corneille's plays. Kirsch examines the argument for placing this work in the sentimental genre, noting that it is actually a continuation of Dryden's interest in "the ethos of *gloire*."

Powell, Jocelyn. *"Almanzor and Almahide: Or, The Conquest of Granada by the Spaniards."* In her *Restoration Theatre Production*. London: Routledge & Kegan Paul, 1984.
Powell's study of the style and form of productions of Restoration plays manages to extract this play from its literary confines to show how it "worked" onstage. Some illustrations of gestures of "supplication and veneration" and a careful analysis of the play's structure as it unfolds before the audience, taking popular ideals and playing upon the spectators' "awareness of the gap between those ideals and actual human behaviour." This study helps see the play as a viable stage piece, at least in its own time.

Waith, Eugene M. *"The Conquest of Granada."* Chapter 6, part 1, in his *The Herculean Hero in Marlowe, Chapman, Shakespeare, and Dryden*. New York: Columbia University Press, 1962.
Waith sees the central character of Almanzor surrounded by the large cast as a way of emphasizing his importance, because "a chaos of conflicting energies is turned, at least temporarily, into order by the lone might of Almanzor." Discusses the love relationship's importance and the dramatic comparisons possible among Almanzor and the three lords at Boabdelin's court. He is a "recreation of an ideal," not just a disguised seventeenth century gentleman.

The Indian Emperour

Loftis, John. "Exploration and Enlightenment: Dryden's *The Indian Emperour* and Its Background." *Philological Quarterly* 45, no. 1 (January, 1966): 71-84.
Subtitled *The Conquest of Mexico by the Spaniards*, this early heroic drama (1665) provides a clear vision of Restoration attitudes toward exploration, primitivism, and "the validity of traditional assumptions." The central character Montezuma "has the combination of strong natural reason and emotional distance needed to expose irrationalities in European beliefs" and is an early example of the "citizen of the world," an eighteenth century convention in literature. A strong discussion of the Spanish sources for this play and the Dryden-Davenant version of *The Tempest*.

The Indian Queen

Barbeau, Anne T. "A Reading of the Heroic Plays." Part 1, *"The Indian Queen."* In her *The Intellectual Design of John Dryden's Heroic Plays*. New Haven, Conn.: Yale University Press, 1970.
    Writing in collaboration with Sir Robert Howard, Dryden introduces a number of themes and characters that he will deal with in his next four plays. The character of Acacis is seen by Barbeau as the source for two different types: His "sense of doom" is representative of one type, while his "precise virtue develops into such patterns of virtuous behavior" as are displayed by the central characters in his next four plays. Dryden's plays identify a "heavenly justice" bringing the world toward its redemption.

Hughes, Derek. *"The Indian Queen."* In his *Dryden's Heroic Plays*. Lincoln: University of Nebraska Press, 1981.
    Previous scholars, in criticizing the erratic nature of Dryden's schematic of characters, have overlooked "the intricate and ironic shifts of character by means of which the schematism is subsequently invalidated." Major themes are analyzed in three subsections: "The Quest for Divinity," "Enslavement to Passion," and "The Hero and his 'Normative' Mentors." While not a great play, *The Indian Queen*, Hughes contends, occasioned Dryden's discovery of his *métier* and "a dramatic imagery commensurate with the scale of his intellectual ambitions."

Kirsch, Arthur C. "The Rhymed Plays from *The Rival Ladies* to *The Conquest of Granada*." Part 3, *"The Indian Queen."* In his *Dryden's Heroic Drama*. Princeton, N.J.: Princeton University Press, 1965.
    The geometric intricacy of Dryden's previous plays is continued here, working among the four principal characters with "correspondingly symmetrical and contrived" action. Kirsch cites lines that delineate the grandeur of Montezuma and Zempoalla's contempt for weak monarchs, noting that the creation of "a passionate, if not raging female, became a staple of the plays of Dryden and his contemporaries," due in large part to the novelty of the presence of actresses on the Restoration stage.

Marriage à la Mode

Auburn, Mark S., ed. *Marriage à la Mode* by John Dryden. London: Edward Arnold, 1981.
    The last of the thirty-five-volume Regents Restoration Drama series. Dryden's play was performed by the King's Company in 1671; Auburn details its recep-

tion and the original cast, and identifies two lines of action (each with its own source) in the introductory essay. The unity of the piece can be seen in "demonstrations of contrasts between the behavior and values of the characters in the comic action, and those of the characters in the romantic heroic action." Notes and chronology.

Beaurline, L. A., and Fredson Bowers. *"Marriage à-la-Mode."* In *John Dryden: Four Comedies*, edited by Beaurline and Bowers. Chicago: University of Chicago Press, 1967.
The geometric design of this comedy is like an English garden in its intricacy and symmetry, "the maximum amount of artifice than can be attained with material drawn from nature." Alternating scenes of contrasting kinds of love and "complementary episodes with their exquisitely defined tones" make this comedy one of the best contrived in the Restoration. The authors discuss the ways Dryden manipulated his sources to heighten the design; the play's production history and record in the Stationers' Register is outlined. Strong footnotes throughout.

Kalitzki, Judith. "Versions of Truth: *Marriage à la Mode.*" *Restoration* 4, no. 2 (Fall, 1980): 65-70.
This most popular of Dryden's comedies has been misunderstood by modern critics, who "presume a basic incompatibility between the genres which Dryden combines in this split-plot tragicomedy." Kalitzki treats the heroic plot with the same seriousness and attention to detail that the comic plot has received from others, noting the shared theme in both halves: "the need to follow one's instincts rather than the rule of fashion or convention, to be sensitive to context and occasion." A good example of genre study, especially in the light of tragicomic tendencies in many modern plays.

Sir Martin Mar-All

Beaurline, L. A., and Fredson Bowers. *"Sir Martin Mar-All."* In *John Dryden: Four Comedies*, edited by Beaurline and Bowers. Chicago: University of Chicago Press, 1967.
First performed in 1667, and introducing a character much imitated in later Restoration drama, this flawed comedy reveals discrepancies in the times of the two plots, an error possibly attributable to Newcastle, who had translated Molière's *L'Étourdi*; borrowed passages are, nevertheless, "much changed, particularized, and made slightly more subtle." Details of textual history; footnotes throughout.

The Spanish Friar

Milhous, Judith, and Robert D. Hume. *"The Spanish Fryar (1680)."* In their *Producible Interpretation: Eight English Plays, 1675-1707*. Carbondale: Southern Illinois University Press, 1985.
The "production analysis" approach designed by these two scholars works best for less frequently produced plays such as this double-plot Dryden work. Special problems of performance of split-plots are analyzed, and four kinds of multiple plots in theatre history are identified. A scene plan and a good discussion of "place conventions" help to understand the "strong sense of place-consciousness" in the play. A casting history shows that the original intention was equal sympathy for characters in both plots, but notes that there is more opportunity for variety of interpretation in the comic characters. Are the plots parallel or antagonistic? "The play is eminently producible as either a celebration of a heroic ethos . . . or . . . an ironic reconsideration of the heroic drama code."

Tyrannic Love

Barbeau, Anne T. "A Reading of the Heroic Plays." Part 3, *"Tyrannic Love."* In her *The Intellectual Design of John Dryden's Heroic Plays*. New Haven, Conn.: Yale University Press, 1970.
Dramatizes a spiritual rather than a military victory of Christian over non-Christian kingdoms. Barbeau discusses the contrasting, even antithetical pair of Maximin and St. Catharine in the play, the first "a murderer and usurper of the throne of his benefactor," the other a humble saint who "makes religion a matter of private conscience," obedient "to the promptings of faith rather than reason just prior to her martyrdom."

Hughes, Derek. *"Tyrannick Love."* In his *Dryden's Heroic Plays*. Lincoln: University of Nebraska Press, 1981.
Composed in haste (1669), this work is uneven, failing to gather its multiple plots under a unifying structural principle. Hughes does not agree with previous critics that Sir Robert Filmer's political philosophy is embodied in this work; a more important view is the "villain/saint" duality of Maximin, "the passionate aspirant to divinity, engaged in an implacable rebellion against the restrictions of mortality and moral responsibility," and Catharine, his nemesis. In a lighter note, Hughes observes that her martyrdom will earn for her "the privilege of seated bliss" in heaven, while her servant Apollonius is confined to "respectful hovering."

Kirsch, Arthur C. "The Rhymed Plays from *The Rival Ladies* to *The Conquest of Granada*." Part 5, *"Tyrannick Love."* In his *Dryden's Heroic Drama*.

Princeton, N.J.: Princeton University Press, 1965.

Dryden himself compared the poetry of *Tyrannic Love* with a painting, in the careful placement of its characters in the space. Kirsch perceives as artificial and external the arrangements of events and persons; Dryden's "fascination with the possibilities of hyperbolic rhetoric" transforms Maximin's speech into rant; in his "perversion of *gloire*," Maximin "is akin to the numerous lustful tyrants of Jacobean drama, from whom he may have been initially derived."

GEORGE ETHEREGE

General Studies

Birdsall, Virginia Ogden. "The Beginnings in Etherege." In her *Wild Civility: The English Comic Spirit on the Restoration Stage*. Bloomington: Indiana University Press, 1970.
  Etherege was a thoroughly conscious artist, a developing writer with a consistent comic philosophy, like his rake-heroes, measuring other worlds against the mode of life he has chosen "in all its devilish vanity." The historical importance of *A Comical Revenge: Or, Love in a Tub*, has been stressed rather than its intrinsic qualities. A structural analysis of the play concentrates on the function of Sir Frederick as the central figure through which the experience of the play can be seen. Notes warfare metaphors in *She Would If She Could*, and Etherege's chief occupation of writing characters in pairs, "taking the air."

Boyette, Purvis E. "The Songs of George Etherege." *Studies in English Literature 1500-1900* 6, no. 3 (Summer, 1966): 409-419.
  Just as Shakespeare's songs inform the dramatic work in which they are embedded, a close examination of Etherege's use of songs can demonstrate his dramatic predilections. The Restoration was a musical age, and Etherege's name "appears a sufficient number of times in the bibliography of musical miscellanies" to warrant the present study. Songs serve many dramaturgical functions—to delineate character, to reveal emotional attitude, to distinguish themes, or to satirize ideologies; Etherege, who chose his songs carefully, is revealed as "a more conscious and deliberate artist than one might suspect from a cursory reading of his comedies."

Brett-Smith, H. F. B. "Sir George Etherege." In *Restoration Drama: Modern Essays in Criticism*, edited by John Loftis. New York: Oxford University Press, 1966.
  Etherege taught both Congreve and Wycherley, and his contemporaries were struck by the novelty of his characters and his methods. *The Comical Revenge* was "the first play to hold the mirror up to Covent Garden and the Mall." Dorimant, in *The Man of Mode*, trusts his head more than his heart, and Harriet is "given enough heart to make her lovable, and enough head to win our respect." Protracted notes outline Etherege's structural practice and alternation of prose and verse for comic and heroic scenes, respectively.

_____ , ed. *The Dramatic Works of Sir George Etherege*. 2 vols. Boston: Houghton Mifflin, 1927.
  More than one hundred pages of preface, introduction, and textual documenta-

tion precede this edition, considered the authoritative text for all subsequent scholarship. The introduction corrects A. Wilson Verity's assumptions (1888), traces Etherege's ancestry, reviews the original productions and casts of the three plays, and outlines the salient features of the *Letterbook* from (in Brett-Smith's view) "the snobbery of Ratisbon . . . this world of politics, anxicty and petty squabbles" in which Etherege maintained his good taste (a problematic statement) and his love of literature. Valuable textual notes at end of the second volume.

Cordner, Michael, ed. *The Plays of Sir George Etherege.* Cambridge, England: Cambridge University Press, 1982.
The introduction to this strongly annotated edition reviews Etherege's early life, London dissipation, and eventual knighthood, marriage, and service to James II as envoy to Austria. Besides his light verse, the three stage works have received considerable modern criticism, summarized here in brief. Additional notes after the texts refine the editor's comments and offer other directions for inquiry; a thoroughly scholarly but usable edition.

Dobrée, Bonamy. "His Excellency Sir George Etherege." In his *Essays in Biography, 1680-1726.* Oxford, England: Oxford University Press, 1925.
A condensed study of Etherege's life, in essay form, succinct and articulate, but dealing with his theatre contributions only in very brief retrospect, since the thrust of the essay is his fitness or unfitness for ambassadorships, especially Ratisbon. John Dryden, the London life, the theatre wits, and the good taste of the Town are nothing but fond reminiscences among his correspondence.

Fujimura, Thomas H. "Sir George Etherege." In his *The Restoration Comedy of Wit.* New York: Barnes & Noble Books, 1952.
Etherege submits to a biographical approach because of the existence of the *Letterbook*, official and personal letters from his late years as ambassador. A clear picture of Etherege prevents dismissing him as a "butterfly" or "rake." Fujimura sees him as an amateur man of letters, anticlerical, with the wit's opinion of women: "affected, hypocritical, vain and dissembling creatures, used principally for venereal pleasures." Agrees with most critics that *Love in a Tub* is inferior early work, *She Would if She Could* an improvement, and *The Man of Mode* the best example of the Truewit in action.

Gosse, Edmund. "Sir George Etheredge." In his *Seventeenth Century Studies: A Contribution to the History of English Poetry.* New York: Dodd, Mead, 1897.
Misinformed regarding Etherege's death, but anxious to print "mainly for the first time, and from manuscript sources, a mass of biographical material which makes this dramatist . . . perhaps the poet of the Restoration of whose life and character we know the most," Gosse launches into his revelations with the

confident voice of a seasoned scholar. Contains some brief discussion of his plays but concentrates on the *Letterbook* material, state papers, and his own imagination.

Huseboe, Arthur R. *Sir George Etherege*. Boston: Twayne, 1987.
Adding some new record searches to Etherege scholarship, Huseboe looks closely at his disrupted family life, his circle of relatives, an inheritance under dispute, his brief time in law as a solicitor's clerk (all before his brilliant but brief moment in the theatre), and his unfortunate stint as envoy to Austria. Each play is given a close examination, character by character, in its own chapter; remarks on the minor works and an epilogue follow, assessing Etherege's place today. A select bibliography and index round out this rather more scholarly work than the series usually offers.

Kronenberger, Louis. "Etherege." In his *The Thread of Laughter: Chapters on English Stage Comedy from Jonson to Maugham*. New York: Alfred A. Knopf, 1952.
Characterizes Etherege as well-born, into a society that valued wit. "They led shocking lives and wrote shocking plays. But equally they led stylish lives and wrote stylish plays." The easy Kronenberger style moves through the canon: *The Comical Revenge* has the honor of ringing up the curtain on the Restoration stage; *She Would if She Could* is a criss-crossing of pairs of equally matched lovers— "a true duet of the sexes"; *The Man of Mode* is "as interesting for what is aesthetically wrong with it as for what is right . . . a handbook on smart London life." Sir Fopling Flutter "must be all affectation and absurdity, yet somehow float, not mince." Praises Etherege's accomplishments as a portrait-painter of London social life.

Lynch, Kathleen M. "The Period of Etherege." Chapter 6 in her *The Social Mode of Restoration Comedy*. New York: Macmillan, 1926.
The period from 1664 to 1676 firmly established the comedy of manners and separated out the artistically successful work of Etherege and William Wycherley from the scores of second rate imitators. This chapter examines the relation of this period to the earlier English drama, notably the *précieuse* tradition, whose study is the center of Lynch's book. *The Man of Mode* is singled out as most influenced by earlier traditions. "Where Etherege led the way, his contemporaries followed," even, Lynch adds, "the greatest plagiarists of the period."

Mann, David D. *Sir George Etherege: A Reference Guide*. Boston: G. K. Hall, 1981.
After an introductory essay on the biography, theatre history, and textual history of Etherege's plays, Mann provides a year-by-year list (with brief annotation) of Etherege scholarship. Designed "for scholars, graduate students, and

advanced undergraduates," this guide continues the study of Etherege into doctoral dissertations, specialized journals, tabloids, and less accessible publications. Index.

_____ , comp. and ed. *A Concordance to the Plays and Poems of Sir George Etherege*. London: Greenwood Press, 1985.

A computerized entry into the work of Etherege by key word. Speaker, line, page, title, act, scene, and line number are provided for every word in the H. F. B. Brett-Smith edition of 1927 (and James Thorpe's 1963 edition of the poems). Interestingly, "wit" has 44 entries, "woman/women" has 158, "lady/ladies" has 263, and "love" has 335. Much thematic information can be gleaned from concordances, by tracing images from play to play, noting dominant linguistic patterns, and documenting recurring subjects dear to the playwright. Etherege's modest canon of three plays makes him particularly eligible for this kind of analysis.

Mignon, Elisabeth. "Etherege." In her *Crabbed Age and Youth: The Old Men and Women in the Restoration Comedy of Manners*. Durham, N.C.: Duke University Press, 1947.

Sir Frederick and Lady Cockwood, in *The Comical Revenge* and *She Would If She Could*, begin to advance the portraits of old age, but "the parents who look back on a better age" appear fully as Old Bellair and Lady Woodvil in *The Man of Mode*, both standing "in ignominious defeat" at the end of the play. Mignon's theories will be better demonstrated in Etherege's imitators, by whom his "concentrated scorn" will be exaggerated even further.

Muir, Kenneth. "Sir George Etherege." In his *The Comedy of Manners*. London: Hutchinson University Library, 1970.

An amateur with only three plays to his credit, Etherege was "indolent by nature." Muir ranks the plays by quality, with *She Would If She Could* "more successful" than *Love in a Tub* (*The Comical Revenge*), which lacks realistic dialogue and plot, and *The Man of Mode* "the masterpiece" that gave the world Sir Fopling Flutter. Devoting most of the chapter to a close reading of central scenes in this work, he takes exception to some scholars' opinion that Dorimant is a model of conduct and defends the language on grounds that the licentious dialogue mirrors the age.

Palmer, John. "The Life and Letters of Sir George Etherege." In his *The Comedy of Manners*. London: G. Bell & Sons, 1913.

The first of two chapters, this essay deals sympathetically with the questionable conduct of Etherege as an ambassador and reviews the Ratisbon correspondence as evidence. Palmer investigates "the habit of thought and of temperament in which the comedy of manners was formed and developed" by

looking closely at Etherege's relations with the court, the nature of his acquaintance with the stage, and "the delicate urbanity, smoothness, felicity, and
balance" of the style (not the content) of his letters.

_____ . "The Plays of Sir George Etherege." In his *The Comedy of Manners*. London: G. Bell & Sons, 1913.
Clearly speaking for his own time and breaking with the traditions of John
Fletcher and Ben Jonson, Etherege cannot be judged by any other fashion than
his own. *She Would If She Could* "was the first finished example of the new
comedy of manners." Palmer sees "honest knavery," not personal immorality,
in Etherege's writings: ". . . style was the man. There was form, and there
was bad form. The whole duty of man was to find the one, and to eschew the
other."

Perry, Henry ten Eyck. "Sir George Etherege." In his *The Comic Spirit in Restoration Drama*. New York: Russell & Russell, 1925, reprint 1962.
The considerable interval between the composition of his plays indicates how
casually Etherege took his profession. *The Comical Revenge* turns on Betty's
trick on Dufoy, but it is his own falseness that prompts the comical revenge.
The uneven "complications are diverting and ingenious." Dorimant in *The
Man of Mode* is a "real gentleman of fashion," and Sir Frederick and Oliver
from the earlier plays anticipate Etherege's skill in the later characterizations.
Each piece is really dominated by "the figure of a charming woman," and the
plots deal with "meeting our match in the opposite sex."

Powell, Jocelyn. "George Etherege and the Form of a Comedy." In *Restoration
Dramatists: A Collection of Critical Essays*, edited by Earl Miner. Englewood
Cliffs, N.J.: Prentice-Hall, 1966.
Comic devices are analogies that enable Etherege to explore the real world
through "heightened images" (play-ending marriages are an example of this
property). Insofar as images provide distinct views of the subject and an
appreciation of disparate attitudes among the characters and actions, they are
effective comic tools. The essay moves rather quickly through the canon,
making several points worthy of continued discussion, such as the observation
that Etherege's use of characters like Sir Frederick and Sir Fopling gives us
"not one man but eight . . . and translates into pure spectacle the empty
emotionless forms" in these plays.

Rosenfeld, Sybil, ed. *The Letterbook of Sir George Etherege*. New York: Benjamin
Blom, 1928, reprint 1971.
The introduction to this edition serves as a portrait of Etherege the fop,
sometime writer, and envoy to Austria, but in a larger sense it is a review of
the age itself: the low social position of the actor, the generosity of the idle and

well-mannered, the censoriousness of the sober. Hugh Hughes, secretary to Etherege at Ratisbon, sums up Etherege's transgressions (and the age's follies) in his complaints published with Etherege's correspondence. Maps, index, and catalog of Etherege's books.

Underwood, Dale. *Etherege and the Seventeenth-Century Comedy of Manners*. New Haven, Conn.: Yale University Press, 1957.
Generated out of a study of Etherege alone, the study gradually incorporates the larger subjects of genre, society, and the comic tradition. After setting forth the problem in a preliminary section, Underwood devotes a chapter each in part 2 to comic view (*The Comical Revenge*), comic form (*She Would If She Could*), and comic values (*The Man of Mode*). The final section places Etherege firmly in the Lyly-to-Shirley progression of the comedy of love and the comedy of manners. A thorough and thought-provoking study. Index.

Verity, A. Wilson, ed. *The Works of Sir George Etheredge: Plays and Poems*. London: John C. Nimmo, 1888.
Verity began modern scholarship of "Etheredge" with this edition, from which all subsequent scholarship begins. The introduction summarizes the facts of his life, reporting "unfortunately" his personal pranks and dissolute behavior, in London and Ratisbon. *The Man of Mode* "aimed . . . at a realistic representation of contemporary society," culminating in Congreve's masterpiece, *The Way of the World*. Historically interesting, Etherege's "plays possess considerable merit."

Wilcox, John. "Sir George Etherege." In his *The Relation of Molière to Restoration Comedy*. New York: Columbia University Press, 1938.
Wilcox attacks Gosse's notion that Etherege was indebted to Molière's work for the foundation of the English comedy of manners. Despite Etherege's possession of the French language and a copy of Molière as early as 1689, there is no internal evidence of the influence in the plays themselves. The "British products" are his alone, and "Etherege secured little or nothing from Molière and hence transmitted nothing to his successors."

The Comical Revenge

Birdsall, Virginia Ogden. "The Beginnings in Etherege." Part 1, "*The Comical Revenge: Or, Love in a Tub*." In her *Wild Civility: The English Comic Spirit on the Restoration Stage*. Bloomington: Indiana University Press, 1970.
Sir Frederick Frollick is treated by critics as "a golden mean" and as the masquerader through whom the audience perceives the play's "world." There

are two modes of life in the play: down-to-earth, Falstaffian life; and idealized, poetic life, represented by Beaufort and Graciana. Sir Frederick moves between these modes but despite his birth is more "at home" in Wheadle and Palmer's world. Birdsall notes disease imagery and war imagery but claims for Sir Frederick a sexual and artistic creativity. When he and Dufoy join the Widow and Betty, the audience can foresee a constructive unity even among these perpetual adversaries. "Sir Frederick leaves the play with four marriages to his credit, one of them his own."

Holland, Norman N. *"The Comical Revenge: Or, Love in a Tub."* In his *The First Modern Comedies: The Significance of Etherege, Wycherley, and Congreve.* Cambridge, Mass.: Harvard University Press, 1959.
 "Easy" Etherege wrote "the gentlemanly number of three plays," examined here with William Wycherley's and William Congreve's four comedies each. Holland's approach is dialectic, "right" and "wrong" perceptions being divided between characters relying on "appearance" and characters with "natural understanding." Sir Frederick's "appearance" as a dead man and his coming alive at Dufoy's uproarious entrance, are examples of conversion from one to another. Holland concludes this brief but penetrating look with the discovery of "three characteristic devices of language and action."

Huseboe, Arthur R. *"The Comical Revenge: Or, Love in a Tub* (1664)." In his *Sir George Etherege.* Boston: Twayne, 1987.
 A study of this first play, which owed its success in large part to "the combination . . . of social comedy with serious heroic play and lively farce." Huseboe supplies a plot summary, a close look at Sir Frederick Frollick, and an analysis of the "gay couple who begin their relationship as antagonists and who retain their prickly defensive outer shells to the very verge of matrimony itself." A final look at the pairing of "Hyperbolical Joy and Outragious Sorrow" in the play justifies the audience's enthusiasm for this writer of "A New Tone and Attitude."

Underwood, Dale. "The Comic View: *The Comical Revenge.*" In his *Etherege and the Seventeenth-Century Comedy of Manners.* New Haven, Conn.: Yale University Press, 1957.
 Sir Frederick Frollick is seen here as the principal character, and the work "a dramatic hodgepodge, a confused mixture . . . of old and new elements." Sir Frederick's wit is both casual and "studied"; this and other evidence of "circularity and inconsistency" become a source of the comic hero's strength. Contestants "conceal and otherwise control their mutual feelings of attraction." The Dufoy-Betty plot "supports and expands" the central themes, presenting another perspective on the comic view.

The Man of Mode

Barnard, John. "Point of View in *The Man of Mode*." *Essays in Criticism* 34, no. 4
    (October, 1984): 285-308.
    In the continuing discussion/debate revolving around the relation of text to
    performance, this interesting study notes that John Dryden, when he wrote the
    epilogue to *The Man of Mode*, had some sort of performance in mind, directly
    from which the printed play-text was taken. His awareness of political, social,
    even theatrical tensions currently vibrating in his audience must be taken into
    account in modern productions, even in the reading of the play today. The
    point of view of an audience (for instance, in its attitude toward Dorimant)
    may or may not be the same point of view entertained by the playwright. An
    important essay for modern theatre also, as witnessed by the references to Tom
    Stoppard and T. S. Eliot.

Berman, Ronald. "The Comic Passions of *The Man of Mode*." *Studies in English
    Literature 1500-1900* 10, no. 3 (Summer, 1970): 459-468.
    The passionate poetry of Edmund Waller accompanied the prevailing Restora-
    tion sensibilities and was the subject of satire in Etherege's masterpiece. Dori-
    mant, the hero, quotes Waller in mocking tones throughout, because, accord-
    ing to this study, Etherege is mocking the lyrical passions of traditional love,
    "the Restoration model for affairs of the heart." Harriet affects Dorimant in a
    way that is neither sensual nor passionate; consequently they must invent their
    own vocabulary of love. Berman concludes: "Repose is perhaps . . . deeply
    sought in a time of demoralizing freedom."

Birdsall, Virginia Ogden. "*The Man of Mode: Or, Sir Fopling Flutter*." In her *Wild
    Civility: The English Comic Spirit on the Restoration Stage*. Bloomington:
    Indiana University Press, 1970.
    Etherege has been "insistently tough-minded and unremittingly open-eyed and
    honest." The larger theme running through all of Etherege's plays— "a dead
    world . . . being exposed by juxtaposition to a living one"—is here drama-
    tized through contrasting characters Fopling Flutter and Dorimant. Both are
    fashionable, but Fopling's "artifice" is rejected by both Dorimant and Harriet
    on grounds of "style as manifestation of self." Fopling has advanced from the
    earlier "*précieux* mode," a development that Etherege perceived in Charles II's
    court since writing his two earlier works. A long analysis concludes that the
    "ridiculous posturings of the human animal" should not be misinterpreted as
    taste and style. The play ends with clever conceits on country life and a
    promise that Harriet and Dorimant will avoid the deadliness of sterility.

Carnochan, W. B., ed. *The Man of Mode*, by George Etherege. London: Edward
    Arnold, 1966.

Noting the use of French throughout Etherege's canon and the difficulties the play poses for a modern editor, Carnochan stays sober in this discussion of the "pervasive religious imagery" of *The Man of Mode*, consigning Mrs. Loveit "to the darkness of her own tormented spirit" and placing the "ironic themes of the fall, of grace, of redemption" at the play's center. Good footnotes; chronology in appendix.

Hawkins, Harriett. " 'Vice Under Characters of Advantage': Dramatic and Social Success in *The Man of Mode*." In her *Likenesses of Truth in Elizabethan and Restoration Drama*. Oxford, England: Clarendon Press, 1972.
Reviewing recent opinion on Etherege and noting the appeal to universal audiences of characters who "not only outrage accepted moral standards but (what is worse) seem to enjoy themselves thoroughly in the process of doing so," Hawkins defends Etherege's comic organization, "designed to excite admiration for the ability to dissemble successfully." Dorimant is a model of the kind, treated here at length.

Holland, Norman N. "*The Man of Mode: Or, Sir Fopling Flutter*." In his *The First Modern Comedies: The Significance of Etherege, Wycherley, and Congreve*. Cambridge, Mass.: Harvard University Press, 1959.
Holland's method is dialectic: "the contrast between two parallel lines of intrigue, one 'high' and one 'low.' " Dorimant and Sir Fopling act as a pair whose actions demonstrate the "appearance/nature" duality; using the critical vocabulary established in the opening chapters, Holland works toward the "reformed rake" interpretation of Dorimant, aligning the play with sentimental drama, but "variously undercut by irony," Etherege's distinct signature in this period.

Huseboe, Arthur R. "*The Man of Mode: Or, Sir Fopling Flutter* (1676)." In his *Sir George Etherege*. Boston: Twayne, 1987.
A play by a middle-aged writer with middle-aged actors, it may have presumed a different audience from that of earlier work. A plot summary is followed by an examination of Dorimant, his relation with Medley, and his love-combat with Harriet. It is "The Great Creature" Sir Fopling Flutter, however, who takes the play away from the love pair, drawing the audience to him in his final scene with Mrs. Loveit. This shift of attention may explain the play's popularity in its own time, a popularity not justified in the light of later criticism.

Langhans, Edward A. "An Edinburgh Promptbook from 1679-80." *Theatre Notebook* 37, no. 3 (1983): 101-104.
The promptbook referred to is Etherege's *The Man of Mode*, discovered in Scotland's National Library, indicating from the style of note-taking and other evidence that it belonged to the King's Company, or rather a dissenting group

from the company which played in Edinburgh in these years. More than just another detail in Langhans' lifelong study of the period, this short report demonstrates the scholarly procedures necessary to glean historical information from the smallest clues, and the value of close reading of the text along with the flotsam of theatre history. Langhans was even able to deduce that one actor's costume had no belt.

Underwood, Dale. "The Comic Values: *The Man of Mode*." In his *Etherege and the Seventeenth-Century Comedy of Manners*. New Haven: Yale University Press, 1957. (Reprinted in *Restoration Drama: Modern Essays in Criticism*, edited by John Loftis. New York: Oxford University Press, 1966).
This play gave "a certain definitive and final form to lines of interest" in earlier seventeenth century drama. Two interlocking values emerge: a traditional value mode and a "libertine Machiavel" mode. The characteristic conflict between passion and reason is present in all the major roles, with Dorimant perhaps taking a more Machiavellian attitude than previously seen. Emilia's awareness of the frailty of life is essential to seeing the pattern of values throughout. Sir Fopling Flutter's "chief offense" is his lack of "restraint to keep decorum or degree." Notes review previous scholarship and tie in Etherege's later correspondence.

Zimbardo, Rose A. "Of Women, Comic Imitation of Nature, and Etherege's *The Man of Mode*." *Studies in English Literature 1500-1900* 21, no. 3 (Summer, 1981): 373-387.
Setting out "to consider briefly what in the nature of the comic perspective makes the role of women crucial," Zimbardo dissects *The Man of Mode*, with its interesting variety of female characters (among them Mrs. Loveit, Bellinda, the perplexing Harriet, and, in the subplots, Emilia and Lady Woodvill), to conclude that the play is "a comedy *about* comic perspective." The perceptive Harriet "tries to bring Dorimant to self-knowledge," who, like the hero of the bygone age, "tries again and again to employ all the extravagant language, oaths, and posturings of heroic love in wooing Harriet."

She Would If She Could

Birdsall, Virginia Ogden. "The Beginnings in Etherege." Part 2, "*She Wou'd If She Cou'd.*" In her *Wild Civility: The English Comic Spirit on the Restoration Stage*. Bloomington: Indiana University Press, 1970.
In a protracted analysis of this often neglected play, Birdsall traces the pairs of "walkers" taking the air of Mulberry Garden and the Exchange. Lady Cockwood and Sir Oliver follow the male-female standards of the "*précieux* mode," an unnatural stance that collapses in the realities of physical and sexual ap-

petites. Strategies of youthful "players" are mapped out in act 1, and the language maintains the tension between haughty formalization and the high spirits of youth. Add to it the religious vocabulary and Courtall's manipulation, and the play proceeds through amazing psychological complexities. Birdsall uses some modern terminology— "Freudian" defenses of Lady Cockwood's "fortress," and the possibility (denied here) that Gatty is a "divided personality."

Holland, Norman N. *"She Wou'd If She Cou'd."* In his *The First Modern Comedies: The Significance of Etherege, Wycherley, and Congreve.* Cambridge, Mass.: Harvard University Press, 1959.
Working from Pepys's dismissal of the play's worth in 1668, Holland applies his "appearance and nature" criteria to Etherege's least known play. The central theme revolves around liberty/restraint, contrasting town and country. Holland's analytical method consists of dipping into the text for dualities of character and action, to support an interesting conclusion regarding social appearance versus personal nature: "Folly is the confusion of the two; wisdom is their separation and balance."

Huseboe, Arthur R. *"She Would If She Could* (1668)." In his *Sir George Etherege.* Boston: Twayne, 1987.
The two pairs of lovers introduced in Etherege's first play are lowered somewhat in class here, but put in the center of the action with realistic prose dialogue. After a plot summary, Huseboe examines the relation of "Pretty Heiresses and Witty Rakes," noting that Gatty and Ariana really move the story forward. Sir Oliver, Sir Joslin Jolly, and Lady Cockwood are treated in turn. The young ladies will accept the rakes, but only after a test, "a month's experience of your good behavior"; Freeman remarks "a month is a tedious time." A readable and clearheaded review of this neglected play.

Taylor, Charlene M., ed. *She Would If She Could,* by Sir George Etherege. London: Edward Arnold, 1973.
Part of the Regents Restoration Drama series, this edition is generated from the 1668 quarto, with "few textual problems." While its first performance was not particularly successful, the play's significance is great for its qualities reflecting "the brilliant if sometimes debauched society" of Charles II. Satiric characterizations—"a combination of idealism and skepticism" which produced a "double vision" onstage—made intellectual demands on the audience, as does the unraveling of its "three elements of social, romantic, and artificial comedy."

Underwood, Dale. "The Comic Form: *She Would If She Could.*" In *Etherege and the Seventeenth-Century Comedy of Manners.* New Haven, Conn.: Yale University Press, 1957.

Outlining a "diagrammatic balance" in comic form, with the added character of the "female dupe, Sir Oliver's wife," Underwood designs the shape of all comedies of manner with a careful examination of Etherege's middle play. The play's concerns are defined in character, in action, and even in the structure of the scene changes, "this bipartite division in thc physical world of the play." The final comic balance leaves some questions, resolved in Etherege's final stage piece.

GEORGE FARQUHAR

General Studies

Archer, William, ed. *George Farquhar*. London: T. Fisher Unwin, n.d. (after 1904).
Archer offers four plays (*The Constant Couple*, *The Twin Rivals*, *The Recruiting Officer*, and *The Beaux' Stratagem*) in this no longer scholarly but still handy edition. The introduction is divided equally between biographical and critical material. Archer sees the early death of Farquhar as "among the cross accidents" of English stage history: "As this is not the view commonly taken by literary historians, I will try to give my reasons for it." Thus Archer demonstrates once more his insight, his good grace, and his innate sense of theatrical genius.

Boas, Frederick S. "George Farquhar." In his *An Introduction to Eighteenth-Century Drama, 1700-1780*. Oxford, England: Clarendon Press, 1953.
Treated here as a comic bridge between Restoration and sentimental drama, Farquhar is briefly described in his early years, translating French novels, from which he learns the art of writing "amourous entanglements with disguises and mistakes of identity," a skill which he employs in the badly misnamed *The Constant Couple*. By his death in 1707, Farquhar had reflected his own domestic troubles in the unhappy situation of Sullen and his wife in *The Beaux' Stratagem*. A good general introduction to the Restoration's last comic writer.

Burns, Edward. "The Last Restoration Comedies: Farquhar, Centlivre, and Steele." In his *Restoration Comedy: Crises of Desire and Identity*. New York: St. Martin's Press, 1987.
From Farquhar's "light, modish, daring, but rather glibly 'pure' comedies" to Richard Steele's "studied badness" in *The Conscious Lovers*, "Restoration comedy is simply the falling away of the contingencies that had shaped it." *Love and a Bottle*, *The Constant Couple* ("very much a Drury Lane piece"), *The Recruiting Officer*, and *Beaux' Stratagem* are compared with the plays of Susanna Centlivre and Steele.

Connely, Willard. *Young George Farquhar: The Restoration Drama at Twilight*. London: Cassell, 1949.
A warmhearted biographical novel of Farquhar, the well-liked, impoverished, and sickly epilogue to a comic age. Connely's style allows the human figure to emerge from the background of a busy historical period, drawing an accurate portrait of London life and the theatre sub-society at the same time. With his uncanny abilities as "diarist of drama" whose "impulse was to write down what he apprehended," Farquhar never suffered from the ennui and cynicism

of Restoration playwrights past their peak. His early death in 1707, at age thirty, essentially brought the "Restoration period of drama" to a close.

Ewald, Alex. Charles, ed. *The Dramatic Works of George Farquhar*. 2 vols. London: John C. Nimmo, 1892.
A "Life of George Farquhar" introduces this two-volume set, very lightly footnoted. *Love and a Bottle* must be recognized as a first effort. Ewald provides few critical comments other than noting the plays' receptions in premiere. In his closing years, "embittered by poverty," Farquhar married a lady who pretended to more wealth than she had. *The Beaux' Stratagem* is described in more detail ("deals with vicious subjects" but "wit is not always allied with profanity"). The author, says Ewald, was "not so completely enamoured of darkness as to refuse to admit the light."

Farmer, A. J. *George Farquhar*. London: Longmans, Green, 1966.
This valuable series of supplements to *British Book News*, on writers and their work (this is number 193) treats Farquhar as a more three-dimensional writer, devoting one chapter to his plays and another to his novel, poems, and letters. Farquhar is praised not for the intricacy of his plots but for his timing (the juxtaposition of Cherry's monologue and Archer's entrance is cited as an example from *The Beaux' Stratagem*) and dialogue, which "has an unaffected ease and naturalness often lacking in the work of [contemporaries]." Selected bibliography.

Kenny, Shirley Strum. "George Farquhar and 'The Bus'ness of a Prologue.' " *Theatre Survey* 19, no. 2 (November, 1978): 139-154.
In addition to prologues and epilogues to his own plays, Farquhar supplied several for plays of his contemporaries and a few occasional prologues as well. Kenny mines the ore for three riches: biographical information, knowledge of the writer/theatre relationship, and "information about the commissioning and writing of prologues and about their remarkable value in the early eighteenth century." Indications are found of a warm and friendly relationship with other playwrights (although only one was a close friend), a concentration on additions for one company only, and an indifference to the actual content of the play for which he was offering an introduction. An appendix lists the prologues and epilogues, with notes.

Kronenberger, Louis. "Farquhar." In his *The Thread of Laughter: Chapters on English Stage Comedy from Jonson to Maugham*. New York: Alfred A. Knopf, 1952.
Farquhar is definitely the last Restoration playwright, and Kronenberger ranks him lower than William Congreve but admits to uneasiness about his place in

history. Farquhar is difficult to appraise; his limitations may arise from the transitional nature of the period: ". . . caught between two sets of antagonistic values [wit and sentiment], he necessarily formulated no harmonious values of his own." All of Farquhar's plays except for *Love and a Bottle* receive Kronenberger's characteristic light touch, but with little substantive penetration of the real critical problems they present to the more careful reader.

Mignon, Elisabeth. "Farquhar." In her *Crabbed Age and Youth: The Old Men and Women in the Restoration Comedy of Manners*. Durham, N.C.: Duke University Press, 1947.
"Admirable old men return to the stage, and the hitherto unviolated Restoration code is cast aside" when Farquhar begins his brief career. Alderman Smuggler, in *The Constant Couple*, is typical of earlier old men (such as William Wycherley's Alderman Gripe), but admits his own iniquity; Old Mirabel in *The Inconstant*, however, is "a thoroughly admirable old man, one with few predecessors in the comedies already examined" in Mignon's study. Justice Balance, in *The Recruiting Officer*, is also amiable and rare, a father "who remembers his youth without undue reminiscence or garrulity."

Palmer, John. "George Farquhar." In his *The Comedy of Manners*. London: G. Bell & Sons, 1913.
"The comedy of manners, reaching perfection in Congreve, perceptibly droops in Vanbrugh, and in Farquhar is extinguished. . . . [He] killed the comedy to which he contributed the last brilliant examples." The conditions of wit and the relation of the playwright to the audience dictated a change of style; "English comedy is at point of becoming a business," and that transformation is anathema to comedy. Never quite succeeding in reconciling his own moral convictions with the conventions of the theatre, Farquhar is "perhaps the lightest of foot of all our comic authors."

Perry, Henry ten Eyck. "George Farquhar." In his *The Comic Spirit in Restoration Drama*. New York: Russell & Russell, 1925, reprint 1962.
Farquhar was a new ally to William Congreve and John Vanbrugh after Jeremy Collier's attack in the *A Short View of the Immorality and Profaneness of the English Stage*. Lifts "English Comedy from the Centre of Indifference . . . to set it down in the freer aether of eighteenth-century sentiment." Scenes in the plays are often "inconsistent" but always "amusing." In *The Beaux' Stratagem*, the Archer/Mrs. Sullen bedroom scene is "one of the most straightforward scenes in Restoration Comedy." Farquhar's treatment of wild young heroes (Roebuck, Wildair, Mirabel, and Plume are examples) is closest to revealing his own soul; they "represent his constant attempt to paint the laughable and, at the same time, the admirable."

Rogers, J. P. W. "The Dramatist vs. the Dunce: George Farquhar and John Oldmixon." *Restoration and Eighteenth Century Theatre Research* 10, no. 2 (November, 1971): 53-58.

An interesting report on the reception of Farquhar's second play, *The Constant Couple*, produced and published in 1699. The coffee-house wits of the time included one John Oldmixon, who made the mistake of mocking Farquhar in print (and in disguise); Farquhar's "spirited, witty and crushing retort" took the form of a new prologue for the last night of the play. A valuable sketch of London theatre life and the immediacy of critical communication during the period. Oldmixon also gets his just desserts in rhymed couplets in Alexander Pope's *The Dunciad*.

Rothstein, Eric. *George Farquhar*. New York: Twayne, 1967.

Rothstein claims to be the first to take a close look at Farquhar's plays, but he intentionally omits discussion of stage histories and acting companies. Farquhar was neither a good student nor a good actor, but he impressed actor and theatre manager Robert Wilks, who offered him a lifelong friendship. "The External Facts" of the opening chapter and "The External Meaning" of the last bracket strong discussions of the canon, with *The Twin Rivals* as a turning point. The penultimate *The Stage Coach* "makes one hungry for the work he did not do" from 1702 to 1706. Notes, bibliography, chronology, index, and a chapter on his nondramatic writing.

Wilcox, John. "Congreve, Vanbrugh, and Farquhar." Part 3, "George Farquhar." In his *The Relation of Molière to Restoration Comedy*. New York: Columbia University Press, 1938.

Wilcox finds no debt to Molière in Farquhar's work, in a brief glance as part of a larger dismissal of Edmund Gosse's contention that English comedy has its roots in Molière. The "Irish impudence" of such a character as Sir Harry Wildair is Farquhar's own and appears in all of his plays. "Farquhar holds his secure place in literature because of his fertile genius for originating comic figures," not from adroit borrowings.

The Beaux' Stratagem

Fitzgibbon, H. Macaulay. Preface to *The Beaux-Stratagem*, by George Farquhar. London: J. M. Dent & Sons, 1914.

Thoroughly Irish Farquhar, in poverty even after writing a series of "bright, rattling comedies" from 1698 to 1706, was encouraged to write one more, by his friend, actor Robert Wilks. The result is *The Beaux-Stratagem* (as this edition styles it), and "the plaudits of the audience resounding in his ears, the destitute, broken-hearted dramatist passed to the bourne where stratagems avail not any longer." Noting that Archer and Aimwell improve as the play

progresses ("they set out as mere intriguers, but prove in the end true gentlemen"), Fitzgibbon cites the details of the first performance and subsequent
stage history.

Jeffares, A. Norman. Critical introduction to *The Beaux Stratagem*, by George
Farquhar. Edinburgh, Scotland: Oliver & Boyd, 1972.
A long and thorough introduction that begins with Farquhar's debt to John
Milton in the Sullen/Mrs. Sullen plot. Using as a basis for his discussion the
review of the play's critical reception and a geographically delineated outline
of its stage history, Jeffares offers an excellent checklist of scholarship on the
play and playwright. Textual notes, commentary, and a strong bibliography are
added.

Milhous, Judith, and Robert D. Hume. "*The Beaux' Stratagem* (1707)." In their
Producible Interpretation: Eight English Plays, 1675-1707. Carbondale: Southern Illinois University Press, 1985.
One of the first plays to which these authors applied their "production analysis" methodology, it reveals its accessibility. The major interpretive problems
are: How do Aimwell and Archer play to each other in the presence of others?
Who does Archer get, Mrs. Sullen or Cherry? Is the play about something?
Should the bed be real or painted (thus defusing the tension of the scene)? The
complicated business of money is straightened out, and the over-tidy ending is
explained as a convention of the comic genre. The country values and the
social differences between inn and house are part of the question of "romp
versus satire."

Rothstein, Eric. "*The Beaux' Stratagem*." In his *George Farquhar*. New York:
Twayne, 1967.
Two earlier plays which assaulted assumptions about Restoration comedy set
the stage for Farquhar's audience to be "eased unwittingly into the new dimension of judgment" and an innovative structure in his last work. A long discussion of resolution of the Sullen/Mrs. Sullen plot. With Lady Bountiful at the
hub of activity, the play's point is made: Give freely, not from contractual
obligation. Archer cannot go off with Mrs. Sullen (in this interpretation); only
Sir Charles has the power to reward him. Farquhar died with his apprenticeship
finally over and the tools for greatness in his hands.

The Constant Couple

Rothstein, Eric. "The Years of Apprenticeship." Part 2, "*The Constant Couple*." In
his *George Farquhar*. New York: Twayne, 1967.
The invention of Sir Harry Wildair marks an advance from Roebuck, Sir

Harry's success warranting a sequel in his own name next for Farquhar. Lurewell, whose thematic importance extends to Vizard, Smuggler, and Clincher ("all might find congenial ground in a society that deifies appearances, lust, and money"), is contrasted with Angelica Darling, at sixteen "unassailed because unassailable." Farquhar handles the moral resolution with a surer hand of someone learning his art.

Love and a Bottle

Rothstein, Eric. "The Years of Apprenticeship." Part 1, "*Love and a Bottle*." In his *George Farquhar*. New York: Twayne, 1967.
This is one of the first close looks at Farquhar's first play, discussing the success with which he incorporated the conventions of his age into "a kind of dramatic grammar for reading Farquhar's comedies and tracing his development." In the treatment of Roebuck, especially against Mockmode, "style is by-passed, and personal and social virtue justifies itself in terms of morals, not manners." He works at being as broadly appealing as Colley Cibber but has something to learn artistically.

The Recruiting Officer

Dixon, Peter. Introduction to *The Recruiting Officer*, by George Farquhar. Manchester, England: Manchester University Press, 1986.
The Revels Plays series (which includes John Vanbrugh's *The Provok'd Wife* and William Wycherley's *The Country Wife*) introduces this play, second in contemporary and current popularity only to *The Beaux' Stratagem*, with a well-designed recapitulation of the playwright, the play, the stage history, and the text. Long glosses and commentary accompany the text page for page and are made even more useful by an index to notes at the end of the edition. Appendices outline textual and theatrical variants and give the score of the music for the play. A complete edition in every respect.

Ross, John. Introduction to *The Recruiting Officer*, by George Farquhar. New York: W. W. Norton, 1977.
A comprehensive edition with protracted support material, including appendices of songs, textual variants, a map of Shrewsbury, and extracts from the Articles of War which inform the humor and the social setting of the play. Ross's introduction is more scholarly than most, surrounded by exhaustive stage histories, lists, notes, and suggestions for further reading; his best efforts, however, cannot recover the source of "the song of chickens and asparagus" mentioned in the first quarto but deleted in the second quarto.

Rothstein, Eric. *"The Recruiting Officer."* In his *George Farquhar*. New York: Twayne, 1967.
>
> The uncomplicated play is "a fertile situation, rich in dramatic conflict and skulduggery upon which comedy could thrive." Farquhar's plays, especially this one, do not turn upon individual reform but exhibit "an ideal system of social relationship in tune with reason and moral law." The playwright is moving "toward a kind of comedy that went beyond the individual to the relational patterns of law."

Shugrue, Michael. Introduction to *The Recruiting Officer*, by George Farquhar. London: Edward Arnold, 1965.
>
> Farquhar's own experiences as a Lieutenant of Grenadiers in 1704, summarized here in a detailed and interesting introduction, form the basis for this and his last play (he was posted to Lichfield in 1705, where *The Beaux' Stratagem* takes place). "Financially successful marriages" were a central theme in Restoration comedy: "No other activity counted so much as the search for wealth and station in a mate." Farquhar's greatest contributions to the period were "his use of a country setting and his appreciation of rural life." Footnotes; chronology in the appendix.

The Twin Rivals

Rothstein, Eric. "Jeremy Collier and *The Twin-Rivals*." In his *George Farquhar*. New York: Twayne, 1967.
>
> In an interesting series of arguments Rothstein claims that the passion of Farquhar's characters actually recommends fidelity to the audience. "Libertine roving is disavowed not because it is immoral but because its superiority, in a libertine's terms, has been empirically disproved." The play is "corseted" by the camps of loyal and disloyal servants, pairs of lovers, etc. Why the play failed is not clear, but possibly Farquhar's moral stand did not answer the audience's desire for simple "social propriety and tender feelings. In short, they wanted sentimental comedy . . . [moral] for the sake of tears."

NATHANIEL LEE

Armistead, J. M. "Writings About Nathaniel Lee, 1677-1980." In his *Four Restoration Playwrights*. Boston: G. K. Hall, 1984.
Of the four playwrights of the "second water" featured in this annotated bibliography, Nathaniel Lee is the most neglected, despite the several hundred mentions gathered here. His collaboration with John Dryden on *Oedipus* and his masterpiece, *The Rival Queens*, has perhaps saved him from the oblivion many of his contemporaries have suffered. His work is described in various centuries and by various critics as "lurid," inept," and (in Armistead's interpretation of Jeremy Collier's famous opinion) "full of smut and profanity." When Lee is paired with Thomas Otway, the term "baroque" is often applied to his style and the age. Armistead's critical biography (1979) is given the most complete annotation and serves as a summary statement of the general critical profile.

Brown, Richard E. "Nathaniel Lee's Political Dramas, 1679-1683." *Restoration* 10, no. 1 (Spring, 1986): 41-52.
Were Lee's plays part of the political efforts of the Whigs to promote arguments "attacking the English monarchy and supporting the establishment of a constitutional republic"? Some plot and character parallels were suspicious, and buzzwords such as "commonwealth" and "tyrant" were not to be ignored. Nevertheless, Brown finds evidence to argue otherwise as well, concluding that Otway's "political temperament combined conservatism with experimentation" in a unique way. This article can be used as an introduction to this little-read playwright.

Hume, Robert D. "The Satiric Design of Nat. Lee's *The Princess of Cleves*." In his *The Rakish Stage: Studies in English Drama, 1600-1800*. Carbondale: Southern Illinois University Press, 1983.
A detailed examination of the structure of this adaptation from the French novel by Madame de La Fayette, the essay pays tribute to Lee's dramaturgy in this eclectic form, not entirely tragedy but possibly proto-sentimental, even satiric comedy. Shocking changes in the character of Nemours transform the gentle novel into a deliberately "nasty, ugly, degrading" work, not "a comfortable sermon from a superior vantage point, but rather a brutal exposé whose author can find *no* meaningful positive norm."

Vieth, David M. "Nathaniel Lee's *The Rival Queens* and the Psychology of Assassination." *Restoration* 2, no. 2 (Fall, 1978): 10-13.
A short but information-packed graphic review of the structure of this heroic

play, outlining "the social psychology of assassination" of any world leader and how the character relations—split between the loyal insiders and the bitter outsiders—work as a device for the gradual intensification of the drama. The article is accompanied by a graph of the play's relationships.

THOMAS OTWAY

Burns, Edward. "Thomas Otway." In his *Restoration Comedy: Crises of Desire and Identity*. New York: St. Martin's Press, 1987.

The most uncompromising of the professional writers, who had a "more disabused view" of political events, was Otway, writing the play of "apparently casual ironies that articulates wit comedy's fascination with the unsaid." Comedy's conventional description of life differs darkly from life itself, and "there is no really adequate language for the irrational fears and gratuitous cruelty below the surface of comically mundane lives." Attention is paid to Otway's comedies *Friendship in Fashion*, *The Soldier's Fortune*, and *The Atheist*.

Dobrée, Bonamy. "Thomas Otway." In his *Restoration Tragedy, 1660-1720*. Oxford, England: Clarendon Press, 1929.

After a glance at Otway's comedies (*The Soldier's Fortune* offers "an insight . . . into the emotional material which forms the basis of his later tragedy"), Dobrée turns his attention to the tragedies on which Otway's reputation rests. *Venice Preserv'd*, according to Dobrée's approach (the playwright's life reflected in his work), "is continually marred by his preoccupation with his personal troubles" and is not quite redeemed by "a higher poetic potential."

Gosse, Edmund. "Thomas Otway." In his *Seventeenth Century Studies: A Contribution to the History of English Poetry*. New York: Dodd, Mead, 1897.

Remarking on the odd proliferation of professional playwrights from 1670 to 1675 and again from 1693 to 1700, Gosse proposes calling this latter group the Orange dramatists. Otway, in the elder school, was a master of the tragic and his language "vigorous, muscular verse." Ranks him below John Dryden in comedy but finds qualities in Otway's tragedies (describing *Venice Preserv'd* as a noble and solid masterpiece) to rank him with Pierre Corneille and Jean de Rotrou, a lesser known French playwright whose life was, according to Gosse, as sad as Otway's.

Harth, Phillip. "Political Interpretations of *Venice Preserv'd*." *Modern Philology* 85, no. 4 (May, 1988): 345-362.

A review and reassessment of critical approaches to Otway's play, especially those treating the political implications, this essay is a response to Harry M. Solomon's on the same subject (see below). Most valuable here is Harth's larger project, an attempt to "consider some of the problems involved in the political interpretation of Restoration plays." Contemporary audiences "could be expected to recognize the striking similarities between many of the details in his play and in their own recent experience," but to view Otway's play as an allegorical or parallel "political document" requires, Harth maintains, critical flexibility to work against the responses of readers and spectators over the years. It has not been viewed as a primarily political play, but simply as one based on a historical source.

Hauser, David R. "Otway Preserved: Theme and Form in *Venice Preserv'd.*" In *Restoration Dramatists: A Collection of Critical Essays*, edited by Earl Miner. Englewood Cliffs, N.J.: Prentice-Hall, 1966.
Otway, in this view, reanimated the genre of heroic tragedy by overcoming some of the obstructions of the heroic conventions. Hauser defends the play's structure and craft against past critics, identifying Jaffeir with "the sin and redemption motif" and Belvidera "with angels, goodness, and faith," taking on the sins of her husband before being destroyed herself. The texture of the images in the play speaks for a finer craftsmanship than previously detected.

Hume, Robert D. "Otway and the Comic Muse." In his *The Rakish Stage: Studies in English Drama, 1600-1800*. Carbondale: Southern Illinois University Press, 1983.
Otway's accomplishments in tragedy are well known, but his comedies, "works which require a strong stomach," put him in the same league with William Wycherley, George Etherege, and William Congreve. *Friendship in Fashion*, *A Soldier's Fortune*, and *The Atheist* get particular consideration. Brutal, agonizing, very dark views of the world emerge from his comedies, seen from a cynic's eye, a world "onto which he foists a harsh, macabre gaiety which scarcely distracts from the savage picture."

Milhous, Judith, and Robert D. Hume. "*Venice Preserv'd* (1682)." In their *Producible Interpretation: Eight English Plays, 1675-1707*. Carbondale: Southern Illinois University Press, 1985.
This play, analyzed in the "production analysis" method introduced by these scholars, has a long stage history. There are four analytical centers: as topical political commentary, as a pathetic vehicle, as political manifesto, and as pessimistic satire. A good demonstration of what a director/reader can learn from the stage history of a work. It can be a manifesto for Tory politics (1682), a vehicle for the plaintive Jaffeir (1707), a vehicle for a violent Jaffeir (1713), a vehicle for Pierre as a republican idealist (1721), or a pathetic vehicle for Belvidera (1782). The authors identify five key scenes and add an appendix of the scene-plan.

Munns, Jessica. "Daredevil in Thomas Otway's *The Atheist*: A New Identification." *Restoration* 11, no. 1 (Spring, 1987): 31-38.
The atheist in the title of this satire, Otway's last play (1683), has long been

assumed to be a stage caricature of Thomas Shadwell. Munns maintains that internal and external evidence points to John Wilmot, second Earl of Rochester, who made a famous death-bed repentance in 1680. Once the Earl's friend but ridiculed in Rochester's posthumously published poems, Otway had a "passionate commitment to the ideal of friendship and [a] horror of betrayal." The value of this close study is in the demonstration of the methods for finding historical information embedded in this fictional, but highly topical, genre.

Parker, Gerald D. "The Image of Rebellion in Thomas Otway's *Venice Preserv'd* and Edward Young's *Busiris.*" *Studies in English Literature 1500-1900* 21, no. 3 (Summer, 1981): 389-407.
Noting the tendency on the part of tragic dramatists to seek foreign models rather than undertake "the more arduous task of discovering and releasing their own 'voice,' " Parker observes the difficulty of separating a dramatic treatment of political themes from a personal partisan statement by the playwright. Otway solves the problem (partly) by reaching for a higher, more cosmological conscience, especially in the fate of Jaffeir. The essay continues in a comparison of Otway's play with the lesser known *Busiris: King of Egypt* (1719) by Edward Young.

Powell, Jocelyn. "*Venice Preserv'd: Or, A Plot Discover'd.*" In her *Restoration Theatre Production*. London: Routledge & Kegan Paul, 1984.
The question of whether Otway was exploring new forms or simply compromising the conventions of the times with "his own need for personal expression" moves this study through the production considerations of Powell's major thesis. The rhythms of the lines as spoken are analyzed, contrasting with John Dryden's "pristine couplets." Based on formal patterns but filled with "sensual emotionalism," the play must be seen in the context of the political aftermath of the Popish Plot.

Solomon, Harry M. "The Rhetoric of 'Redressing Grievances': Court Propaganda as the Hermeneutical Key to *Venice Preserv'd.*" *ELH* 53, no. 2 (Summer, 1986): 289-310.
Taken together with Phillip Harth's article (see above), the extended discussion of the political purposes behind Otway's most famous play demonstrates the value of literary studies married to historical/sociological analysis. Solomon's view, that the play "should be interpreted as court propaganda designed to discredit inflammatory Whig rhetoric and to win moderate Whigs to the Tory cause," is carefully argued, from the historical context and from an examination of the play's inner workings. Whether the argument holds water is best judged from reading it in conjunction with Harth's response. A good example of the function of scholarly journals as forums for the exchange of ideas.

Taylor, Aline MacKenzie. *"Venice Preserv'd."* In *Restoration Drama: Modern Essays in Criticism*, edited by John Loftis. New York: Oxford University Press, 1966.

A long section from a whole work on this "second light" of Restoration drama, adumbrated by John Dryden's genius in the same genre. Taylor reviews the low opinions put forth by Bonamy Dobrée and others, especially critics in the nineteenth century, then reconsiders what is "irritating" about this play. A brief biographical recapitulation, comparing the events of history during Otway's time, fails to explain the absence of point of view. The greatest characters are villains and traitors, and no defense of their ignobility justifies the rebels. Jaffier is damned in modern eyes, despite Otway's articulation of his motives. Massive notes struggle to tie this extract into the longer scholarly work from which it is taken.

Wilcox, John. "The Minor Borrowers." Part 6, "Thomas Otway." In his *The Relation of Molière to Restoration Comedy*. New York: Columbia University Press, 1938.

Wilcox holds that Otway is more important for tragedy than comedy. His effort to Anglicize *The Foibles of Scapin*, called *The Cheats of Scapin*, is an example of competent workmanship as translator and adjuster of plot and character "to a nominally British scene at Dover." *The Soldier's Fortune* makes one "unmistakable" use of Molière: the duped messenger. Otway "seems to have learned nothing of technique" from his contact with the French master.

THOMAS SHADWELL

Alssid, Michael W. *Thomas Shadwell*. New York: Twayne, 1967.
This critical study attempts to show "how highly conscious an artist Shadwell was and how intelligently and perceptively he translated into his plays many of the profound and ironic views of man, society, and art which he and his age held." After examining his work, from three early comedies to the last plays, Alssid adds an interesting coda on Shadwell's place in Restoration drama ("I believe that we can call most of Shadwell's plays impressive"), comparing it to the place of Jean Giraudoux, Samuel Beckett, Harold Pinter, Edward Albee, the Marx brothers, and W. C. Fields in their respective worlds. Notes, bibliography, and index.

Armistead, J. M. "Writings About Thomas Shadwell, 1668-1980." In Armistead's *Four Restoration Playwrights*. Boston: G. K. Hall, 1984.
Often Shadwell is dealt with by critics in parts of chapters or in protracted discussions of larger topics, rather than in chapters or books devoted entirely to him. Here, these discussions are unearthed, arranged by year of publication, and annotated, giving a much clearer view of the value of Shadwell scholarship over three centuries. Annotations, from whole paragraphs to one-sentence explanations, help the reader find the pertinent information embedded in longer articles, unpublished dissertations, foreign publications, and other difficult sources. Most critics cited see Shadwell's work as an early indication of the eventual trend toward sentimental drama.

Borgman, Albert S. *Thomas Shadwell: His Life and Comedies*. New York: New York University Press, 1928.
An early study, chronological in format. The table of contents serves as a detailed index to topics; the first six chapters move from "Early Life" through the literary conflicts of 1668-1680, to his reputation after his death. Chapters 7 through 19 treat major plays individually; a conclusion claims that Shadwell may have been surpassed in polish by George Etherege and William Wycherley, but he "surpasses them in presenting a larger gallery of character . . . [and] in using greater novelty in setting." Index.

Burns, Edward. "Professional Dramatists: Shadwell and Crowne." Part 1, "Shadwell and the Wits." In his *Restoration Comedy: Crises of Desire and Identity*. New York: St. Martin's Press, 1987.
The professional dramatists "provide an impressive roster of still underrated plays." They lack "gentlemanly virtues of poise and perfect finish," but as "outsiders of the court ethos" they bridged the gap between George Etherege and Thomas Southerne. Shadwell's work is discussed in overview, appre-

ciatively described despite "the short-windedness of his inventions." *A True Widow* was an "ambitious synthesis of the available comic styles."

Gilde, Joseph M. "Shadwell and the Royal Society: Satire in *The Virtuoso.*" *Studies in English Literature 1500-1900* 10, no. 3 (Summer, 1970): 469-490.
Contrary to all previous interpreters of this play, Gilde maintains that the Royal Society, a newly formed group dedicated to scientific inquiry, provided an honorable standard of scientific practice against which the follies of Sir Nicholas and Sir Formal are to be judged, rather than to be seen as the brunt of the joke of the play. In three specific areas—the utilitarian nature of all experiment, sanctions against pretenders to science (such as the Rosicrucians), and language in the service of reason—the Royal Society's pronouncements underline the folly of the comic characters' actions. A valuable essay when contrasted with Albert S. Borgman's earlier opinion (see entry above) and that of Marjorie Hope Nicolson and David Stuart Rodes (below).

Hamilton, Walter. "Thomas Shadwell." In his *The Poets Laureate of England.* London: Elliot Stock, 1879. Reprint. Detroit: Gale Research, 1968.
Besides presenting a biographical outline of the facts of Shadwell's life, his brief study of law and poetry ("In that art he was also unsuccessful"), and his eventual success and fame for his drama, the entry notes his controversy with John Dryden (another poet laureate), who made a lifelong career of criticizing him. Hamilton considers it "unfortunate that the coarseness of Shadwell's language banishes his plays from our modern stage, where loose expressions are only tolerated when veiled in poetical diction."

Kronenberger, Louis. "Thomas Shadwell." In his *The Thread of Laughter: Chapters on English Stage Comedy from Jonson to Maugham.* New York: Alfred A. Knopf, 1952.
A brief chapter in the Kronenberger style notes Shadwell's place between two generations. *The Squire of Alsatia* is a "useful and picturesque social document" for its tour of London's criminal sanctuary. Compares Shadwell to Ben Jonson unfavorably. *A True Widow* "exposed the practice of wellborn men keeping—instead of marrying—girls of decent family," a remonstrance too close to home to be popular onstage. Kronenberger admires Shadwell's poet, who "weighs himself before he sits down to write, and again when he gets up." Concludes with a brief mention of *Bury Fair*.

Kunz, Don R., Jr. *The Drama of Thomas Shadwell.* Salzburg, Austria: Institut für Englische Sprache und Literatur, 1972.
"More remarkable for variety than consistency," Shadwell deserves to be rescued from John Dryden's critical portraiture in *MacFlecknoe.* Kunz argues his thesis through a close examination of Shadwell's work, especially noting his

transition from neoclassicism to "romanticism": "He acted out in miniature that transition from classic to romantic which England continued long after his death." Extended bibliography.

_____ . "Shadwell's *A True Widow*: 'Promis'd a Play and Dwindled to a Farce?' " *Restoration and Eighteenth Century Theatre Research* 10, no. 1 (May, 1971): 43-54.
Shadwell was known for his Restoration interpretation of Ben Jonson's comedy of humours, and this play is considered one of his better works in the genre. Kunz defends the play as "an original, useful satire by a professional with taste and aesthetic convictions," not an imitation. Shadwell did have a tendency to attempt to instruct his audience and readers, and this play is a step toward convincing them that farce was "vulgar, anti-intellectual, and anti-moralistic." The play-within-a-play presented by the character Prickett is Shadwell's way of separating false wit from true (his own).

Mignon, Elisabeth. "Dryden, Shadwell, and Aphra Behn." Part 2, "Shadwell." In her *Crabbed Age and Youth: The Old Men and Women in the Restoration Comedy of Manners*. Durham, N.C.: Duke University Press, 1947.
Shadwell's theory of characterization, derived from Ben Jonson's "humours" as well as from George Etherege, gives a different cast to his treatment of old age. Lady Loveyouth in *The Humorists*, the senile English parallel of Harpagon, Goldingham (in *The Miser*), and Oldwit and his wife, Lady Fantast (in *Bury Fair*) represent the great number of aged personages and demonstrate the varieties of senescence portrayed on Shadwell's stage, influenced by the standards of his contemporaries as well as by the inheritance of Elizabethan humours.

Nicolson, Marjorie Hope, and David Stuart Rodes, eds. *The Virtuoso*, by Thomas Shadwell. London: Edward Arnold, 1966.
A critical edition of Shadwell's satire on science. The introduction outlines the nature of the target, the Royal Society of London, and compares his "light artillery" to Ben Jonson's similar attack on pseudoscience in *The Alchemist*. Many of the allusions are lost to those who do not read Latin; others are still lively: "Like Boyle, Gimcrack has spent much time in weighing the air" but finally must admit to having invented nothing of value, "not even an engine with which to pare cream cheese." Chronology added.

Saintsbury, George, ed. *Thomas Shadwell*. London: T. Fisher Unwin, n.d.
An edition of four plays (*The Sullen Lovers, A True Widow, The Squire of Alsatia,* and *Bury Fair*), introduced with an odd, halfhearted defense of Shadwell's professional skills: "One can pardon desultoriness, dulness, coarseness, want of critical power, tediousness, ineptitude, when any of these amiable

qualities appears by itself . . . but when they all appear together it is rather trying." Nevertheless, the edition appears, risking "the danger of utterly disgusting the reader," because "his very bareness of literary gift makes him faithful and true" to the times he depicts.

Smith, John Harrington. "Shadwell, the Ladies, and the Change in Comedy." In *Restoration Drama: Modern Essays in Criticism*, edited by John Loftis. New York: Oxford University Press, 1966.
Smith sees 1688-1689 as a point of change in spirit and method for Restoration comedy, when new attitudes finally held their own against the old. "The ladies"—respectable female patrons of the theatre—called for a change from "non-exemplary" behavior (a wonderful understatement) of characters onstage. Shadwell believed the business of comedy was to encourage virtue and discourage vice, and he found an audience for his ideas. Oddly, indications are that "the ladies" boycotted Aphra Behn's *Sir Patient Fancy* in 1678. Jeremy Collier's written objections were part of a response already felt among the theatergoers themselves, reflecting publicly the sentiment that "cuckolding cannot go unchallenged."

Towers, Tom H. "The Lineage of Shadwell: An Approach to *MacFlecknoe*." *Studies in English Literature 1500-1900* 3, no. 3 (Summer, 1963): 323-334.
Ironically, Shadwell is better known from John Dryden's satirical portrait of him in *MacFlecknoe* than for his own work, largely a series of translations and adaptations. Arguing that the company Shadwell keeps in Dryden's parody reveals much about Dryden's attitude toward the older theatrical tradition represented by Christopher Beeston and others, this essay demonstrates the genre of biographical criticism which enjoyed popularity in an earlier decade. Towers' point is that Dryden's satire is "a document more theatrical than critical."

Wilcox, John. "John Dryden and Thomas Shadwell." Part 2, "Thomas Shadwell." In his *The Relation of Molière to Restoration Comedy*. New York: Columbia University Press, 1938.
Shadwell incurred an unmistakable debt to Molière, as he did to Jonson, as he pursued the profession. His debt is acknowledged in the preface to *The Sullen Lovers*; a direct adaptation of *L'Avare* becomes *The Miser*. The list of borrowings is extensive, but *The Squire of Alsatia*, according to Wilcox, seems to be "as original as anything in the period." Shadwell actually "set forth social ideas contrary to the Restoration notions," under Molière's influence, but was nevertheless "sturdily British."

JOHN VANBRUGH

Dobrée, Bonamy. "The Architect of Blenheim." In his *Essays in Biography, 1680-1726*. Oxford, England: Oxford University Press, 1925.
The first part of this long study of Vanbrugh deals with his early years and his theatre career; subsequent sections summarize his experiences at Blenheim. Vanbrugh "was able to make fruitful the long months spent in the company of the comic musc in the depths of the Bastille," says Dobrée, referring to his imprisonment in 1690 in Paris, during which time he wrote *The Provok'd Wife*. Anecdotes of the Kit-Cat Club and remarks on the possibly ill-chosen site of the opera house take up the rest of the chapter.

_____ , ed. *The Complete Works of Sir John Vanbrugh*. 4 vols. New York: Nonesuch Press, 1927.
All plays, including the adaptations from the French, dedicatory epistles, poetry, letters, and other material, are gathered here in the first definitive edition of Vanbrugh's works. Dobrée supplies long descriptions of sources, stage history, and biographical facts. The Letters are edited by Geoffrey Webb. Extended commentary appears in the notes, which also serve as a bibliography.

Harris, Bernard. *Sir John Vanbrugh*. London: Longmans, Green, 1967.
Number 197 in the bibliographical series of supplements to *British Book News*, on writers and their work, this brief overview of Vanbrugh looks at his mind as a model of its kind, his "matchless spirit of impudence," and finally the writer as "a poet as well as an architect." Vanbrugh is depicted as "manfully resis-tant" to refinement and sentimentality of the kind advocated by Colley Cibber. A fair assessment of Vanbrugh's art is that his "basic themes appeal to com-mon sense and to the common senses alike." He died "choked by a quinzey"; his unfinished play became Cibber's *The Provok'd Husband* and thus (Harris remarks) "a compliment was returned, and comedy extinguished." Short bibliography.

Huseboe, Arthur R. *Sir John Vanbrugh*. Boston: Twayne, 1976.
This critical biography concentrates on Vanbrugh's literary (that is, dramatic) achievements rather than his business or architectural ones, giving a chapter each to his two hits, *The Relapse* and *The Provok'd Wife*. A chapter on his career in the theatre serves as an overview of the theatrical world of the late Restoration; Vanbrugh's "translations" from the French (actually adaptations) are given separate treatment. Reviewing Vanbrugh's posthumous reputation, Huseboe notes that Sir John Brute and Lord Foppington were "the most coveted acting roles of the eighteenth century." Notes, bibliography, and index.

Kronenberger, Louis. "Cibber and Vanbrugh." In his *The Thread of Laughter: Chapters on English Stage Comedy from Jonson to Maugham*. New York: Alfred A. Knopf, 1952.

The Relapse is a sort of sequel to Colley Cibber's *Love's Last Shift*, but "we miss a certain tone," because Vanbrugh "lacks the right mixture of urbanity and brutality." It is really two plays, while *The Provok'd Wife* (Kronenberger modernizes contractions in titles) is only one. In the final analysis, Vanbrugh is "adequate, a wine of a good year, only not in itself a very notable wine." A footnote points out that Vanbrugh was more innovative as an architect than as a playwright.

Mignon, Elisabeth. "Vanbrugh." In her *Crabbed Age and Youth: The Old Men and Women in the Restoration Comedy of Manners*. Durham, N.C.: Duke University Press, 1947.

The "aging participant" in *The Relapse* is Sir Tunbelly Clumsey (with Coupler and the Nurse as secondary examples), borrowed with alterations from Colley Cibber's *Love's Last Shift*. The complaints of Sir John Brute in *The Provok'd Wife* "reverberate through the play," in a language memorable enough to promote him into a classic comic figure. In his adaptations, Vanbrugh "misses no opportunity to make an old man more despicable by heightening his ugliness and his delusions."

Milhous, Judith. "New Light on Vanbrugh's Haymarket Theatre Project." *Theatre Survey* 17, no. 2 (November, 1976): 143-161.

What had appeared as a simple partnership of Vanbrugh, William Congreve, and Thomas Betterton, with the possibility of the Kit-Cat Club as investors, has, in Milhous' study, become a much more complicated financial affair involving some thirty Haymarket subscribers. With typical careful but creative scholarship, she presents an explanation for the haste with which the company moved into, and quickly out of, a theatre not yet ready for occupancy. Finally, the evidence points to the possibility that, contrary to all prevailing notions, the theatre was not even built to accommodate Betterton's troupe in the first place. A fascinating example of critical scholarship's ability to realign itself in the face of new evidence.

Palmer, John. "Sir John Vanbrugh." In his *The Comedy of Manners*. London: G. Bell & Sons, 1913.

The successor who brings the style into decline, Vanbrugh reflects the new conscience and philosophical changes voiced by Collier. Vanbrugh's association with the Haymarket, and his architectural contributions to Blenheim are summarized. Vanbrugh might have started a renaissance in comedy with his best passages in *The Provok'd Wife*, but his place in history is clear: "He is a dramatist of the fall." He made a breach for George Farquhar to enter and change the sense of the comedy of manners altogether.

Perry, Henry ten Eyck. "Sir John Vanbrugh." In his *The Comic Spirit in Restoration Drama*. New York: Russell & Russell, 1925, reprint 1962.

Vanbrugh offers a longer canon, not uniform in genre; many were adaptations of French works. At first, in *The Relapse*, Vanbrugh "achieves a philosophical detachment . . . which assures him of power and ability as a comic writer." Summarizes *The Provok'd Wife* and compares Amanda and Worthy to other combatants of wit in Restoration comedy. Sees great contrast in women's "loftiness and pettiness"; Vanbrugh's work "helps to define . . . the narrow sphere allotted in the world of art for the exclusive possession of the Comic Spirit," Perry's central topic in these chapters.

Smith, James L., ed. *The Provoked Wife*, by John Vanbrugh. London: Ernest Benn, 1974.

A long introductory essay on the author, play, and stage history prepares the reader for this "marriage comedy," whose main plot derives "from marital imprisonment, with a pair of witty lovers to round out supporting scenes." Particularly interesting is the long list of modern revivals and Smith's conclusions regarding the shift of emphasis onto Sir John Brute and Lady Fancyfull, balancing "the academic emphasis upon the play's more 'intellectual' debates" with the "hearty fun derived from . . . bestial appetites in action."

Swain, A. E. H., ed. *Sir John Vanbrugh*. London: T. Fisher Unwin, 1896.

The editor supplies a bibliography of Vanbrugh's works and a biographical notice, but defers to Leigh Hunt for the introductory essay. The playwright's "double success as author and architect" is detailed, with special attention to his arrangement with William Congreve and others in the building of a new company of actors and a new theatre. Four plays—*Virtue in Danger* (*The Relapse*), *The Provok'd Wife*, *The Confederacy*, and *A Journey to London*—are printed here; the edition, in the Mermaid series, offers "literal reproductions of the old text, with etched frontispieces."

Whistler, Laurence. *Sir John Vanbrugh: Architect and Dramatist, 1664-1726*. London: Cobden-Sanderson, 1938.

This biography treats as less important Vanbrugh's theatre writings, detailing instead his architectural accomplishments and his political allegiances, in eighteen chapters and five appendices. A thorough but staid account; of the fourteen plates accompanying the text, thirteen are of buildings. Bibliography and index.

Wilcox, John. "Congreve, Vanbrugh, and Farquhar." Part 2, "Sir John Vanbrugh." In his *The Relation of Molière to Restoration Comedy*. New York: Columbia University Press, 1938.

Lord Foppington's dressing scene in *The Relapse* may owe something to Molière's *Le Bourgeois Gentilhomme*, and *The Mistake* is a conscious translation of *Le Dépit amoureux*, reproducing the gaiety "by the masterly paraphrasing of the sense of each speech into the colloquial prose of which Vanbrugh had a ready command." Wilcox also remarks as "baffling" the relation of an anonymous quarto (but connected with Vanbrugh), revised and produced as *The Cornish Squire*, which is clearly an adaptation from Molière's *Monsieur de Pourceaugnac*.

Zimansky, Curt A., ed. *The Provoked Wife*, by Sir John Vanbrugh. London: Edward Arnold, 1969.

Noting the moral questionability of this play in a brief introduction, Zimansky corrects some eighteenth century additions and deletions in this edition, part of the Regents Restoration Drama series. Possibly written during his imprisonment, but showing influences from plays by Thomas Otway and George Etherege, the play did not lead to a theatre career for Vanbrugh. Strong footnotes, with added songs and revisions in an appendix, along with a chronology.

——————— . *The Relapse*, by Sir John Vanbrugh. London: Edward Arnold, 1970.

Working from the quarto of 1697 ("about as inept a piece of typesetting as can be found in a Restoration play") but recording variants from three other editions, Zimansky provides a brief introduction dealing with the play's reception, its place in Restoration theatre history, and its share of Collier's attack. The analysis of the plot and characters is kept short, except for Lord Foppington, his stage predecessors, his importance in the subplot, and his portrayal by Colley Cibber. Notes and chronology.

GEORGE VILLIERS

Coffin, Robert P. Tristram. *The Dukes of Buckingham: Playboys of the Stuart World*. New York: Brentano's, 1931.
Only after "the empty and cooling clay of the [first] Duke of Buckingham sagged over the table, crumpled, fell, and lay sprawled out under the table legs" does Coffin's dual biography get to the Restoration playwright of *The Rehearsal*, but even then the concentration is on affairs of state and bedroom, not on the stage. His greatest achievement of statesmanship in 1671 (also the year of his "packed election" as Chancellor of Cambridge), says Coffin, was his comic attack on the tragic genre, at Drury Lane. List of books consulted; index.

Crane, D. E. L., ed. *The Rehearsal*, by George Villiers, Duke of Buckingham. Durham, England: University of Durham Press, 1976.
Collaborating with at least three others and working over a number of years, Villiers meant this satire, finally seeing the stage in 1671, to be leveled at John Dryden; his playwright-hero Bayes parodied the then poet laureate in unmistakable fashion. Crane analyzes not only this play but also the play in rehearsal, "itself so occupied with immediate theatrical effect upon the audience that it never achieves any really internal coherence of purpose." The complexities of the play-in-play, along with the topical allusions, require all the commentary the editor supplies at the end of the text, along with a glossary, bibliography, and thorough textual notes.

O'Neill, John H. *George Villiers, Second Duke of Buckingham*. Boston: Twayne, 1984.
About half of this study deals with Villier's dramatic work, and one chapter is devoted to *The Rehearsal*. O'Neill supplies a biography, a review of his reputation and influence, and a selected bibliography and index. Of the minor dramatic works, O'Neill says "probably no living person has ever seen a performance of any of them." Discusses *The Chances* at some length, as a revision (produced in 1667) of John Fletcher's adaptation (1617) of a novella by Miguel de Cervantes (published in 1613). *The Rehearsal*, O'Neill notes, "is a burlesque—that is, a humorous imitation—of a form of drama which today is almost never seen on the stage, the Restoration heroic drama."

Wilson, John Harold. *A Rake and His Times: George Villiers, Second Duke of Buckingham*. New York: Farrar, Strauss & Young, 1954.
From the imaginary journey by boat along the banks of the Thames, which opens the book, to "Buck's" disgrace before the House of Lords for loving the same woman too long, this racy biography moves quickly through Restoration

intrigues, the affairs of court, and (incidentally) the flourish of theatrical and extratheatrical activities that marked Villiers' life as both extraordinary and typical of the times. A strong visual style in the narrative more than makes up for the absence of illustrations (save the frontispiece). Notes and index.

WILLIAM WYCHERLEY

General Studies

Birdsall, Virginia Ogden. "Wycherley's Early Plays." In her *Wild Civility: The English Comic Spirit on the Restoration Stage*. Bloomington: Indiana University Press, 1970.
If George Etherege's comedy was an "early morning mood," Wycherley's is "a nighttime world whose occupants are more frequently preoccupied with bedrooms than with drawing rooms." The satirized characters are mainly in minor positions, representing a "variety of affectation, dishonesty, hypocrisy with regard to their own basic natures." Not exclusively a satirist, Wycherley makes sure the main character disguises himself or herself to get behind the hypocritical fronts of others, but is not self-deceived. Discusses *Love in a Wood* and *The Gentleman Dancing-Master* at length, the latter distinguished by its comic heroine, Hippolita, as opposed to typically male "heroes."

Burns, Edward. "William Wycherley." In his *Restoration Comedy: Crises of Desire and Identity*. New York: St. Martin's Press, 1987.
St. James's Park at nighttime "stands for an anarchy of desire wiser than self-conscious wit" in his first effort; Wycherley is fascinated by "disguise and the *Doppelgänger* plot." Burns's larger theme, "the crisis of desire and identity," is well demonstrated throughout Wycherley's canon, but especially in *The Gentleman Dancing-Master* and *The Country Wife*. "If there is one ache at the heart of Wycherley's plays, it is the fear of isolation."

Chadwick, W. R. *The Four Plays of William Wycherley: A Study in the Development of a Dramatist*. The Hague, Netherlands: Mouton, 1975.
Avoiding the mistake of treating plays purely as literature, this study is a detailed "look at Wycherley's plays as stage pieces," concentrating on their generic basis, dramatic form, and (the major thrust) the development of the playwright's thought and dramatic technique. Individual chapters move from the "first step" of *Love in a Wood*, drawing on his observation of earlier models, to *The Plain Dealer*, a "problem play" in that potential directors must deal with "the major difficulty of assessing accurately the moral standpoint from which the play is written." Chadwick adds a concluding chapter, a stunning portrait of Wycherley by Sir Godfrey Kneller, an appendix on problems of establishing the performance chronology, and a strong bibliography.

Connely, Willard. *Brawny Wycherley: First Master in English Modern Comedy*. New York: Charles Scribner's Sons, 1930.
In the informal, almost novelistic biographical style that sacrifices sober an-

notation for lively reconstruction of the atmosphere of the subject. Connely has done his scholarship, but he immerses the facts in conjecture, stylistic color-atura, and rhetoric: "Such were the scenes, the happenings, which caught the eye and thought of the brawny young student of law," or "Wycherley . . . again put his hand, not too steadily, across the banister at the Widow Hil-ton's . . . his brawny step, once so graceful and positive, was shorter, slower, measured . . . he could still stand proudly, even though not quite erect." Lists "Readings for Wycherley and his Times"; index.

Friedman, Arthur, ed. *The Plays of William Wycherley*. Oxford, England: Claren-don Press, 1979.
The chronology of the composition of Wycherley's plays introduces the edi-tion; each play is preceded by a summary of information on composition, sources, production and stage histories, reception, publications, and editions. The edition contains excellent footnotes, leading to more detailed articles in journals, comparisons with other plays, etymological notes, and comments on phraseology.

Fujimura, Thomas H. "William Wycherley." In his *The Restoration Comedy of Wit*. New York: Barnes & Noble Books, 1952.
Largely a comparison/contrast with George Etherege, in which Fujimura ques-tions Wycherley's reputation as somehow morally superior to other Restora-tion comic dramatists. The "serious moral purpose" seen by earlier critics, who even dubbed Wycherley as Puritan and Quaker, is a misconception by apologists of Restoration drama struggling to justify its sexual frankness. Here Wycherley is simply a playwright who "desired a faith compatible with rea-son," and he differs from his contemporaries only in the skill with which old ideas are inserted into the dramatic action, in a world not as carefree as Etherege's but not as malicious either.

Holland, Peter, ed. *The Plays of William Wycherley*. Cambridge, England: Cambridge University Press, 1981.
Part of a series of plays by Renaissance and Restoration dramatists, with introductory biographical details, lists of works, textual notes, and bibliogra-phies. Each play is introduced as well, with a two-page summary placing the play in its historical and canonical context. Footnotes are confined to glossings.

Kronenberger, Louis. "Wycherley." In his *The Thread of Laughter: Chapters on English Stage Comedy from Jonson to Maugham*. New York: Alfred A. Knopf, 1952.
Wycherley and Etherege were unlike the other playwrights, yet the best of the kind. Wycherley led a life of pleasure and possessed a "vigorous talent mixed with violent emotions." Comparing him with Jonathan Swift, Kronenberger

believes "he displays [the same] self-consuming, self-poisoning rage." *The Gentleman Dancing-Master* is "airier than most farces [but] the air is not fresh air." Defends Wycherley's satire because "it was so much the age of leisure that the joke is at the expense of those who lacked leisure." A long discussion of *The Country Wife* and *The Plain Dealer*; Manly was "created out of [Wycherley's] black thoughts and lacerated moral emotions."

McCarthy, B. Eugene. *William Wycherley: A Biography*. Athens: Ohio University Press, 1979.
A complete biography, with only one chapter on Wycherley the playwright, an inclination that remains "one of the persistently unanswerable biographical questions." Treated as a gentleman, courtier, politician, with "ancestry and parentage," the playwright seems far removed from the liveliness of the Restoration stage. Rather than supplement his work with theatrical lists and chronologies, McCarthy supplies an appendix detailing the fire in the village of Wem, which affected Wycherley's family, and law cases concerning Daniel Wycherley, the playwright's father. An index helps the reader to find theatre-related activities.

Mignon, Elisabeth. "Wycherley." In her *Crabbed Age and Youth: The Old Men and Women in the Restoration Comedy of Manners*. Durham, N.C.: Duke University Press, 1947.
In a stage world in which "nine-and-thirty was an age advanced enough for abhorrence," Wycherley draws satirical portraits of doddering aldermen, Puritan ladies, rich old Spanish merchants, and husbands too old for their wives. Old Lady Squeamish in *The Country Wife* is passed over too quickly, but Pinchwife's follies are analyzed in more detail. "Wycherley's attitude toward old age is [George Etherege's] intensified and enlarged in the direction of blunt realism."

Muir, Kenneth. "William Wycherley." Chapter 5 in his *The Comedy of Manners*. London: Hutchinson University Library, 1970.
Reviews contemporary and current critical attitudes towards the plays, from *Love in a Wood* ("some tolerably effective repartee but very little wit") to *The Plain Dealer*. The central question of all Wycherley scholarship— "Is Wycherley immoral?"—is answered here in the negative: bad marriages (Pinchwife, Sparkish) are balanced with good (Harcourt and Alithea) in *The Country Wife*, and for every Horner there is a Manly.

Palmer, John. "William Wycherley." In his *The Comedy of Manners*. London: G. Bell & Sons, 1913.
Wycherley, unlike George Etherege, added satire to his mix, so that the characteristics of his age were exaggerated, isolated from reality, and held up to

ridicule in an endistancing way. Biographical information from Thomas
Babington Macaulay's report is corrected; Wycherley's second marriage not
necessarily as "scandalous" as Macaulay suggests. Palmer cites Horace Wal-
pole's dictum that "life is a comedy to the man who thinks, a tragedy to the
man who feels," defending Wycherley's distance as "making the comic appeal." A strong argument for defusing the argument of immorality leveled
against Wycherley by Jeremy Collier.

Perry, Henry ten Eyck. "William Wycherley." In his *The Comic Spirit in Restoration Drama*. New York: Russell & Russell, 1925, reprint 1962.
Typical of the confusion of literary analysis, the dates of composition of
Wycherley's plays are not clear, although production dates are a matter of
record. The first two plays "are frankly prentice work," but with the later plays
"satire—and satire was undoubtedly Wycherley's forte—assumes its true
importance as the backbone of plot." Sees Alithea as "soft and sentimental," a
view at odds with most interpretations since Perry's; he considers Horner, who
is without illusions or emotions, "the ideal hero for a Restoration comedy."
Manly, in *The Plain Dealer*, is "either a brute or a hero, as you choose to take
him."

Righter, Anne. "William Wycherley." In *Restoration Dramatists: A Collection of
Critical Essays*, edited by Earl Miner. Englewood Cliffs, N.J.: Prentice-Hall,
1966.
In the process of abandoning the Etheregean model, Wycherley brought sentimentalism and a darker form of comedy to the Restoration stage, to be "joined
by the less certain but even more disturbing talents of Otway, Crowne, and
Lee." That abandonment was not abrupt; the construction of *The Country Wife*
seems similar to his two previous efforts but enlarges his interest in presenting
"that savage vision of society which is being revealed all the time on the
outskirts of the play" in the Horner plot. *The Plain Dealer* "prefigured a
change in the temper of the age."

Rogers, Katharine M. *William Wycherley*. New York: Twayne, 1972.
Following the format of the Twayne series of English authors, this study
outlines Wycherley's background and his rise to London notoriety with his
first two efforts; separate chapters on *The Country Wife* and *The Plain Dealer*
examine the plays by character and theme. Rogers sees Wycherley's illness,
memory loss, and secret first marriage as a turning point from which Wycherley never recovered. An epilogue argues for "the operation of a nemesis—
as he brought to happen in his own life the very things he had despised or
laughed at in youth." Bibliography, index, chronology.

Summers, Montague. Introduction to *The Complete Works of William Wycherley*.
Vol. 1. New York: Nonesuch Press, 1924.

Provides a full genealogy and extended biographical information on Wycherley, details of the casts of each play (and the critical receptions), a review of all borrowings, sources, and adaptations, and a description of the playwright's final years, marriages, and death. Wycherley's poetry and his argument with Alexander Pope are also discussed. A thorough and scholarly reprise of Wycherley's life and work, to which all subsequent scholarship owes a debt. Each play also has its own introduction, on source and history; explanatory notes accompany the plays.

Thompson, James. *Language in Wycherley's Plays*. Tuscaloosa: University of Alabama Press, 1984.
Part of a series on seventeenth century language theory and drama, this study tries to distinguish Restoration philosophies and ethics of language and identify their manifestations in the texts. By establishing the age's attitude toward eloquence, the reader can become more sensitive to variations in linguistic choices made by playwright and by characters. While there is no coherent "world-view" of Restoration language, understanding the range of ethical and philosophical stances will help penetrate this language-conscious society in its theatrical mode. Unfortunately, except for some discussion of "asides," the author virtually ignores the texts' function as anything except literature.

Vernon, P. F. *William Wycherley*. London: Longmans, Green, 1965.
Number 179 in the series of *British Book News* supplements, the monograph follows Wycherley's "unhappy" life through his brief rise and prolonged fall, noting that in the forty years between his last play and his death, he had "adopted the habits and outlook of the wealthy gentlemen whose lives centred on the theatres," without the financial resources to sustain the style. Of his plays, Voltaire's praise of Wycherley's wit is cited; of the poems, "his dotages . . . works created in need," Vernon remarks, "He was no poet, and he knew it." Brief bibliography.

Ward, W. C., ed. *William Wycherley*. London: Vizetelly & Co., 1888.
The introduction to this edition (as well as the individualized introductions to each play) set out the articles of contention for subsequent generations of scholars. "The characters of Wycherley . . . we neither love nor detest; we are interested not in what they are, but only in what they say and do." For Ward, the characters have no realistic counterpart except insofar as they embody the follies of the times. "Their laughing outrages upon decency are infinitely less harmful, because more superficial, than the sentimental lewdness which . . . instills a more subtle venom." Ward places Congreve above him in every regard.

Weales, Gerald, ed. *The Complete Plays of William Wycherley*. New York: Doubleday, 1966. Reprint. New York: W. W. Norton, 1971.

Weales's introduction points out the tendency of critics to use the playwright as a kind of Rorschach, seeing either Horner (the amoral libertine of *The Country Wife*) or Manly (the rampaging idealist of *The Plain Dealer*) as an expression of Wycherley's philosophy. Reviews scholarship, noting the difficulties in pinning Wycherley down to any generalizations, and discusses whether the actor or the reader is better served in the texts, concluding that Wycherley had a good sense of the theatre. Bibliography.

Wilcox, John. "William Wycherley." In his *The Relation of Molière to Restoration Comedy*. New York: Columbia University Press, 1938.
Wycherley's debt is in the form of "borrowings of matter and in suggestions for artistic procedure." The question is not whether there is a debt to Molière, but rather the nature of that debt. At least three characters in *The Country Wife* came from *The School for Wives*, in which Molière discusses how to turn a girl into a proper wife. However indebted to Molière for his beginnings, Wycherley "ends with a brilliant reflection of the fashionably corrupt society of his own country."

The Country Wife

Birdsall, Virginia Ogden. "*The Country Wife*." In her *Wild Civility: The English Comic Spirit on the Restoration Stage*. Bloomington: Indiana University Press, 1970.
Birdsall agrees that this play is wholly successful. Wycherley's ironies "play unsparingly over the whole." Thinks Wycherley owes a debt to Ben Jonson, citing parallels to Jonson's *Volpone*. Examines Horner's morality in the eyes of the other characters, especially Alithea's, whose notion of ideal marriage involves truth and freedom. Sparkish will be a Pinchwife eventually. Concludes oddly: "The dance of life derives its rhythmic tensions, in effect, from the struggle of wild things to be free."

Fujimura, Thomas H., ed. *The Country Wife*, by William Wycherley. London: Edward Arnold, 1967.
Fujimura spends most of the introduction justifying his opening remark that it is Wycherley's best comedy. "The clarity and unity of the dramatic action" should not obscure its genre, which is farce; Horner's announced impotence is a standard device which calls for suspension of disbelief and marks the farce genre clearly. Wycherley's notion of marriage pervades the play; "though the play is not licentious, its tone is libertine, cynical, and earthy." Fully footnoted, with brief bibliography and a chronology.

Holland, Norman N. "*The Country Wife*." In *Restoration Drama: Modern Essays in Criticism*, edited by John Loftis. New York: Oxford University Press, 1966.

Reprinted from Holland's 1959 study, *The First Modern Comedies*, this literary analysis of plots reveals a "wrong way"/ "right way" scheme as the play discusses intrigue and strategy. Holland goes through each character's "disguises," including the *quid pro quo* of the letter scene. Horner's state "satirizes the importance of pretense in the town" that claims that sexual desire does not exist. Alithea is educated through the play's actions, to the lesson of giving one's loyalty only to a deserving object. An interesting diagram of the personal world/social world structure (with Mrs. Margery Pinchwife straddling both) closes the essay.

Mann, David D. "The Function of the Quack in *The Country Wife.*" *Restoration* 7, no. 1 (Spring, 1983): 19-22.
Hardly a fully formed character, but rather a "functionary" in the precipitation of the plot, Quack nevertheless works well as a representative of the audience, both from the point of view of knowing the ironies of the play and as a moral gauge for the enormities of the plot's developments. The character raises questions of "appearance versus reality, double dissimulation, and rumors triumphing over truth." Potentially, Quack could provide a quite different ending to the play, but Wycherley chooses to keep him as part of the conspiracy against virtue.

Matalene, H. W. "What Happens in *The Country-Wife.*" *Studies in English Literature 1500-1900* 22, no. 3 (Summer, 1982): 395-411.
As a curative to scholarship of a self-justifying kind, the method of this essay is a close reading of a single dramatic device—Horner's announced impotence—and the scrutiny of the evidence as embedded in the play's overall structure rather than as isolated thematic moments. Matalene separates text from subtext, direct utterance from ironic or implicit expression, and actual event from modern re- and mis-interpretations based on pet theories, to conclude that Freudian approaches to Horner's latent homosexuality, emotional impotence, and the like, are ungrounded and unfruitful.

Milhous, Judith, and Robert D. Hume. "*The Country-Wife* (1675)." In their *Producible Interpretation: Eight English Plays, 1675-1707*. Carbondale: Southern Illinois University Press, 1985.
A fresh and valuable "production analysis" of Wycherley's most often produced play. Reviews "astonishing" controversy of critical opinion. "The Critical Muddle" can be resolved by asking, "What is the play about?" What was Wycherley's view of marriage? What assumptions were brought to the play by its audience? Identifies four cruxes: the degree of realism; the production's attitude toward the Harcourt/Alithea plot; the presentation of the Pinchwifes; and the staging of the finale. These are the points on which a specific perfor-

mance will turn. Charts the character treatments available to the director, leading to three interpretations: comedy, farce, or satire.

Morrissey, L. J. "Wycherley's *Country Dance.*" *Studies in English Literature 1500-1900* 8, no. 3 (Summer, 1968): 415-429.
A graceful study of the structure of *The Country Wife*, based on the figures and formations of baroque cotillion dances of the period. The dance patterns give clues to the play's "comic buoyancy," and explain the complex final scene, in its reestablishment of pairings originally introduced in the opening acts. Morrissey sees patterns of "danse-contredanse" repeated through the piece, which on one level serve as "preparations for cuckoldry in this play." An interesting comparison between two related arts, especially valuable in the light of the social formality of both.

Powell, Jocelyn. "*The Country Wife.*" In her *Restoration Theatre Production.* London: Routledge & Kegan Paul, 1984.
From its first lines, this play is direct and active in its pursuit of the audience's participation in Horner's "fiction." Its stage history is witness to its subtle and intricate design, "certainly the best organised of Wycherley's comedies." The audience-actor contract begun at the play's opening is brought to fruition in the "china" scene, with the same set and the same device of Quack's witness to the action. Even Margery's *quid pro quo* at the play's climax is shared with the audience; the play is "a carefully constructed fiction, playing with the real world to discover its inner truth."

Rogers, Katharine M. "*The Country Wife.*" In her *William Wycherley.* New York: Twayne, 1972.
A slightly biased examination of the play. Horner's character can be seen either as one "reduced . . . to an object instead of a free agent" in the china scene or as a totally independent libertine "who gratifies his natural impulses without inner scruples or outward restraints." Compares Sparkish and Pinchwife as two kinds of satirical portraits, neither a true wit. The two women, Alithea and Margery, are treated as "virtuous" and "natural" respectively. Wycherley here "laid bare the selfishness of the proprietary husband, the man absorbed in business, and the fashionably indifferent fop." Rogers blames the marriage laws, which treat women as property, for the play's immoral tone.

Thompson, James. "Figurative Language in *The Country Wife.*" In his *Language in Wycherley's Plays.* Tuscaloosa: University of Alabama Press, 1984.
A study that discusses social attitudes toward language as reflected in Wycherley's work. Subtlety of language has been much remarked on in previous scholarship, especially the number of similitudes in act 1. Much of the action of the play is generation of figurative language, part of the larger disguise

motif—things are "like" things. Oaths, vows, deliveries of oral and written mis-messages, and rumor are all language-oriented activities that move the play forward at every point. The false report of the town regarding Horner is the precipitant; Lady Fidget misunderstands figurative speech but uses it well in the china scene, as do the other linguistic disguisers. Finally, "honor" and "reputation" are empty words that reconcile the play's moral contradictions.

The Gentleman Dancing-Master

Birdsall, Virginia Ogden. "Wycherley's Early Plays." Part 2, "*The Gentleman Dancing-Master.*" In her *Wild Civility: The English Comic Spirit on the Restoration Stage*. Bloomington: Indiana University Press, 1970.
   The play is closer to *The Country Wife* than others have observed, despite weaknesses, but indicates a "failure of inventiveness," causing the playwright to "prolong single scenes unnecessarily and to fall back on the same farcical proceedings again and again." It is simpler and more unified than *Love in a Wood* and unique in its heroine, Hippolita, "who makes the rules and devises the challenges," demonstrating a feminine boldness that Wycherley questions in other plays. Examines the structure of act 5 in relation to Hippolita's split of focus between comic and romantic heroine. Wycherley "loses his nerve" at the play's end, not letting Hippolita express the carpe diem philosophy lurking around the edge of the play.

Holland, Norman N. "*The Gentleman Dancing-Master.*" In his *The First Modern Comedies: The Significance of Etherege, Wycherley, and Congreve*. Cambridge, Mass.: Harvard University Press, 1959.
   The title's hidden contradiction begins Holland's examination of "disguise, comic and cosmic," an approach outlined in the preceding chapter and carried through the discussion of dualities. "Right" and "wrong" ways of behaving— each with its own divisions—inform the play, in which "from the wrong way" of one set of characters "we infer the rightness of the way represented by Gerrard and Hippolita." Wycherley presents clearly the proper action (while Etherege leaves the audience to infer it). However, "The hero does what the villain does, and one must look inside to see the difference."

Marshall, W. Gerald. "The Idea of Theatre in Wycherley's *The Gentleman Dancing-Master.*" *Restoration* 6, no. 1 (Spring, 1982): 1-10.
   Here Marshall tries to rescue Wycherley's second play from its critical obscurity, by noting the prevailing *topos* of "man as actor, as player on the world stage." Contrasts Hippolita's "positive" use of "natural" theatricality with its antithesis, embodied in the roles of Don Diego and Paris, who "function in their own dramas of madness, play-worlds of illusory perception in

which they are able to make of themselves and everything about them mere
fiction or play." This study declares, rather typically, that such an approach
"makes *The Gentleman Dancing-Master* a much richer play than critics have
heretofore perceived."

Rogers, Katharine M. "The Rise to Fame." Part 3, *"The Gentleman Dancing-
Master."* In her *William Wycherley*. New York: Twayne, 1972.
Less successful than his first play, partly due to a new cast and new location.
Wycherley in this work "focused on a single situation, one which was not
sufficiently substantial to carry out a whole play." Borrowing the central situation from Calderón, the playwright enhances the character of Hippolita,
enlightened and charming, witty and resourceful, self-reliant and honest.
Wycherley's army experiences interrupt his writing until 1675, when his
masterpiece appears at Drury Lane.

Thompson, James. "Clothing Thought with Language in *The Gentleman Dancing-
Master."* In his *Language in Wycherley's Plays*. Tuscaloosa: University of
Alabama Press, 1984.
A study of language as used in the dramatic work of this period. For "the right
use of words" (the book's central concern) this play offers several strong
examples. Questions of "honor" and the status of "gentlemen" dwell in proof
by words. Dress and speech are identical; characters put on a speech "habit,"
and "Monsieur's and Don Diego's attitude toward language is the same as their
attitude toward clothing." The "trial" relationship of the lovers (as in *Love in a
Wood*) is one of proper language conduct, and language reflects extremes
between levity and gravity.

Love in a Wood

Birdsall, Virginia Ogden. "Wycherley's Early Plays." Part 1, *"Love in a Wood: Or,
St. James's Park."* In her *Wild Civility: The English Comic Spirit on the Restoration Stage*. Bloomington: Indiana University Press, 1970.
This play has not aroused much critical enthusiasm, possibly because it lacks
comic focus. Wycherley had yet to marry Jonsonian humours with the more
realistic comic figures centered on the Restoration notion of the libertine.
Birdsall takes earlier studies to task for their pastoral interpretation, suggesting
that the title should be taken in a reductive way. In the portraits of the lower
characters, the difference between Wycherley and other, earlier playwrights is
clear: Unpleasantness of action is something unique to Wycherley; these are
not merely fools but dangerous fools. The Ranger fails to make his world (the
park) dominate the play because he is not dynamic himself. The three levels—
pastoral romance, realistic comedy, "humourous" comedy—do not come
together here.

Holland, Norman N. "*Love in a Wood: Or, St. James's Park.*" In his *The First Modern Comedies: The Significance of Etherege, Wycherley, and Congreve.* Cambridge, Mass.: Harvard University Press, 1959.

Third in order of performance among these eleven samples, Wycherley's first effort demonstrates the double-plot convention, and Holland's larger theme of "appearance/natural understanding." The argument outlines the low-plot intrigue, in which appearance and nature are confused by Dapperwit and Sir Simon, and the high-plot action, in which Christina and Valentine reconcile deceptive appearance with a reliance "on what should be [Valentine's] knowledge of Christina's impeccable character." "In a wood," Holland points out, means "confused" and gets its reference from the confusing and "unconfusing" episodes in the park. Holland is at his best in these kinds of comparison/contrast efforts.

Marshall, W. Gerald. "Wycherley's *Love in a Wood* and the Designs of Providence." *Restoration* 3, no. 1 (Spring, 1979): 8-16.

A study of themes and structure: "There is an overall dramatic structure in which the secret schemes of the play's characters are revealed through unexpected and unusual events," leading to precisely timed retributive justice. This essay is part of the inquiry of Restoration critics regarding the place, if any, of a universally shared idea of "providence," the notion that events are guided by a higher order, from which mere human activities can only deviate temporarily and ineffectively. Such inquiries combine literary analysis with examination of religious and sociological precepts in the Restoration audience and readership.

Rogers, Katharine M. "The Rise to Fame." Part 1, "*Love in a Wood.*" In her *William Wycherley*. New York: Twayne, 1972.

Wycherley sought merely to produce an amusing example of the already identified form, the Restoration comedy of manners, in his first play. Dapperwit is a model of the would-be wit, conscious of his "parts" and "so proud of his similes that he pauses to complete one while he is eloping with Martha." Unlike its less inspired counterparts, the play "demonstrates a moral point of view; for Wycherley reforms or punishes selfish and heartless behavior." Rogers supplies a colorful description of the opening night, partly from theatre history and partly from conjecture.

Thompson, James. "*Love in a Wood* and Decorum." In his *Language in Wycherley's Plays*. Tuscaloosa: University of Alabama Press, 1984.

Part of a linguistic study of Wycherley's plays. There is more comic than satiric language in this play. Decorum is the outward indicator of character, and speech the sign of it. Dapperwit's speech calls attention to itself and serves as "a false standard against which others' linguistic skills can be measured." Heroes and lovers are natural in speech, but "if wits use language to slander others, their praise is equally slanderous." Language as social strategy is discussed, the dialogue being characterized as an ongoing combat of "trust and trial." Worthiness is equal to "consideration of others, the quintessential right use of speech."

The Plain Dealer

Birdsall, Virginia Ogden. *"The Plain Dealer."* In her *Wild Civility: The English Comic Spirit on the Restoration Stage*. Bloomington: Indiana University Press, 1970.

Is it a comedy at all? What is the audience to make of Manly? Is he contradictory to the play in which he appears? Is he a spokesman or a dupe? Birdsall sees the play as a debate between comedy and satire, and points to the debate tradition in that time, especially in John Dryden. Claims that Manly himself is not satirized by Wycherley, and therefore he is asking for our understanding, not our acknowledgment of Manly's folly. We are not asked to condemn Manly but to recognize the behavior of "a tormented man." At play's close, comedy is winning the debate.

Holland, Norman N. *"The Plain-Dealer."* In his *The First Modern Comedies: The Significance of Etherege, Wycherley and Congreve*. Cambridge, Mass.: Harvard University Press, 1959.

In a more detailed examination than given to earlier Restoration plays, Holland applies to this last play in his study his dialectic of "right" and "wrong" action based on appearances versus natural understanding. In Holland's view, Manly is a dupe, not a hero, because he distrusts the "natural" world and lives the appearance of the heroic, with "his raging furious honesty." Fidelia, too, seems borrowed from heroic drama, and her unreality lends credence to her interpretation as an idealistic figure. In the "education" of Manly and Fidelia, they are dragged "through the very mire they despise."

Hughes, Leo, ed. *The Plain Dealer*, by William Wycherley. Lincoln: University of Nebraska Press, 1967.

The introduction to this work gives a recapitulation of its stage history, a brief review of Jonsonian comedy leading to the borrowings here, along with Molière's influence on the playwright; John Dryden's opinion of the play, leading to modern views of its "savagery"; and overviews of Restoration comedy using specific details from the play as examples. As such, it is much more an essay for those familiar with the period than an introduction to the play itself. Full notes throughout; chronology in appendix.

Rogers, Katharine M. "Fatal Inconsistency: Wycherley and *The Plain-Dealer*." *ELH* 28, no. 2 (June, 1961): 148-162.

A character study of Manly, with an extended discussion of how he should be interpreted. Taken as pure literature here, the text and its inconsistencies "can be explained only as the result of a blurring of artistic purpose" between Wycherley's intentions and "what part of his nature was compelling him to do." Too far removed from a sense of theatrical intentionality, this essay finally reduces to chambered speculation: "Probably when Wycherley was not deeply involved in his work. . . ." Or this: "Possibly the autobiographical references . . . betray an excessive involvement of the author in his material." This same scholar clarifies her views some years later (see below).

—————————. *"The Plain-Dealer."* In her *William Wycherley*. New York: Twayne, 1972.
By transforming Molière's Alceste (in *The Misanthrope*), who retreated from a society he despised, into Manly, "a romantic hero with whom the audience is invited to identify," Wycherley gets closest to drawing a self-portrait. Examines the play in detail, identifying the inconsistencies in Manly, and giving to Freeman and Olivia credit for good sense and "real wit." Rogers believes Wycherley's own disenchantment with the Restoration world prompted him to abandon Freeman and turn to Manly as a hero, resulting in an inconsistent characterization somewhere between realistic portrait and Jonsonian "humours."

Smith, James L., ed. *The Plain Dealer*, by William Wycherley. London: Ernest Benn, 1979.
A brief overview of the author's life, a long and careful summary of the play's plot and characters, and the stage history of the play introduce this edition, fully footnoted, with a portrait of Wycherley, a facsimile of the 1677 title page, and an engraving of Westminster Hall's interior, lined with books. "The play does more than hold up to our scrutiny the complex, contradicting attitudes that surround the ideal of plain dealing. It flings Manly head first into the intriguing world, and waits to see if he will sink or swim."

Thompson, James. "Correctness and *The Plain-Dealer*." In his *Language in Wycherley's Plays*. Tuscaloosa: University of Alabama Press, 1984.
A study of language in the theatrical literature of the Restoration. Manly is a problem character, "surly" and difficult to accept. Lawyers and the law use words here to explain words—"self-referential." Petulant's name and actions are signals of a character who uses language with "masterful indifference." Manly's diction and predilection for etymologies mark his plain-dealing approach to language—a stripping of disguises through "correctness" of actions and speech—in contrast to lawyers who use words to obfuscate and abuse, "subordinating meaning to effect."

Zimbardo, Rose A. "The Satiric Design in *The Plain Dealer*." In *Restoration Dramatists: A Collection of Critical Essays*, edited by Earl Miner. Englewood Cliffs, N.J.: Prentice-Hall, 1966.

Examines Wycherley's last play against the framework of the classical satiric form, which Zimbardo reduces to thesis and antithesis, represented by the satirist and the adversarius, "a kind of combative hollow man." Entering the lists regarding Manly's place in the design, she sees him as the satirist, with Freeman as the adversarius, "who detaches himself from the crowd and draws near to the satirist, where he plays the role of the devil's advocate." Manly's reduction to hypocrisy, which threatens to ruin him, is finally itself reversed by Fidelia, an "expanded allusion" to the Juvenalian values of virtue and generosity.

RESTORATION DRAMA

INDEX

Alssid, Michael W.   127
Andrew, N. J., ed.   91
Anthony, Rose   8
Archer, Stanley L.   8
Archer, William   9
Archer, William, ed.   114
Armistead, J. M.   10, 53, 121, 127
Armstrong, Cecil Ferard   61
Arundell, D. D., ed.   83
Ashley, Leonard R. N.   58
Atkinson, Brooks   22
Attridge, Derek   83
Auburn, Mark S., ed.   98
Avery, Emmett L.   10, 61, 72
Avery, Emmett L., Arthur H. Scouten, George
   Winchester Stone, Jr., Charles Beecher Hogan,
   and William Van Lennep, eds.   31

Balch, Marston Stevens   53
Barbeau, Anne T.   83, 93, 96, 98, 100
Barker, Richard Hindry   58
Barlow, Graham   10
Barnard, John   11, 70, 77, 109
Bax, Clifford   11
Beaurline, L. A., and Fredson Bowers   91, 94, 99
Beaurline, L. A., and Fredson Bowers, eds.
   83, 84
Berman, Ronald   109
Bernbaum, Ernest   11
Birdsall, Virginia Ogden   12, 61, 71, 73, 75, 78,
   102, 107, 109, 111, 137, 142, 145, 146, 148
Black, James   12
Blashfield, Evangeline Wilbour   53
Boas, Frederick S.   12, 114
Booth, Michael R.   12
Borgman, Albert S.   127
Boswell, Eleanore   13
Bowers, Fredson, and L. A. Beaurline   91, 94, 99
Bowers, Fredson, and L. A. Beaurline, eds.
   83, 84
Bowyer, John Wilson   13
Boyette, Purvis E.   102
Braumiller, A. R., and J. C. Bulman, eds.   13, 69
Brett-Smith, H. F. B.   102
Brett-Smith, H. F. B., ed.   102
Brooke, Iris   13
Brown, John Russell, and Bernard Harris,
   eds.   13, 67, 87
Brown, Laura   14
Brown, Richard E.   121
Bruce, Donald   14
Bulman, J. C., and A. R. Braumiller, eds.   13, 69

Burner, Sandra A.   15
Burns, Edward   15, 53, 58, 61, 82, 114, 123,
   127, 137
Burns, Landon C.   15
Butter, Francelia, ed.   42

Cameron, Kenneth M.   15, 16
Canfield, J. Douglas   16
Carnochan, W. B., ed.   109
Case, Arthur E., and George H. Nettleton,
   eds.   37
Cecil, C. D.   16
Chadwick, W. R.   137
Chisman, Isabel, and Hester Emilie
   Raven-Hart   17
Cibber, Colley   58
Coffin, Robert P. Tristram   135
Collier, Jeremy   17
Connely, Willard   114, 137
Cope, Kevin L.   17
Cordner, Michael, ed.   103
Corman, Brian   17
Cox, James E.   18
Crane, D. E. L., ed.   135
Crawford, Bartholow V.   18
Crawford, Patricia   54
Cunningham, John E.   18
Cunningham, Peter   18

Davis, Herbert   62
Davison, Peter   18
Deane, Cecil V.   19
DeRitter, Jones   54
Dixon, Peter   119
Dobrée, Bonamy   19, 62, 84, 85, 103, 123, 131
Dobrée, Bonamy, ed.   19, 131
Doran, Dr. [John]   20
Downes, John   20
Doyle, Anne   85
Drinkwater, John, ed.   18

Edgar, Irving I.   63
Ellenhauge, Martin   20
Elwin, Malcolm   21
Evans, Gareth Lloyd   63
Ewald, Alex. Charles, ed.   115

Fairholt, F. W.   21
Farmer, A. J.   115
Fink, Laurie A.   21
Fitzgibbon, H. Macaulay   117
Foakes, R. A.   63

153

Fone, B. R. S.   59
Freehafer, John   22
Friedman, Arthur, ed.   138
Fujimura, Thomas H.   22, 63, 78, 103, 138
Fujimura, Thomas H., ed.   142

Gagen, Jean   78
Gibbons, Brian   22, 75, 78
Gilde, Joseph M.   128
Goreau, Angeline   54
Gosse, Edmund   64, 103, 123
Gosse, Edmund, ed.   22
Grace, Joan C.   85
Granville-Barker, Harley   23
Guffey, George R.   54, 85

Hamilton, Walter   59, 86, 128
Harbage, Alfred   23
Harris, Bernard   131
Harris, Bernard, and John Russell Brown,
   eds.   13, 67, 87
Harth, Phillip   123
Harwood, John T.   23
Hathaway, Baxter   86
Hauser, David R.   124
Hawkins, Harriett   23, 73, 79, 110
Heilman, Robert B.   24
Henderson, Anthony G.   71, 73, 76, 79
Henderson, Anthony G., ed.   64
Hersey, George L.   80
Hinnant, Charles H.   79
Hodges, John C.   64, 76
Hodges, John C, ed.   64
Hogan, Charles Beecher, William Van Lennep,
   Emmett L. Avery, Arthur H. Scouten, and
   George Winchester Stone, Jr., eds.   31
Holland, Norman N.   24, 71, 73, 76, 79, 108, 110,
   112, 142, 145, 147, 148
Holland, Peter   24
Holland, Peter, ed.   138
Hook, Lucyle   24
Hopper, Vincent F., and Gerald B. Lahey,
   eds.   80
Hotson, Leslie   25
Hughes, Charlotte Bradford   82
Hughes, Derek   86, 94, 96, 98, 100
Hughes, Leo, ed.   148
Hume, Robert D.   25, 26, 86, 121, 124
Hume, Robert D., ed.   26
Hume, Robert D., and Judith Milhous   35, 74, 92,
   100, 118, 124, 143
Hume, Robert D., and Judith Milhous, eds.   20
Huseboe, Arthur R.   104, 108, 110, 112, 131

Jackson, Allan S.   26
Jalali, R. K.   87
James, E. Nelson   27

Jantz, Ursula   27
Jeffares, A. Norman   118
Jefferson, D. W.   87
Jenkins, Annibel   27
Jones, Howard Mumford, and Dougald
   MacMillan, eds.   33
Jones, Marion, A. H. Scouten, John Loftis, and
   Richard Southern   31
Jordan, R.   27

Kalitzki, Judith   99
Kalson, Albert E.   59
Kelsall, Malcolm   65, 74
Kenny, Shirley Strum   28, 115
King, Robert L.   92
Kirsch, Arthur C.   87, 92, 94, 96, 98, 100
Kroll, Richard W.   80
Kronenberger, Louis   28, 55, 59, 65, 88, 104, 115,
   128, 132, 138
Krutch, Joseph Wood   28, 65
Kunz, Don R., Jr.   128, 129

Lahey, Gerald B., and Vincent F. Hopper,
   eds.   80
Langbaine, Gerard   29
Langhans, Edward A.   29, 110
Langhans, Edward A., ed.   30
Larson, Richard Leslie   88, 92, 95
Law, Richard   88
Leech, Clifford   65
Le Gallienne, Richard, ed.   30
Lincoln, Stoddard   66
Link, Frederick M.   55
Link, Frederick M., ed.   95
Loftis, John   30, 97
Loftis, John, ed.   30, 62, 65, 87, 94, 102, 111, 126,
   130, 142
Loftis, John, Richard Southern, Marion Jones, and
   A. H. Scouten   31
Love, Harold   66, 71, 74, 76, 80
Lowe, Robert W., ed.   58
Lynch, Kathleen M.   31, 32, 66, 80, 104

McAfee, Helen   32
McCarthy, B. Eugene   72, 139
McCollum, John I., ed.   32
McComb, John King   77
McDonald, Margaret Lamb   33
McHenry, Robert W., Jr.   88
MacMillan, Dougald, and Howard Mumford
   Jones, eds.   33
McMillin, Scott, ed.   33
Mann, David D.   104, 105, 143
Markley, Robert   33
Marshall, Geoffrey   34
Marshall, W. Gerald   145, 147
Martin, Lee J.   34

Matalene, H. W.   143
Mendelson, Sara Heller   56
Mignon, Elisabeth   34, 56, 67, 89, 105, 116, 129, 132, 139
Miles, Dudley Howe   34
Milhous, Judith   35, 132
Milhous, Judith, and Robert D. Hume   35, 74, 92, 100, 118, 124, 143
Milhous, Judith, and Robert D. Hume, eds.   20
Miner, Earl, ed.   35, 78, 87, 93, 94, 106, 124, 140, 150
Moore, Cecil A.   36
Moore, Frank Harper   89
Morris, Brian, ed.   63, 65, 67, 68, 69, 70, 75, 81
Morrissey, L. J.   144
Mudrick, Marvin   36
Muir, Kenneth   36, 67, 68, 105, 139
Mullin, Donald C.   36
Munns, Jessica   124
Musser, Joseph F., Jr.   56
Myers, William   68

Nettleton, George H., and Arthur E. Case, eds.   37
Newman, Robert S.   95
Nicoll, Allardyce   37
Nicolson, Marjorie Hope, and David Stuart Rodes, eds.   129

O'Neill, John H.   135
Orrell, John   38
Oxenford, Lyn   38

Palmer, John   38, 68, 105, 106, 116, 132, 139
Parfitt, George   69
Parker, Gerald D.   125
Pendlebury, F. J.   90
Perry, Henry ten Eyck   38, 69, 106, 116, 133, 140
Persson, Agnes V.   39
Potter, Elmer B.   75
Powell, Jocelyn   39, 81, 97, 106, 125, 144
Prior, Mary, ed.   54
Pry, Kevin   39

Radaddi, Mongi   39
Raven-Hart, Hester Emilie, and Isabel Chisman   17
Restoration and Eighteenth-Century Drama   40
Restoration Plays   40
Reverand, Cedric D., II   90
Ricks, Christopher, ed.   11, 50
Righter, Anne   140
Roberts, Philip   81
Rodes, David Stuart, and Marjorie Hope Nicolson, eds.   129
Rogers, J. P. W.   117
Rogers, Katharine M.   140, 144, 146, 147, 148, 149

Roper, Alan   40
Rosenfeld, Sybil, ed.   106
Ross, J. C.   72
Ross, John   119
Ross, Julian L.   40
Rothstein, Eric   117, 118, 119, 120

Sackville-West, V.   56
Saintsbury, George, ed.   90, 129
Salgado, Gamini   41
Schlegel, Augustus William   41
Schneider, Ben Ross, Jr.   41
Scouten, A. H.   42
Scouten, A. H., John Loftis, Richard Southern, and Marion Jones   31
Scouten, Arthur H., George Winchester Stone, Jr., Charles Beecher Hogan, William Van Lennep, and Emmett L. Avery, eds.   31
Shafer, Yvonne Bonsall   42
Sherwood, Margaret   90
Shipley, John B.   42
Shugrue, Michael   120
Silvette, Herbert   42
Singh, Sarup   43
Smith, James L., ed.   133, 149
Smith, John Harrington   43, 130
Solomon, Harry M.   125
Sorelius, Gunnar   44
Southern, Richard, Marion Jones, A. H. Scouten, and John Loftis   31
Staves, Susan   44
Stone, George Winchester, Jr., Charles Beecher Hogan, William Van Lennep, Emmett L. Avery, and Arthur H. Scouten, eds.   31
Styan, J. L.   44
Sullivan, Maureen   60
Summers, Montague   20, 45, 140
Summers, Montague, ed.   90
Swain, A. E. H., ed.   133

Taney, Retta M.   45
Taylor, Aline MacKenzie   126
Taylor, Charlene M., ed.   112
Taylor, D. Crane   69, 72, 74, 77, 81
Taylor, Ivan E.   45
Thompson, James   46, 141, 144, 146, 147, 149
Thorndike, Ashley H.   46, 47
Towers, Tom H.   130
Traugott, John   47

Underwood, Dale   107, 108, 111, 112

Van Lennep, William   47, 48
Van Lennep, William, Emmett L. Avery, Arthur H. Scouten, George Winchester Stone, Jr., and Charles Beecher Hogan, eds.   31
Vance, John A.   60

Verity, A. Wilson, ed.   107
Vernon, P. F.   48, 141
Vieth, David M.   121
Vieth, David M., ed.   93
Visser, Colin   48

Wain, John   48
Waith, Eugene M.   91, 93, 96, 97
Walsh, Martin W.   49
Ward, W. C., ed.   141
Weales, Gerald   81
Weales, Gerald, ed.   141
Webb, Geoffrey, ed.   131
Weber, Harold   49

Wertheim, Albert   69
Whistler, Laurence   133
White, Eric Walter   49
Wickham, Glynne   50
Wilcox, John   50, 57, 69, 82, 91, 107, 117, 126, 130, 133, 142
Wilkinson, D. R. M.   50
Williams, Aubrey L.   70
Wilson, John Harold   50, 51, 135
Wilson, John Harold, ed.   82
Wimsatt, W. K., Jr., ed.   36, 52

Zimansky, Curt A., ed.   134
Zimbardo, Rose A.   52, 111, 150